Going Places

Going Places

SLOVENIAN WOMEN'S STORIES ON MIGRATION

Mirjam Milharčič Hladnik
and Jernej Mlekuž, editors

The University of Akron Press
Akron, Ohio

Copyright © 2014 by The University of Akron Press
All rights reserved • First Edition 2014 • Manufactured in the United States of America.
All inquiries and permission requests should be addressed to the Publisher, the
University of Akron Press, Akron, Ohio 44325–1703.

18 17 16 15 14   5 4 3 2 1

ISBN: 978-1-937378-71-4 (paper)
ISBN: 978-1-937378-75-2 (ePDF)
ISBN: 978-1-937378-74-5 (ePub)

LIBRARY OF CONGRESS CATALOGING-IN-PUBLICATION DATA
Going places : Slovenian women's stories on migration / Mirjam Milharčič Hladnik and
Jernej Mlekuž, editors. — First edition.
    pages cm
  Includes bibliographical references.
  ISBN 978-1-937378-71-4 (pbk. : alk. paper) — ISBN 978-1-937378-75-2 (epdf) —
ISBN 978-1-937378-74-5 (epub)
 1. Slovenes—Foreign countries—Biography. 2. Women—Slovenia—History.
3. Slovenes—Foreign countries—History. 4. Slovenia—Emigration and immigration—
History. I. Milharčič Hladnik, Mirjam. II. Mlekuž, Jernej.
  DR1375.G65 2014
  305.48'8918400922—dc23
                                            2014002919

∞ The paper used in this publication meets the minimum requirements of ANSI/NISO
z39.48–1992 (Permanence of Paper).

Cover: The Rand-McNally New Library Atlas Map of Europe, courtesy of the Library of
Congress. Postcards courtesy of Marjan Drnovšek. Cover design by Amy Freels

Going Places was designed and typeset in Minion by Amy Freels and printed on sixty-
pound natural and bound by Bookmasters of Ashland, Ohio.

Contents

Introduction
Mirjam Milharčič Hladnik   1

I | Transnational Emotions: Those Who Left and Those Who Stayed
  1 | A Slovenian Bride in Cleveland: Emotions in Letters
    Mirjam Milharčič Hladnik   21
  2 | A Wife at Home: Longing and Writing
    Marjan Drnovšek   68

II | Silenced Stories: Emancipatory Experiences
  3 | Aleksandrinke in Egypt: Between Condemnation and Adoration
    Daša Koprivec   105
  4 | Dikle in Italian Cities: Personal Experiences, Public Interpretations
    Jernej Mlekuž   136

III | Active, Skilled, Ambitious
  5 | Slamnikarice Abroad and at Home: Ladies and Entrepreneurs
    Saša Roškar   171
  6 | Eurocrats in Brussels: Contemporary Career Women
    Tatiana Bajuk Senčar   213

Conclusion
Jernej Mlekuž   235

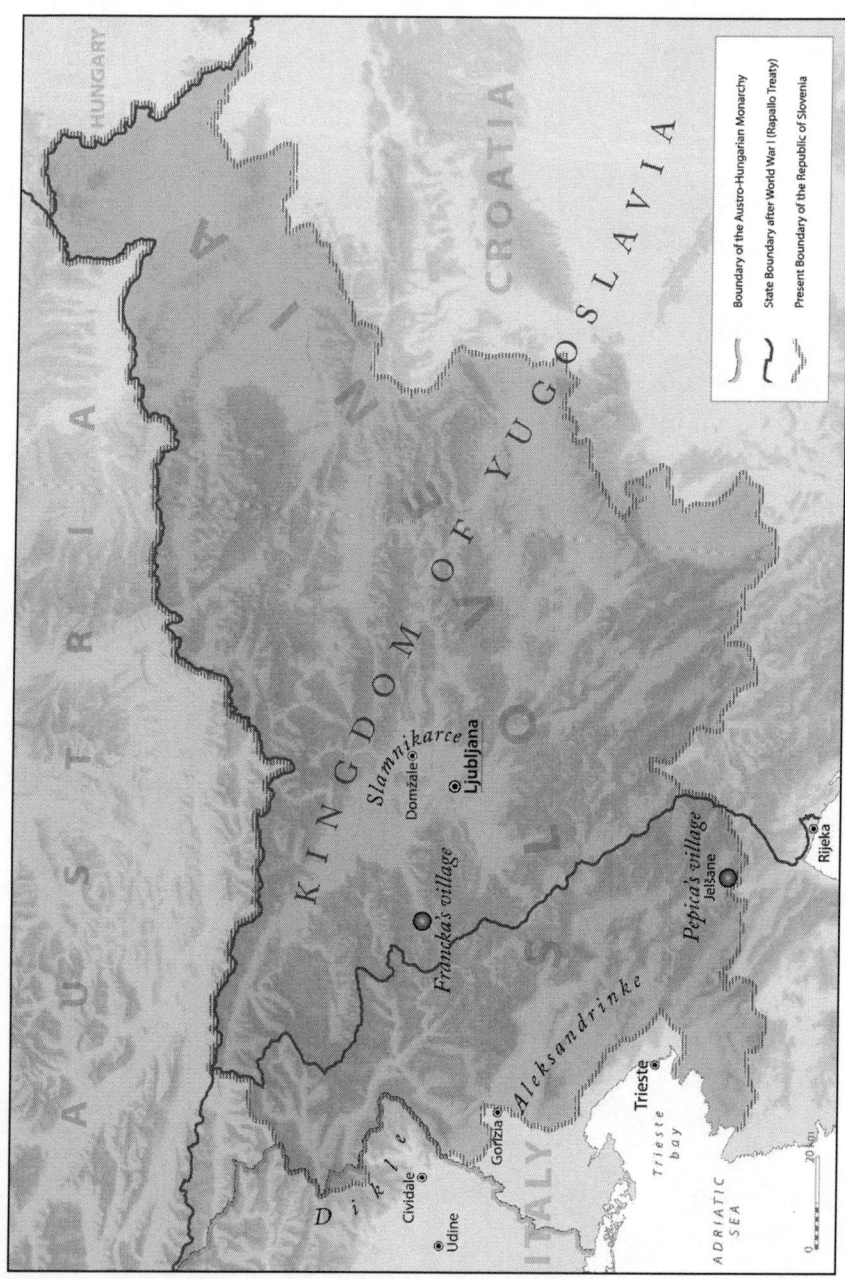

Figure 1. Map of Slovenia through history with regions of women's emigration. *Map by Mateja Rihteršič*

Introduction
Mirjam Milharčič Hladnik

This book is based on the written and oral records of the personal experiences of women migrants from a small land in Central Europe. The letters, narratives, life stories, and testimonies cover a span of three to four generations of women who faced an unknown world, conquered fear, gained control over their minds and bodies, and began the age of self-determination. They represent a record of the interpretation of national identity and gender roles through a female migrant perspective during a time when national identity and gender roles were challenged by two world wars, in turbulent times before World War I, and in the unique moment after the independence of Slovenia in 1991. Slovenia is a small triangle of land where the Slavic-speaking world that stretches as far as Moscow and Vladivostok meets the Latin universe that starts in Italy. The borderline between the Slavic and Latin cultures is joined by the German-speaking Austrians in the north. The three cultures contact, penetrate each other with words and expressions, exchange culinary experience, and sometimes intermarry but always stay separate as cultural and linguistic groups. In the second half of the nineteenth century when mass emigration began, no more than a million people spoke the Slovenian language; today, barely two and a half million speak it. When we put a century of Slovenian women migrants' experience in a brief historical context, we see their land—the Slovenian ethnic territory—subject to fast and dynamic trajectories in that period.

Places of Departure: Shifting Boundaries

A part of the Austro-Hungarian Empire for centuries, the territory encompassing Slovenia was divided into three parts after World War I. The largest part became a constitutional entity of the new Kingdom of Serbs, Slovenes and Croats; the name was changed to the Kingdom of Yugoslavia in 1929. The smallest part, Koroška in the north, became part of Austria as a result of a referendum. The much bigger western part, known as Primorska, became part of Italy as a result of the Rapallo Treaty. For Slovenians, this decision never meant anything except occupation. The population in Primorska, the region where three of the chapters in the book take place, suffered under the fascist regime from 1921 to 1943. This involved economic, social, and ideological measures that the Italian regime used to force the population to "become" Italian. When the measures stirred revolt, the answer was state brutality, forced migration, killings, imprisonments, and devastating tax policies. Among the population, the reaction was armed resistance and exodus. People left for Yugoslavia, Argentina, the United States, and Egypt; the latter destination was especially true for women. After World War II, most of the Primorska region returned to Slovenia, which became part of the socialist federation of Yugoslavia. Slovenia became an independent state in the process of the breakup of Yugoslavia in 1991.

Accurately determining how many people migrated from Slovenian territories is difficult. The reason is obvious: the statistics in countries of origin and in host countries usually used citizenship as the most important factor for defining migrants. In the period of mass migration, from the late nineteenth to the mid-twentieth century, Slovenians from different regions of the ethnic territory were citizens of many states: the Austro-Hungarian Empire, the Kingdom of Yugoslavia, Italy, Hungary, and the Republic of Yugoslavia. Between 1901 and 1910, the Austro-Hungarian Empire was ranked first in Europe by the number of immigrants to the United States. Slovenians were part of Slavic-speaking peoples from Central and Eastern Europe who formed "one of the largest and newest groups of immigrants at the turn of the century."[1] American immigration authorities put Slovenian and Croatian immigrants in the same category. For the period between 1889 and 1914, some 450,000 Slovenian and Croatian migrants were reported. The U.S. census included a category about mother tongue and thus provided more accurate numbers. In the 1910 census, around 183,000 people declared Slovenian as their mother tongue. Using this data, we can estimate that more than 250,000 Slovenians migrated to the United States during this time.

Slovenians were also leaving for Argentina and Brazil in South America as well as for other European countries. After World War I, the biggest emigration wave swept through Primorska, which was annexed to Italy. Between 1920 and 1940, fascist repression and poverty forced between sixty thousand and ninety thousand Slovenians to leave for Yugoslavia, Argentina, the United States, and other countries. In the interwar time of the Kingdom of Yugoslavia and after the restrictive American immigration legislation, Slovenians migrated to European countries such as France, Belgium, Germany, the Netherlands, and Switzerland.

In May 1945, approximately seventeen thousand Slovenians fled the country and were settled in refugee camps in Austria. Some of them collaborated with the German and Italian occupiers, some were afraid of communism or were against it, some were ordinary people or family members, and some were prewar politicians. Approximately five thousand migrated to the United States, while five thousand three hundred went to Argentina, three thousand went to Canada, and two thousand went to Australia. They were defined as displaced persons and later labeled as Slovenian political emigrants. From 1960 to 1975, Slovenians migrated mainly to Germany, Sweden, Switzerland, France, and England. After that the migration almost stopped, and Slovenia—like most European countries—changed from a land of emigration to a land of immigration.

The number of women migrants is even more difficult to determine. It is estimated that the share of women in Slovenian migration processes was approximately 38 percent. There were a few exclusively women migration flows that are also covered in this book. *Slamnikarice* ("straw hat makers") from the central part of Slovenia left mainly for New York and other big cities in the United States and Europe in the first decades of the twentieth century. They left as skilled workers for employment in hat-making factories as seasonal or permanent migrants. At the same time, women from villages in Goriška in the Primorska region were leaving for Egypt. They mostly worked as chambermaids and cooks as well as in various other kinds of domestic help, frequently as nannies and sometimes as governesses, teachers, and wet nurses. Since the most common destination of their migration was Alexandria, at home they were referred to as *aleksandrinke* ("Alexandrian women"), and under this name they remain recorded in the collective memory. Women left from all parts of the Slovenian ethnic territory as domestic workers, but chapter 4 in this book presents *dikle,* those domestic workers who left from Slavia Veneta to work in the big Italian cities. Women were leaving en masse for the United States in the period of European mass emigration. The first Slovenian women in the United States were farmers' wives who settled in central Minnesota in the decades after the American Civil War. Women arrived in greater numbers after 1890 and joined their husbands or sought employment in industrial cities and mining communities. Cleveland, Ohio, became the major Slovenian settlement. It is said that in 1909, nine Slovenians a day arrived in the city. Many among them were women.

Places of Arrival: Changing Identities

Going Places is the narrative of one century of women's migration from one country to multiple destinations, above all to the United

States but also to Egypt, Argentina, and Italy as well as other countries of Europe. In one of the few memoirs written by a Slovenian woman, Marie Prisland described her first impression of America upon arrival at Ellis Island in 1906:

> The day was warm and we were very thirsty. An English-speaking immigrant asked the near-by guard where we could get a drink of water. The guard withdrew and returned shortly with a pail of water, which he set before the group of women. Some men stepped forward quickly to have a drink, but the guard pushed them back saying: "Ladies first!" When the women learned what the guard had said, they were dumbfounded, for in Slovenia, as in all Europe, women always were second to men. Someone dramatically explained it this way: "First comes man, then a long time nothing, then comes the woman." Happy at the sudden turn of events, one elderly lady stepped forward, holding a dipper of water, and proposed this toast: "*Živjo Amerika, kjer so ženske prve!*" (Long live America, where women are first!).[2]

Slovenian immigrants are not often mentioned in the vast literature on American immigration history, and Slovenian women immigrants are paid even less attention. However, Maxine Seller quoted the story about Prisland's arrival to Ellis Island in her influential book, one of the first on women migrants. Seller quoted it at the very beginning of the introduction and added that "For Prisland, who later founded the Slovenian Women's Union of America and created a woman's magazine, *The Dawn*, the American dream became a reality. Not all immigrant women were so fortunate. For many, life in the United States was bitter and the slogan, 'ladies first,' cruelly ironic. 'Ladies' were first to be underpaid, unemployed, and abused."[3]

In general, when Slovenian women and men migrated, they all knew a lot about being underpaid, unemployed, and abused, and they didn't have time for anything but bare survival. However, they made their lives rich with cultural and social activities. Despite poverty, they established societal and social institutions that demanded immense financial input from every member of the community and work in their spare time. To preserve and develop these institutions, volunteer, continuous, and intensive work of the whole community was called for, spanning generations. Churches, schools, national homes, recreation centers, commercial buildings, banks, libraries and reading rooms, newspaper publishing houses, drama groups, choirs, recording studios, and music groups were created, developed, built up, and financed exclusively with the savings of poorly paid Slovenian migrants. Nevertheless, women's responsibilities, opportunities, roles, and experiences at work, at home, and in their communities were different from that of men. Many studies have discovered very much the same as Donna Gabaccia sums up in the following sentences:

> First as community activists and later as socializers of children and organizers of family and religious rituals, immigrant women reproduced and transformed cultural traditions through their labors. Men at first sought women's help in reproducing ethnicity but then abandoned it, leaving it increasingly to women and their domestic roles. It is scarcely surprising that women, more than men, continue to view ethnicity and their immigrant "roots" as an important influence on their lives.[4]

As Christiane Harzig argued, the role of women in this process was crucial: "Not only have women proven to be essential to the community-building process, migration itself has been seen as the terrain where gender relations are renegotiated."[5] These findings are relevant also for the Slovenian migrant women. Women's migration experiences changed their perspective of gender roles in the environment into which they moved and changed their attitudes toward gender roles back home. In addition, permanent or even temporary migration challenged their identities, professional status, parental relations, fashion statements, and the rules of behavior. *Going Places* brings several personal accounts and subjective interpretations about this complicated and dynamic process. They show how Slovenian women migrants were not always underpaid or abused and instead were extremely well paid and were also respected, self-confident, ambitious, and resourceful.

Going Places begins with a young elegantly dressed woman on a transatlantic steamer writing home about her travel to the new world in the 1930s. The book ends with equally elegantly dressed professionals in today's European Union offices sharing their experiences on the virtual universe of the World Wide Web. In between, we meet elegantly dressed nannies in the cosmopolitan Egyptian cities, women entrepreneurs in the straw hat industry, knowledgeable maids in Italian cities, and strong wives and mothers at home taking care of the farms and the families.

From Transnational Emotions to Emancipatory Ambitions

Slovenian women migrants put their personal experiences in many forms of writing: mostly in letters written to family members; often in personal diaries and more seldom in memoirs, and finally in the form of storytelling to the researchers who have only recently become interested in the subjective experiences of the migration process of those who left and of those who stayed.[6] This book tries to assemble all of them in a "human-centered approach," as Dirk Hoerder calls it. He explains the methodological approach that takes into account the economic, cultural, social, and emotional complexity and conditioning of migration decisions and their consequences in the place of origin as well as the place of migration as a "holistic material-emotional approach." Such an approach is extremely important when dealing with women's migrations, because we can use it to argue the widespread popular and academic discourse of women's passive position. With the holistic material-emotional approach, we take into account all the individuals in this migration phenomenon as actors in the process of decision making and the consequences: "Decisions about life-courses, levels of subsistence, and aspirations for betterment involve a conglomerate of traditional cultural norms and practices, of actual emotional and spiritual needs, and of economic rationales," emphasizes Hoerder.[7]

In this sense, the chapters of this book present the infinite series of emotions that decisions of migration triggered. In those who left and in those who stayed, we can follow the life flows of the feelings of loss, abandonment, homesickness, missing, loneliness, alienation, expectations, anger, despair, resentment, and incomprehension but also the feelings of happiness, independence, freedom, achievement, and fulfillment. The holistic material-emotional approach used by the contributors in *Going Places* forces us not to miss anyone in the intertwining of the actors in the migration phenomenon. All of the chapters reveal the contradictions, ambiguities, and complexities of everyday decisions in a dynamic social context of migration. Individual and family decisions, cultural choices, and social experiences are mirrored in each analysis, thus revealing to us the complex picture of Slovenian migration.

The intertwining of the migration actors is presented in chapter 1, where Pepica has the leading role in the seven decades of correspondence of a transnational family that ended only with her death. In addition, her two migrant brothers wrote emotional letters and cared for the family ties across the ocean for as long as they lived, just as much as she did. The analysis of the Udovič-Valenčič-Hrvatin family correspondence is a gendered research in which male and female members of the family provide a comprehensive account of the migration experience of those who stayed and those who left in the complicated social and political context of changing times, borders, homes, and identities. The family correspondence is an important source for understanding migration, because it reveals the subjective reality and intimate experiences of all participants in the migration process as well as their descendants. The collections contain hundreds of letters, postcards, greeting cards, and numerous references to packages that became part of the correspondence in the decades after 1945. All of the mentioned mail traveled between Jelšane, a village in Primorska, Slovenia; Cleveland, Ohio, in the United States; and Buenos Aires, the capital of Argentina.

After reviewing extensive archives of migrant correspondences, Bruce Elliot, David Gerber, and Suzanne Sinke found that "rarely do we have access to both sides of a cycle of correspondence" and that most often we listen to one side of the conversation only, as in migrant correspondence when most often only letters from one side are preserved.[8] In this sense, the correspondence of the Udovič-Valenčič-Hrvatin family is an exceptional source for studying migration: it is extensive in the number of letters and the number of persons taking part in it, and it includes correspondents on three sides.

However, in the case of Francka's letters, presented in chapter 2 by Marjan Drnovšek, we do listen to one side of the conversation only. The bunch of sixty-one letters was acquired at a flea market in Ljubljana many decades after they were posted. During a short period of less than a year from 1929 to 1930, Francka sent them from a village in Slovenia to several places in the Netherlands, where her husband worked as a miner. Here, the author draws attention to the importance of the correspondence of migrants, which reveals what only the eyes of the addressees were supposed to see: the intimate and deeply personal portrait of how the main actors perceived their fates. It is only this intimate perspective that opens the depth of the unknown, the rarely heard, and the seldom seen, which must be handled and presented sensitively and ethically.

Through a family's correspondence we gain a precise insight into a subjective migration process that most studies of migration—historical and sociological—have long excluded. Until recently, the main type of global women migrations—the waged domestic work—was also totally excluded from migration studies and historiography. This is all the more unusual given that waged domestic workers "form the largest single female category of migrant labor, not only in the twentieth and twenty-first century but in fact throughout the history of migration. This is accounted for by economic restructuring processes (mainly agrarian and in the textile industry), by an uneven distribution of wealth between regions and nations, and by changes in the international division of labor."⁹ The reason for the invisibility of the female migrants and their specific work, which is globally expanded and true for the past and the present, is well defined by Sheila Rowbotham:

> One reason for the lack of visibility has been the nature of female migrants' occupation. In many cases they went into domestic service or served as wet nurses—activities which have never been regarded within the prevailing definitions of "work" or the "economy" and have thus defied statistical reckoning. This is a gendered obscurity in a double sense. The women leave no traces because they are female and because the framework of who is to be seen has been biased towards the male.¹⁰

This gendered obscurity is especially relevant for the women headed south from the villages in the Goriška region to the port of Alexandria in Egypt. In chapter 3, Daša Koprivec describes how these women, the aleksandrinke, started a female economic migration to Egypt that spanned almost a century until the 1950s. In Alexandria and Cairo, most of them worked as maids for the affluent bourgeoisie. Some aleksandrinke established independent businesses; some fell in love and married into local families. They left villages in the Goriška region that were not only poor but were also destroyed by World War I and where they only knew how to work the farm and raise children. They came to big metropolises, where they shed their rural identity, adopted an urban style in clothes and table manners, discovered the theater and movies, and experienced the self-confidence of economic independence. When they left, most of them spoke Slovenian and Italian; in Cairo and Alexandria, they learned English, French, and Arabic. Some of them were young mothers who left their children in the care of their husbands, relatives, friends, or neighbors. Some left to breast-feed children of affluent families and sent the money they earned to their husbands to pay the mortgage on the farm. Some stayed as nannies or maids or made it as companions to members of the Egyptian royal families.

As painful as the experience of leaving their offspring was, it was much more painful to return home changed, educated, and experienced. The places to where these women returned were just as conservative and rigid as when they left. The huge sums of money that they had sent home to keep and expand the family propriety were forgotten. On their return, they were often rejected, vilified, and denigrated as fallen women. They were obliged to hide their emancipation and store their city clothes in mothballs, together with their new identities.

In the case of aleksandrinke, the human-centered approach is even more relevant because the phenomenon is so diversified. When we try to understand its material-emotional aspects, we must make a distinction between the women who worked as nannies or wet nurses and the women who did other types of work. We cannot treat single women and those who were married and mothers in the same way. When it comes to children, chapter 3 presents stirring stories of truly abandoned children whom nobody cared for but also testimonies of childhoods that were a lot less dramatic. Some men accepted their wives' absence without any problems, while others had more difficulties. And then there are the testimonies of children cared for by the aleksandrinke that describe how aleksandrinke marked their lives and identities.

Within the female migration, aleksandrinke are a totally specific phenomenon because of the nature of their work. No other form of female migration cut so painfully into gender relationships, family relationships, children's memories, and the collective memory and thus produced interpretations that were emotionally charged, completely opposing, and controversial. Migration studies in Slovenia have only in recent years begun paying more attention to the phenomenon, because it was only recently that female migrants even became the subject of research.

This is also the point in chapter 4, where Jernej Mlekuž describes similar experiences of young women who left the most western part of the Slovenian ethnic territory in the Friuli-Venezia Giulia to work as dikle, or housemaids, in the big Italian cities in order to earn enough money for a dowry and the beginning of married life. As the author notes—and it is relevant also for aleksandrinke—the voice of authority and the public in general has always been and continues to be the voice of contempt. Women domestic labor migrants met with the condemning voice of the Catholic Church, political leaders, writers and poets, and all other important opinion makers in the wider society. To come back to the poor villages, where there was such patriarchal control and orchestrated contempt, was often harder than the work in the comfortable houses of well-off families, where these women were maids and servants but got used to the telephone, electric appliances, and chic clothes and, even more important, got used to earning money and having a sense of freedom.

In the last part of the book, the stage is set for another complex drama of migration that deconstructs the simple perception of division between male and female, the modern and the traditional, the urban and the rural, domestic and foreign, and possibilities and obstacles. By the hundreds, slamnikarice left a small town in central Slovenia to make straw hats in Manhattan hat factories and in several cities of the huge Austro-Hungarian Empire. They left as skilled workers and not necessarily for economic reasons. As Saša Roškar writes in chapter 5, we are rediscovering the stories about the search by young women for better incomes and economic independence. They left because money was better in other countries but also because they wanted to learn languages or improve their education or because they could not resist the invitations of relatives who left before them. The testimonies that Roškar collected show that the treatment of these women migrants was much better abroad than at home. This positive treatment was a common experience of almost all Slovenian women migrants, regardless of their destinations. It is an important revelation that Slovenian women who migrated to America, Italian and Egyptian cities, European countries, and other destinations experienced respect and dignity that they did not experience at home. No matter how difficult it sometimes was to live and work as migrants for economic and emotional reasons, most of the women migrants in the past felt the condemnation and the burden of the patriarchal gender role when they returned home.

This type of condemnation recently disappeared from the public discourse in Slovenia as the role of the Catholic Church diminished and as the country changed from a country of emigration to a country of immigration. Chapter 6 shows a completely different situation and a stark contrast to the migration context of the past. The possibility for young female professionals to move to Brussels is described by Tatiana Bajuk Senčar, who uses Slovenian women's words to portray their own contemporary migration. Slovenia became a member of the European Union in 2004, and most of the women to whom she has spoken started their migration career sometime after that. While a fair number of the women explained that upon looking back they felt as if they wound up in Brussels by chance, their presence in the capital of the European Union can be understood as the result of certain experiences and social connections. Despite the great heterogeneity among the women narrators, one of the things that linked them together was that each of them had a European story before they set out to Brussels, be it in terms of previous travels, previous academic or professional experience, or previous contacts. Chapter 6 illustrates the dynamic history of Slovenian female migration in one century—from straw hat makers, picture brides, maids, servants, and nannies to the Eurocrats—with the similarities of the migration process, which includes social networks, professional experiences, contacts, and courage.

This is one of the most fundamental findings of this book, which mirrors findings of other researchers of global women migrations in the past and in the present: the only common trait of the women within these heterogeneous female migration waves is that they cannot be considered passive victims of the circumstances but instead are active decision makers regarding the options in their lives and in great part also the lives of their families. Although we can still encounter circumstances in which we cannot see positive changes to the position of women,[11] we do, on the other hand, see many situations in which female migrants gained power, influence, and autonomy over their own bodies, work, income, and, above all, freedom that they could not fathom in their country of origin.[12]

A key characteristic discovered by the research of the migration processes as gendered processes in the past and in the present is a fundamental law that says that migration transforms gender roles; migration reorganizes and reconstructs them. In the past, like today, migration gave women variability in roles compared to those they had in places from where they migrated. This is particularly true for migrations into the United States and Egypt. This thinking puts us in the center of the research of the migrant experience of women as an experience of losing, transforming, changing, and rebuilding personal, ethnic, and gender identities. This position is of particular relevance, because it reveals the context of migration as characteristically complex, dynamic, and complicated. Different societies and countries (emigrant and immigrant) are included in these migrations; within them are branched and spread-out transnational family, kinship, and friendship ties. These societies and countries thus represent crossroads of different cultures and religions. This book brings narratives that are each a biographic story of identity under construction, a process of narrating experiences that form that identity. Every identity surpasses what we call ethnic, national identity or belonging and at the same time contains different combinations of its elements in different periods of the narrators' lives. In the dynamic course of life, these elements—preserved, lost, regained—are tied together by memory imbued with transnational emotions. In this way, the book reveals a compelling story of women migrants that is still unfolding around the globe today.

Notes

1. Donna Gabaccia, *Immigration and American Diversity: A Social and Cultural History* (Oxford, UK: Blackwell, 2002), 142.

2. Marie Prisland, *From Slovenia to America: Recollections and Collections* (Chicago: Slovenian Women's Union of America, 1968), 19.

3. Maxine S. Seller, *Immigrant Women* (Albany: SUNY Press, 1994), 2.

4. Donna Gabaccia, *From the Other Side: Women, Gender, and Immigrant Life in the U.S., 1820–1990* (Bloomington and Indianapolis: Indiana University Press, 1994), 131.

5. Christiane Harzig, "Women Migrants as Global and Local Agents: New Research Strategies on Gender and Migration," in *Women, Gender and Labour Migration: Historical and Global Perspectives*, edited by Pamela Sharpe (London: Routledge, 2001), 21.

6. For migrant women's memoirs, see Betty Bergland, "Ideology, Ethnicity, and the Gendered Subject: Reading Immigrant Women's Autobiographies," in *Seeking Common Ground: Multidisciplinary Studies of Immigrant Women in the United States*, edited by D. Gabaccia (Westport, CT: Praeger, 1992), 101–22. For storytelling as oral history methodology, see Alessandro Portelli, *The Death of Luigi Trastulli and Other Stories: Form and Meaning in Oral History* (New York: SUNY Press, 1991).

7. Dirk Hoerder, *Cultures in Contact: World Migration in the Second Millennium* (Durham, NC: Duke University Press, 2002), 20.

8. Bruce S. Elliot, David A. Gerber, and Suzanne M. Sinke, eds., *Letters across Borders: The Epistolary Practices of International Migrants* (New York: Palgrave Macmillan, 2006), 3.

9. Christiane Harzig, "Domestics of the World (Unite?): Labor Migration Systems and Personal Trajectories of Household Workers in Historical and Global Perspective," *Journal of American Ethnic History* 25 (2006): 48.

10. Sheila Rowbotham, "Foreword," in *Women, Gender and Labour Migration, Historical and Global Perspectives*, edited by Pamela Sharpe (London: Routledge, 2001), xvi.

11. For many cases of such circumstances, see Barbara Ehrenreich and Arlie Russel Hochschild, eds., *Global Woman: Nannies, Maids, and Sex Workers in the New Economy* (New York: Henry Holt, 2002).

12. See Floya Anthias and Gabriella Lazaridis, eds., *Gender and Migration in Southern Europe: Women on the Move* (Oxford, UK: Berg, 2000); Tamar Diana

Wilson, *Women's Migration Networks in Mexico and Beyond* (Albuquerque: University of New Mexico Press, 2009); and Luisa Passerini et al., eds., *Women Migrants from East to West: Gender, Mobility and Belonging in Contemporary Europe* (New York: Berghahn Books, 2010).

References

Anthias, Floya, and Gabriella Lazaridis, eds. *Gender and Migration in Southern Europe: Women on the Move*. Oxford, UK: Berg, 2000.

Bergland, Betty. "Ideology, Ethnicity, and the Gendered Subject: Reading Immigrant Women's Autobiographies." In *Seeking Common Ground: Multidisciplinary Studies of Immigrant Women in the United States*, edited by Donna Gabaccia, 101–22. Westport, CT: Praeger, 1992.

Ehrenreich, Barbara, and Arlie Russel Hochschild, eds. *Global Woman: Nannies, Maids, and Sex Workers in the New Economy*. New York: Henry Holt, 2002.

Gabaccia, Donna. *From the Other Side: Women, Gender, and Immigrant Life in the U.S., 1820–1990*. Bloomington: Indiana University Press, 1994.

———. *Immigration and American Diversity: A Social and Cultural History*. Oxford, UK: Blackwell, 2002.

———, ed. *Seeking Common Ground: Multidisciplinary Studies of Immigrant Women in the United States*. Westport, CT: Praeger, 1992.

Harzig, Christiane. "Domestics of the World (Unite?): Labor Migration Systems and Personal Trajectories of Household Workers in Historical and Global Perspective." *Journal of American Ethnic History* 25 (2006): 48–73.

———. "Women Migrants as Global and Local Agents: New Research Strategies on Gender and Migration." In *Women, Gender and Labour Migration: Historical and Global Perspectives*, edited by Pamela Sharpe, 15–28. London: Routledge, 2001.

Hoerder, Dirk. *Cultures in Contact: World Migration in the Second Millennium*. Durham, NC: Duke University Press, 2002.

Passerini, Luisa, Dawn Lyon, Enrica Capussotti, and Ioanna Lalioutou, eds. *Women Migrants from East to West: Gender, Mobility and Belonging in Contemporary Europe.* New York: Berghahn Books, 2010.

Portelli, Alessandro. *The Death of Luigi Trastulli and Other Stories: Form and Meaning in Oral History.* New York: SUNY Press, 1991.

Prisland, Marie. *From Slovenia to America: Recollections and Collections.* Chicago: Slovenian Women's Union of America, 1968.

Rowbotham, Sheila. "Foreword." In *Women, Gender and Labour Migration: Historical and Global Perspectives,* edited by Pamela Sharpe, xvi–xvii. London: Routledge, 2001.

Seller Schwartz, Maxine, ed. *Immigrant Women.* Albany: SUNY Press, 1994.

Sharpe, Pamela, ed. *Women, Gender and Labour Migration: Historical and Global Perspectives.* London: Routledge, 2001.

Wilson, Tamar Diana. *Women's Migration Networks in Mexico and Beyond.* Albuquerque: University of New Mexico Press, 2009.

I | Transnational Emotions
Those Who Left and Those Who Stayed

Chapter 1

A Slovenian Bride in Cleveland
Emotions in Letters

Mirjam Milharčič Hladnik

At noon on Tuesday, November 25, 1930, a young couple disembarked from the steamboat *Saturnia* to Ellis Island. They were elegant, dressed in the latest fashion. The man was relaxed and self-confident, while the woman was obviously facing New York skyscrapers for the first time. He was an American citizen, and she was an Italian, both Slovenians from the same cluster of villages from the Primorska region in Slovenia and recently married. They met in the beginning of the summer and were married as soon as the season of cutting grass in their villages, located a stone's throw from each other, was finished. They were on the way to his home in the steel town of Cleveland, Ohio. The man was taking care of the final details necessary to enter the United States; the woman was holding on to a letter in her pocket, written on a piece of paper imprinted with the crest of the ship. The letter finished with the following words:

> Today on Tuesday the 25th at noon we got off the steamboat.
> Farewell
> I will end for now and send you more from the city.
> I greet you heartily and kiss you all in spirit, you, dear Mother, and you, Ivan,

Don't forget us,
Yours, Pepica and Josip Valencich

Dearest Mother!
Please do not cry and mourn for me, be consoled![1]

The letter was addressed to the Udovič family from the village of Jelšane and marks the beginning of the correspondence and routes of passage, the subject of the analysis in this chapter. The correspondence of the Udovič-Hrvatin-Valencic family is an important source for understanding migration, because it reveals the subjective reality and intimate experiences of all participants in the migration process—those who left and those who stayed at home as well as their descendants. As a source, the correspondence is exceptional not only in its contents but also in its scope and structure.[2] The collections contain hundreds of letters, postcards, and greeting cards and numerous references to packages that became a part of the correspondence in the decades after 1945. All the mentioned mail traveled between Jelšane, a village in Primorska, Slovenia; Cleveland, Ohio, in the United States; and Buenos Aires, the capital of Argentina. The senders and the addressees changed over time. Although the protagonists in this chapter are the mother Helena and her four children Jože, Tone, Pepica, and Ivan, the main focus is on the only daughter and sister, Pepica.[3]

The key to reading the family correspondence is the life story of Pepica's routes of passage—her values, emotions, ambitions, and fears. The routes of passage are without beginning or end, although they are marked with dates and place-names. They are a state, not a path; they are a constant, not a goal. The phrase "routes of passage" describes a migrant's dynamic life: she lived her own life as a person with more than one identity, home, and homeland—in several languages and social milieus—without exchanging, repudiating, or leaving behind any of them. She lived in them and among them, sometimes physically present, sometimes only in thought and emotions, never negligent or one-dimensional, never only there or only here, always in transit. We shall follow her routes of passage through letters but also through the narration of her children in Cleveland and the written testimonies of her niece in Jelšane.

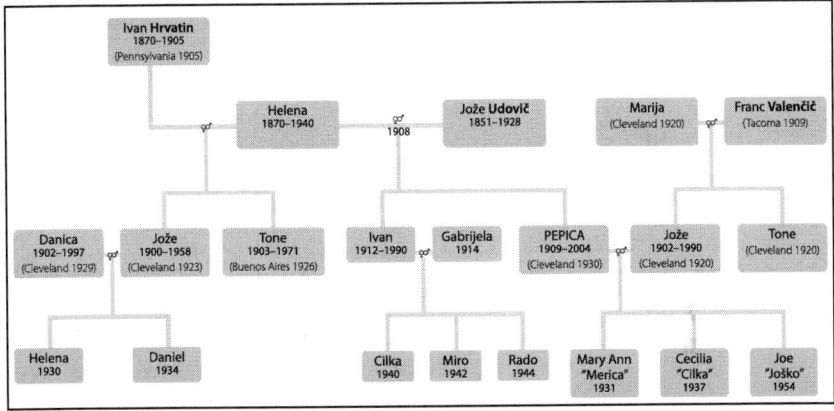

Figure 1. The Udovič-Hrvatin-Valencic family tree. *Image by Mateja Rihteršič*

Those Who Left and Those Who Stayed

The preserved family correspondence was created over a long period of time. Pepica wrote to her mother Helena from 1930 until the mother's death in 1940, to her brother Tone in Argentina until his death in 1971, to her brother Ivan until his death in 1990, and to his wife Elka and their daughter Cilka, her niece, until her own death in 2004. The correspondence of her brother Jože, who also lived in Cleveland, went on between Cleveland, Jelšane, and Buenos Aires until his death in 1958. If we also consider the correspondence between the siblings' descendants, then the family correspondence between Jelšane and the Americas has been continuous since 1923, when Jože settled in Cleveland.

In the studied correspondence, not only do decades and people move across the ocean and letters and packages move in time and space, but the borders of the territory from where they all originate move as well.

In 1905, Helena's first husband Ivan Hrvatin migrated to America from the village of Brgud near Jelšane and died as an Austro-Hungarian citizen in a Pennsylvanian mine mere months later. The two sons from her first marriage, who were adopted by her second husband Jože Udovič, migrated as Italian citizens: Jože Hrvatin in 1923 to the United States and Tone Hrvatin three years later to Argentina. In Cleveland, Helena's son Jože lodged with the Valencic family and became friends with their son, who was also named Jože. Jože Valencic's father had migrated to America from the village of Novokračine near Jelšane in 1909 as a citizen of the Austro-Hungarian monarchy; when his wife and two sons joined him eleven years later, they were Italian citizens. When the young Jože Valencic fell in love with Pepica, seen in the photo that the beautiful sister had sent in a letter to her brother Jože, he was an American citizen, and his last name was Valencich. This was the family name that Pepica received at the end of the summer of 1930 when she married the young man from the neighboring village of Novokračine who was already an American citizen living in Cleveland. When thirty years later she visited Jelšane for the first and only time, she was Josephine, an American citizen visiting Yugoslavia. Just over thirty years later, her son Joe Valencic—the "h" having gotten lost somewhere in time and space—visited Jelšane in the new country of Slovenia, and the village was now an international border crossing between Slovenia and the equally new country of Croatia.

The decades and the people across the ocean and the letters and packages in the time and space are connected by borderless and timeless emotions. When Tone received the news that his sister had gotten married and moved to America in 1930, he wrote from Avellaneda,[4] Argentina:

> We're all complaining how badly we're doing, and I also have nothing to raise ever since I got to this damned Buenos Aires, I am every time worse.... I thought I would send something for Easter, but it looks like I won't be able to. One expects something better, but things continue to go worse, so there's no more life for the poor man. So the separation was difficult for you and mother, oh, I know it was, but what can we do, fate has dispersed us into the wide unknown world.[5]

Figure 2. The newlyweds before leaving for America. *Courtesy of Joe Valencic*

Brother Jože informed the newlywed sister that they were expecting her in Cleveland and tried to console their mother before Pepica's departure:

> Dear Mother! Do not cry too much for Pepica, it could do you harm. I know it is hard for you to lose your only daughter, but may the fact that she got herself a good husband from a good family console you. I know very well that she's always with you in spirit. Maybe she will help you more than she would if she married around there. I am calling out to you again, be consoled. Please receive greetings and warm kisses from your son Josip[6]

After her second husband's death and the departure of her three children into the "wide unknown world," mother Helena remained

Figure 3. Pepica with mother Helena in 1928.
Courtesy of Cilka Udovič

in Jelšane alone with her youngest son Ivan.[7] Everybody was worried that the departure of the only daughter would take a toll on her health. She worried about preserving the farm, about her son's life because he was a military conscript, and about how her children were living around the world. Were they happy, content, well off? A couple of years after her daughter's departure, Helena wrote from Jelšane:

> I still cannot get used to being without you, my daughter. Mostly on Sundays, everything is wrong and everything is empty, dreary and sad, and I remember how it used to be and I cry my eyes out. How easy it was when we could talk about everything, but now I have no one to talk to.[8]

In the mid-1930s Pepica wrote to her brother Ivan, who was drafted into the Italian Army as Giovanni Udovic:⁹

> Your precious letter arrived a couple of days ago. Thank you so very much! But for me it was most sad, today it is the fourth day and my eyes haven't dried yet. Night and day I have you and mother in front of them. Tears keep flowing and I mustn't even think. Even without that my heart is weak and sensitive, and after receiving such a sad message from you, I'm now feeling quite ill. Why, why has fate torn us away from the motherland and forced us to struggle in a foreign world that knows no mercy. Ivan, I see all your pain, I feel what you had to go through when you were separated from the beloved homeland and dear mother and go into the unknown, this is the worst for you and the most grievous stroke that you suffer on your body and your soul.¹⁰

The common thread through all the letters, visible through all the decades despite great distances, remains the strong emotions of love and attachment among family members. The correspondence shows people who played active and dynamic roles in deliberating and making decisions to migrate. In addition, the correspondence shows their modes of adjustment and learning in the new environment, their perseverance, and the strengthening of the social network and the firm family bonds in the old and new milieus. These people live in both worlds, on both sides of the Atlantic, in the old place and the new home. Physically separated, they think of each other, take care of each other, argue, apologize, mourn, regret, love, and work with the thought of their social and family environments here and there. It is clear from the correspondence that the thoughts and emotions are intense, that worries and grudges are earnest, and that lives in fact are subordinated to the needs and ambitions on three sides of the Atlantic. In 1940 Jože sent the following words to his brother Ivan upon learning of their mother's death:

> Fate is cruel! The sadness is bitter! Dearest Mother is no longer with us and never will be again. You have remained orphans and alone, but we, other orphans, have not seen mummy for many

years. Cruel destiny has ripped us from the loving embrace of our most beloved mummy and has thrown us into the cold world. As if one were damned. I know mother cried for us when she stayed almost alone, poor thing. And when you, too, went into this wretched world, I knew her days were ending. When I read that before her death she once more looked at our photos and blessed us all, I cried like a child.[11]

It isn't surprising that the emotional confessions were powerful when mother Helena was still alive, but we could be inclined to ascribe such writing to female members of the family. As we see, the letters surprise us in both our assumptions. The brothers, especially Jože, are just as sincere when expressing emotions as their mother and sister. Besides, the intensity of emotions doesn't decrease with years and in fact is quite the opposite, as we shall see in the extracts. Even after more than thirty years, the letters are still filled with moving memories. In 1953 Jože remembers the anniversary of his departure from home in a letter to his brother Ivan:

Today it has been 30 years since I first left our home, and 24 since I and my Danica bade farewell from all of you, still so dear to me. On such anniversaries I'm still with you in spirit. Every corner of the house, every path, and everything beautiful is still in front of my eyes. These are the memories of the wonderful days of our youth. I shall never forget them. It was beautiful back when dearest mother took care of me, waited when I'd come home and God forbid I'd go hungry. She put a sausage (if only she had one) into a *prhanka* [embers] and baked it and left me a sign that something good was waiting for me. Today, when I could return favors, she's no longer here! May she rest in peace. Our brother Tone wrote me a long time ago, I don't know if he writes to you, I wrote him yesterday, I'm worried about him.[12]

This letter is an example of how those who left and those who stayed kept the bonds through time and space and even through periods of total collapse of communication. Such a collapse occurred in the Udovič-Valencic-Hrvatin family correspondence during World War

II, when not even one letter was exchanged in four years. The time after World War II, when expressions of love and care in letters were supplemented by sending packages to Jelšane, increases the intensity of these decade-long transatlantic relationships. Before I present the mode of communication after 1945, I must introduce the methodological and analytical contexts of studying the epistolary migrant practices and the first decade of Pepica's life in the land of promise.

The Writing Practices of Migrants

Samuel Baily and Franco Ramella, who have published selected correspondence of an Italian migrant family, claim that personal letters are key documents for understanding the subjective reality and social organization of migrants. To understand migrant experience, we must have an insight into the material that represents a subjective perspective of active individuals in a dynamic that is complex and certainly not linear. Baily and Ramella list certain questions that are of special interest in studying subjective processes of migration:

> Why do the individual actors in this great drama decide to migrate when many or even most of the inhabitants from their hometowns do not? How do they choose the destination? How do they find a place to live, a job, and friends? How do they interact with each other and the members of the host society? How do they change as a result of their participation in the migration process? What happens to their traditional culture, their family and village ties, and their personal beliefs and aspirations over time?[13]

Through a family correspondence, we get a precise insight into a subjective migration process that most studies of migration—historical and sociological—have long excluded. Of course, we have to consider the historical, sociological, economic, and political context. For the migration dynamics of the Udovič-Valencic-Hrvatin family, this context is the time after World War I: the war years further deepened the poverty and lack of perspectives for the Jelšane area, which then fell victim to the Italian fascist politics.

Figures 4, 5, and 6. Those who left: Tone, Pepica, and Jože. *Courtesy of Cilka Udovič and Joe Valencic*

However, the mentioned data only become dramatically clear when the experiences of the migration process unfold in those who left and those who stayed, documented in letters, packages, and money orders. Possibilities are opened for a series of questions linked to individuals, especially family members who remained at home and are still also a part of the migrant experience. What does the departure of family members mean to those who stay? How do they organize their lives, how do they fill in the gaps that are left behind, and who helps them with work? How do they retain ties and friendships with those who left? For those who stay, what is their status in the narrow community now that they have migrants in the family? What village bonds do they maintain? How are their personal convictions, strivings, and emotions altered? Nowhere else can we discover the wealth of experience, emotions, suffering, joy, and satisfaction quite as precisely as we can in their own words.

Marta Verginella says that epistolary sources, along with journals and memoirs, became "valuable warehouses of individual memory" when three decades ago the attention of historians and other researchers turned to the individual and her or his emotions in different social environments:

And if at first the relevance of autobiographic sources was obvious particularly when conveying subjective material, social and cultural dimensions of the past, later their ability of conveying the experience became more prominent: experience and emotions of individuals—especially those who didn't excel in shaping politically relevant history, but were its marginal actors and consorts of its most important events.[14]

Bruce Elliot, David Gerber, and Suzanne Sinke edited a relevant anthology on migrants' epistolary practices and named a number of problems with analyzing correspondences in the introduction. After reviewing extensive archives of migrant correspondences, which in some countries are neatly archived,[15] they find that "rarely do we have access to both sides of a cycle of correspondence" and that most often we listen to one side of the conversation only because in migrant correspondence, most often only letters from one side are preserved.[16] The correspondence of the Udovič-Valencic-Hrvatin family is in this sense an exceptional source for studying migration because it is extensive in the number of letters and the number of persons taking part in it and also because of the time frame in which it was conducted. The collections include three sides of correspondents, which is extremely rare and valuable.

The next problem that Elliot, Gerber, and Sinke mention is that we never know how complete the collections of letters are, even where they exist and are archived. This is understandably true for any correspondence, including the one presented here: the family correspondence spanning more than eight decades is not preserved and accessible in its entirety. This is especially true for the part belonging to the brother in Argentina who had no family to save the letters. However, during my research, I had access to the majority of the letters in Jelšane and the letters that Pepica had received in Cleveland.

Elliot, Gerber, and Sinke also say that it is often difficult to understand what the writers want to say, especially when they are uneducated and write in dialect. This is certainly not the case for the writ-

Figure 7. The one who stayed: Ivan as an Italian soldier, Giovanni Udovic, in 1935. *Courtesy of Cilka Udovič*

ers of the studied letters of the Udovič-Valencic-Hrvatin family. Although they weren't educated and they wrote in dialect, usually without punctuation, their expressiveness, clarity, and intelligibility are outstanding. This is particularly surprising when we consider that they were always tired and sleepy when writing, as they made time for writing only when the long workday was over. As we shall see from the sections of the letters quoted, for Jože, who kept an inn, this meant at three or four o'clock in the morning and for Pepica after midnight.

When using migrant correspondence in research, we need to consider how representative particular correspondence is for the general migrant experience and how accurate or verifiable the facts stated in the letters are. Since the letters are most often personal and intimate, the last consideration is often unnecessary, because their value lies precisely in the correspondents' personal perception and emotions. Even more, we need to know that any historic source that originates in human perception is subjective and that both oral history and the correspondence analysis clearly and unambiguously remind us of that. It is also perfectly clear that letters cannot be read as necessarily unbiased, true, and sincere testimonies of thoughts and emotions of the signatory. A letter is always socially contextualized and "shaped by the writer to meet the expectations of its envisaged recipient, whether a political enemy or a political friend, or a lover, or perhaps even the tax inspector."[17] As for correspondence being representative, we must consider that generalization is possible when we have the possibility of analyzing more migrants' correspondences and compare what we have available with the extensive corpus of similar research available in Europe and elsewhere. In any case, migrant correspondence is central to studying migrations as well as to understanding solidarity and bonds and to comprehending the experiences and emotions of individual migrants presented in their own words.

In this way, the migration experiences of nameless crowds are finally being structured into concrete individual and family stories, while the theory and history of migrations are gaining invaluable insight into subjective realities and migrants' social organizations. Besides that, these sources allow us to veer from the established view of migrants as a homogenous group determined by ethnic and class belonging. We are thus able to sharpen our perspective and view the migrants as individuals with completely different reactions to their one common circumstance: the new economic and social order they are facing. As John Bodnar emphasizes and as we shall see in detail in the description of Pepica's arrival in Cleveland, the migrants

> were not clinging together as clusters of aliens or workers but were, in fact, badly fragmented into numerous enclaves arranged by internal status levels, ideology, and orientation. The important implication of group fragmentation is that the real dynamic which explained immigrant adjustment was not simply at the nexus of immigrant and American culture or at the point where foreign-born workers met industrial managers, but it was at all the points where immigrant families met the challenges of capitalism and modernity: the homeland, the neighborhood, the school, the workplace, the church, the family, and the fraternal hall.[18]

In recent decades, research in migration has expanded from countries of immigration to countries of emigration. This expansion complements the perspective of the migration researchers from various social and humanistic fields and enriches their results. Thus, for example, as Bailey emphasizes, historians see

> a more complex, dynamic, and open-ended process that began in the village of origin and continued outward with migration, incorporation into the host society, and sociocultural adjustment. They no longer assume a single outcome such as assimilation, the termination of the process after any given period of time, or the inevitability or irreversibility of specific patterns of interaction. Economic, social, and political structures—as well as the cultures of the villages of origin—become an essential part of the explanation of what happened to individuals abroad. The sending and receiving communities are conceptually linked in a framework of analysis that enables these scholars to explore the simultaneous influence of cultural persistence and change.[19]

In this chapter I show how useful the analytical combination of correspondences and life stories is for the understanding of the conceptual connections between the communities that are sending and communities that are receiving. This allows wide insight into individual migrant experiences from different perspectives: we no longer see migrants as a group of foreigners in an unknown land, defined by their ethnicity and work capability, but instead we see them as individuals who in different circumstances take different personal decisions and achieve different successes in life. Migrant correspondence and oral history turn out to be indispensable sources of relevant information about the intimate perception of the new world and the old place.[20]

The correspondence generally has the same characteristic as narration. Maybe there is no other form of communication in which we would be this acutely aware of the addressees and their expectations as we imagine them, as is the case with letter writing. Paul Thompson

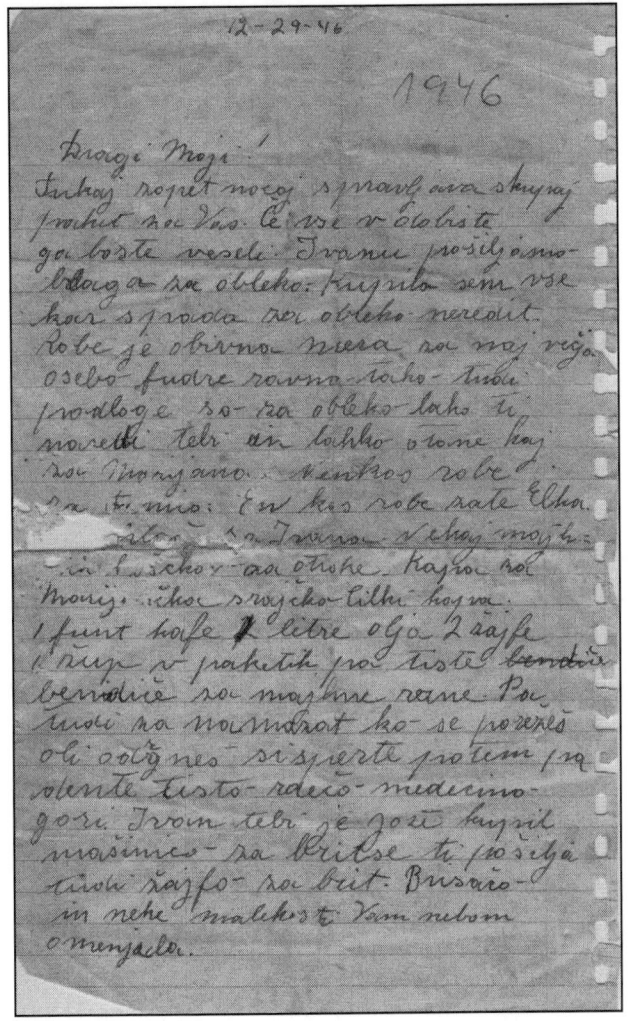

Figure 8. A letter from Pepica to Ivan's family. *Courtesy of Cilka Udovič*

emphasizes that letters are undoubtedly original communication, but this doesn't mean that they are unbiased and show the truth or the actual emotions of the senders. "They are in fact subject to the kinds of social influence which have been observed in interviews, but in an exaggerated form, because a letter is rarely written to a recipient who is attempting to be neutral like an interviewer."[21]

Time plays a special role in this, as there is a time lapse between a letter sent and a letter received, and this can result in an especially dramatic plot. This is what Solveig Zempel, a researcher and collector of Norwegian migrant correspondences, says. She claims that the stories told in letters are characterized by fragmentation:

> By their very existence, letters indicate a separation in time and space between sender and receiver, though at the same time they represent the effort of the sender to bridge that gulf. Fragmentation is inherent in the letter form as well, with long gaps in time between events and the reporting of them, between the sending of a letter and the receiving of a reply.[22]

As we shall see in Francka's letters to her husband in the next chapter, the time between the letter or package sent and the reply received was the most dramatic experience of the senders from Cleveland. This is why the letters so convincingly reveal the complexity, complicatedness, and controversy in constituting the interpersonal relationships and identities of the correspondents. This is undoubtedly a specific analytical problem that David Gerber calls "epistolary masquerade" and describes as a problem of silence and untruths. He stresses that

> immigrant letters are not principally about documenting the world, but instead about reconfiguring a personal relationship rendered vulnerable by long-distance, long-term separation. It is in the service of that goal that the letter develops its content, so that goal, profoundly illusive in its own way because it springs from the most profound recess of human needs and emotions, needs to be understood as the source of the aspirations of the parties involved.[23]

Let me add to this "epistolary masquerade" another problem that a researcher faces that Zempel also emphasized, namely the ethical question of whether a source is publishable or not. As she points out in the analysis of the "America letters,"[24] they tell stories of "migrants made of flesh and blood—or at least as much as the writer wanted to reveal them to friends and family—and can sometimes contain parts that are too intimate or sensitive to share with strangers."[25] It is quite understandable that reading and analyzing letters is a complicated task that demands contextualization and an interdisciplinary approach, but above all the key to comprehending the meanings of the letters stems from the selected thesis and the topic of analysis.

As I have mentioned, the key to the presented reading of the correspondence is the story of Pepica's routes of passages, her values, emotions, ambitions, and fears and the preserving and strengthening of social and family solidarity in the context of translocal life in two worlds, on two shores of an ocean, with a complex cultural and national hyphenated identity.[26] Through the entire family correspondence, the relevance of Gerber's constatation is clearly demonstrated: letters serve to strengthen interpersonal relationships. During decades of separation, the correspondence keeps and strengthens the relationships that all the participants want, in any way possible, to keep as loving, understanding, and loyal, also with the help of silence and untruths, the unwritten and unspoken.

Her Highness, Her Highness

The year 1930 was a milestone for Pepica, although within the family survival strategy it represents merely a continuation of the migration process. Although she did indeed marry a stranger, he was at the same time a boy from the next village and a friend of her brother, who had recommended him in his letters as a man from a good family. With a heavy heart she left her beloved mother, but her two brothers (and her mother's first husband) had done it before her, and one of them was waiting for her impatiently. She moved to another continent and into an unknown environment, but it was an environment where her relatives, fellow villagers, and acquaintances lived. She entered the land of opportunity in a time when the economic crisis and the period of the greatest unemployment in American history began, but the country was still considered a free country full of opportunities. Pepica couldn't speak English, but she knew she would be able to speak Slovenian far more freely than she did at home in Jelšane. She was young, beautiful, and determined. After a long journey, she was welcomed in Cleveland by her husband's mother, dressed in black, her hair covered with a black kerchief. The reception was identical to the one Pepica would have received had she moved from her native village to the neighboring Novokračine and not across the ocean. The family legacy, as summarized by Pepica's son, says:

> When our mother came to Cleveland [she was] wearing a knit suit my father bought for her in Trieste and Spectator shoes, those two-tone shoes with decorative perforations. So she was wearing the latest Italian fashion. She came to Cleveland and Nonna and her friends were wearing dark colors and long skirts. One of them shook her head and said to my mother "her highness, her highness," while a younger friend said she looked like Ingrid Bergman. Nonna didn't let her wear her braid down, saying she should be ashamed to show her hair in front of her husband. After a while mother figured out she couldn't find the right hat, because the ones in fashion were the narrow cloche ones that were tight around her head and left no room to keep a braid underneath. She decided to cut her hair, to be more fashionable. But Nonna revolted saying that she "won't have a girl with sheared hair sleeping under my roof."[27]

From a backward and poor province somewhere in the east of the Italian fascist state, an exquisitely dressed young woman thus arrived in a steel metropolis of the free American urban environment. She moved into a home of traditional rural codices, habits, values, and dress codes. After a long voyage across the ocean, she arrived into a social environment of the land of opportunity, where she encountered the same lack of work that she knew so well from the old place. From a loving and understanding family in a world that wasn't free, she moved to a family of a matriarchal authoritarian regime in the freest country in the world. In this opening scene, the stage is set for a contradictory, ambivalent, and complex drama of passage that we will follow in its continuation. This drama intertwines the simple perceptions of division between the modern and the traditional, the urban and the rural, domestic and foreign, and possibilities and obstacles. What truly sharpens the drama is the perspective in which the routes of passage have no destination because they are life itself. The destinations are merely random places on boat and train tickets.

It seems that Pepica crossed the ocean only to arrive in the well-known cultural environment of the Jelšane area.[28] In Cleveland, there were her husband and her brother's family; there were neighbors and acquaintances from the old Jelšane area, a Slovenian Catholic church and school, and Slovenian shops and banks. The difference was that in the Slovenian community in America, one could speak, sing, recite, shop, gossip, barter, and read in Slovenian without fear of fascist repression, and the Slovenian theater, singing, dance, folkloric, opera, and social functions were plentiful. Although she had her own family now, she didn't have her mother or brothers nearby. In her letters to Jelšane, Pepica is still at home in her thoughts. She worries about the family members and describes her own family life, and when she gets a suitable confidante in Ivan's wife Elka, Pepica also reveals more intimate details. She was a young woman who in her thoughts was always with her mother and was interested in cutting grass, in potatoes, and in the weather. In one letter she had even asked her family in Jelšane to send her lettuce seeds to sow in her garden in Cleveland. But she also had completely different things on her mind. I included the narratives of Pepica's children in the analysis of the family correspondence.[29] From their story, another quite different image emerges. They describe their mother as being very committed to the Slovenian community and culture but on the other hand very much adapted to the American way of life.

Pepica's son Joe Valencic mentioned that she used to always say that her children are what she's most proud of in her life: "then she was most proud that she learned English and could communicate. She was particularly proud that she could talk intelligently to doctors, that she understood them and they understood her, including the specialized expressions."[30] When we add the testimonies of her children to the image from the letters, we can see that Pepica in Cleveland didn't just grow lettuce and *pomidori* ("tomatoes"); she took care of her family, spoke Slovenian, entertained acquaintances from the wider Jelšane area, and wrote letters to her relatives. According to her children, she was a woman who was fashionably coiffed and dressed[31] and who spoke English and occasionally worked in different factories.[32] Pepica lived in the social universe of Jelšane but at the same time lived intensively in the American society, completely different from the native village and its habits.

The simultaneous influence of cultural perseverance and change can be explained with the factors of preserving and changing mentioned by Suzanne Sinke. In her historical analysis of the Dutch women migrants' experience, she emphasized that as far as women migrants and their personal decisions and choices within the context of conservative or innovative approach are concerned, there were several factors of influence. She finds that female migrants were tireless carriers of the conservative preservation of the tradition and gender roles or were the opposite, modernizers who took advantage of the land of the free for public and political participation and rejected anything traditional, from their social roles to their attire. Several different circumstances were decisive for the route that female migrants took, and Sinke classifies them in five factors. The first was the stage of life in which women migrated in addition to their marital status. The decision to adapt to the new environment was completely different for a young single woman than it was for a married woman with a number of children.

> The second [stage] was the degree of ethnic clustering in their new home, particularly of her extended family members. This was a defining feature of whether women could re-create many familial and social networks, and of the degree of control which the ethnic group could place upon its young adults. Third, the proximity to urban areas largely dictated the degree to which women were exposed to "dominant" American roles and various

opportunities. Fourth, class made a major difference in perceptions and opportunities. It translated into education for girls and certain leisure activities for women. Adult women who were already part of bourgeois life in the Netherlands generally did not like migrating, while young women from this background were the ones most likely to take advantage of American educational and career opportunities. Women's place in the ethnic/racial hierarchy of America, the fifth factor, was often invisible, yet it was a striking determinant of opportunities from the ability to migrate at all to marriage options to job possibilities.[33]

If we look at how all these factors influenced Pepica's decisions, we see that she came to America married but young and childless. Although she lived in the traditional structure of her husband's home, she realized her desire to be modern and dressed in the American way. She participated intensely and actively in her tight-knit ethnic community. Pepica took part in cultural and social events and activities as well as religious ceremonies and volunteer work. On the other hand, she was living in a big city that offered possibilities to improve and change traditional life. Pepica took the first opportunity in the mid-1930s, when she and her husband moved away because of the unbearable situation at her mother-in-law's house. The description of the causes was conveyed in the most condensed form in a letter written in the summer of 1934 in which Pepica told her mother the news that they live separately now and that they took off "without an argument."

> Dearest Mother! I never wrote to you before, I preferred to write about the good than about the bad, because I didn't want to cause you any worry, because I know you have more than enough of your own. But not a day passed that I didn't remember you and your words. You helped me a lot that I never had an argument with anybody, but I endured and cried when nobody could hear me. My child was my greatest consolation, I forgot about everything when I was around her. My Jože is also a wretched thing, I feel sorry for him, when he could he consoled me and I him. So

many years he had worked and suffered and given every cent to his mother, and she barely gave anything back, but what she gave he took, and now when he wasn't working it was as if nothing had ever been. But when he started working again she wanted the same thing again, that he would hand over his entire salary to her and then beg when we wanted to go somewhere and when she wouldn't give it she'd say again that she feeds us.[34]

Life was hard, because during the economic crisis Joe Valencich only worked occasionally; the lack of money was felt also because of his poor health and the low unemployment compensation he earned from his union activities as a steel worker. Pepica nevertheless took advantage of the possibilities offered by a big city to improve life. She took occasional employment and bought a house on a very good deal just before World War II began. Despite their working-class environment and a life in the network of family structures that in their case offered no help but only exercised control, in the big-city environment and the opportunities it offered, Pepica and her husband managed to organize their own life and live it autonomously. As can be seen from the letters, the first years were very difficult in the economic, emotional, family, and personal sense. She could help neither herself nor her mother and brother in Jelšane. Pepica's husband was frequently without income, and what he did earn he had to hand over to his mother. Pepica sometimes added a dollar to the letters that she sent to Jelšane. Sometimes this was everything she could send in an entire year. She didn't get on with her mother-in-law, who was very controlling. Pepica missed her mother and brother terribly, especially her mother, with whom she was very close. A couple of years after Pepica's arrival she gave birth to a daughter and then lost a son soon after he was born. She felt lonely, although her letters never show any reproach of her husband or give an indication that they weren't getting along.

Life in a tight-knit ethnic community undoubtedly gave Pepica a sense of security, belonging, and meaning. She raised her children in the Slovenian tradition and consistently taught them the Slovenian language. And yet she enrolled them in art courses at the Cleveland Museum of Art every summer and thus enabled them to have a wider social and educational experience. Her own aspirations were undoubtedly high—we saw that her knowledge of English was not just operational but proficient and that she was thoroughly engaged in the education of her children. The combination of perseverance and change is interesting in Pepica and worthy of attention, even when considering other factors: for example, her rudimentary education, as her schooling in Jelšane was hindered and eventually prevented by Italian fascism; her ethnic and religious loyalty that stemmed from traditional family and community values; her belonging to the working class without protection; and last but not least, her migrant status in the American race hierarchy in which Slavs and Catholics had a lower status. None of this prevented her from aiming high, in the context of a big city and the possibilities that America offered, from exercising her civic rights and duties, and from fulfilling the promise of a better life for her family on both sides of the ocean.

Pleas and Beseeching

Between 1930 and 1940, the entire family correspondence indicates an intimate and emotional yet reserved and formal communication. When it speaks about love and missing it is emotional, be it written by the sister, brothers, or mother. Whenever it talks about difficult or poor life circumstances, it is reserved, regardless of whether it is coming from Jelšane, Cleveland, or Buenos Aires. They all tried to make the decade of the economic crisis and political repression seem controllable, although they didn't hide anything. In my opinion this is an important characteristic, because it shows that they were open with each other. Another interesting fact is that the correspondence doesn't include a lot of descriptions of concrete social circumstances in the United States or Argentina, such as everyday life, habits, and culture. There are plenty more descriptions of meetings of the migrants from the wider Jelšane area, so it sometimes seems that they all live exactly the same life they would have led if they had stayed at home. As for the feelings of the family, they behaved as if they were not separated by the distances but that the communication was hindered by work obligations and lack of time. The letters wove a thick net of family support, such as mother Helena's support of Pepica when her daughter admitted that life with her mother-in-law was unbearable and that she and her husband moved out in 1934.

> I am pleased that your health is getting better and you were right to have moved if there was no peace. But Jože must have felt sad to leave his mother like that and leave behind all the blisters he got working for that house. I would like to know if she let you keep the sewing machine or if she took it from you? Don't gnaw yourself over this, in the end you left, you did it because you need to take care of your health that is easily destroyed by nagging and poking.[35]

In Jelšane, Pepica's niece and correspondent Cilka Udovič contributed to the description of the main actors:[36]

> For as long as I can remember, the name "Pepica" was present in our house. Our parents, Ivan and Elka, told us that Pepica was our father's sister and that she lives far away in a place called America. Where that place could be we didn't know until we went to school. At the same time we were told that one of our father's half brothers, Jože, also lives in America, and the other one, Tone, in Argentina. Rummaging through the old photos our father introduced us to everyone individually, including with the photo of the late Nonna Helena. We had no photos of Nonno Jože. I loved looking at these photos, especially of Aunt Pepica's photo when she was still young and at home, just before she left for America in November 1930. I remember Aunt Pepica's letters, even from before I could read, by her handwriting and the photos of her two small daughters, Merica and Cilka. As a child I felt how eagerly anticipated her letters were. The day the postman brought her letter was always filled with excitement and mirth. Father and mother were the first to read the letters

and then told us what the aunt wrote. When I learned to read, I would read them by myself.

In 1947 I started school. I was really looking forward to it, because I knew I'd learn to read and write. So immediately upon learning the alphabet, I wrote a letter to Aunt Pepica, thanking her for the package, or packages. So our correspondence began. Miran and Rado sometimes wrote a couple of lines. My parents had no time to write because they were in the field from dawn until night. Whenever mother wrote to America, she wrote at night, and father always said he'd write on Sunday, but Sunday was the only free day, a day of rest, so he sometimes put it off even further. But he always congratulated his brothers and sister for name day. As far as I know, the Udovič-Valencic-Hrvatin family correspondence was never interrupted completely. At times, there was a lag for one reason or another, sometimes from one side, sometimes from the other, and sometimes something was said or written because of personal distress. But at the same time it was this distress that joined them, connected them. Love and care for family members on both sides—that was their connection.[37]

In a part of the correspondence after 1945, this connection is present in a particularly interesting manner. It is the time after World War II when the circumstances in the old place were difficult because of the devastation caused by the war and the lack of basic goods and food. There are no letters from the wartime; they begin in the middle of 1945 when it is not even clear if the family in Jelšane has survived. In July 1945, brother Tone wrote from Avellaneda: "Please receive cordial greetings from your brother Anton. Likewise, I send greetings to your wife and children. If you, and them, are lucky to be still alive."[38] In Cleveland, brother Jože wrote to Ivan that he didn't have much time for writing, "as I am overloaded with work, but I'll drop you a few lines here and there. What I hope and expect is that you will describe for me a little your life and your suffering that you went through in those horrible days of cruel war when the homeland was burning and suffering."[39] Sister Pepica wrote in May 1946 "as long as you have survived these horrible times"[40] and immediately started sending packages from Cleveland.

> Here we are tonight, putting together another package for you. If you get all of it, you'll be happy. We're sending Ivan material for a suit. I bought everything needed to make a suit, also the lining for the suit, you can make one for yourself and maybe some will be left for Marijan.... One piece for you, Elka... some small pieces for the children. A cap for little Marijan, a shirt for Cilka.
>
> 1 pound of coffee, 2 litres of oil, 2 soaps, 6 soups in packages and those bandages for small wounds. And also the thing for putting on if you scrape or cut yourself, first you have to wash it and then put that red medicine on. Ivan, for you, Jože sent the machine for shaving, and also soap for shaving. Towels and some trinkets I won't even mention. I got Elka's letter before Christmas but I've not yet written back, because I was about to suffocate before the holidays when I had to work at home, in the factory—we even worked for 5 hours on Christmas Eve. So when you get this don't wait for the letter, because I don't know when I will get the chance to write. Please, write back soon when you get it if you got everything, because I'll worry, I'd so much like you get the things without a problem. I'll finish here, because I have to sew the package tonight.[41]

Tone also sent packages and money from Avellaneda and even sent his photo in 1947. He sent pesos and dollars as well as clothes and food. In a letter from 1947 he writes to Ivan: "As I see you've not yet received either of the two packages, I'm sorry if they got lost. Not because of the value, but because I know you need clothes."[42] And a year later:

> I replied to your letter that I received in June. But I have heard nothing from you. If you've received what I sent you with Brdan, $50 pesos. I sent you three packages, one got lost. In April I sent you 5 kilos of coffee, 5 K of rice and 5 K of sugar. And about all this I still don't know whether you got it or not. When Ivan Surina went home I gave $10 to one Istriano to give to Tepljan who'd give it to you. And you say nothing about it! Write to me if you got all that? Now, Ivan from Brce is going home, I'll send some combs and bits, and needles.[43]

Just like Tone and Pepica, Jože also misses the replies from Jelšane. They all impatiently wait for letters for six months or more. Jože also sends money and packages and writes letters, sometimes desperate, sometimes reconciling, such as the one to his brother Ivan in 1949:

> I received your letter, thank you so very much! You say you wrote three letters, but received no reply. Strange, Ivan, that other people get them, but you don't? I responded to every single letter. But I got no reply to my letters from you. I'm not judging: don't judge me wrongly, either, because in these times, everything's possible. Who knows what the riddle is that you haven't received my letter.[44]

The letters between Pepica and her mother and brother in Jelšane in the decade between 1930 and 1940 are full of emotions, declarations of love, care for health and well-being, and regret that due to the economic crisis Pepica can't send more money. Dollars traveled from America, but sometimes, such as in 1938, Pepica couldn't send a single dollar for the whole year. When two *mastenkas* and some other dried sausages made it to Cleveland in the bags of some migrants from the Jelšane social network sometime in the early 1930s, Pepica and her family were happier than can be described. And Pepica was even happier about the gift that her mother sent with an acquaintance from Rupa some years later: a pair of her earrings for Merica, Pepica's firstborn daughter. Other than these few objects, only words traveled across the ocean without stopping. But in the postwar era, packages began to travel. Joe Valencic describes the ritual of preparing and sewing the packages:

> Mama preserved pieces of white cotton. Once we put everything in a cardboard box, she wrapped the cloth around it and sewed it tight. And then she put a rope around it, so it wouldn't tear and rip open in transit. And the labels for customs were tied to it like on a Christmas tree. When we were sending just clothes we sent a soft package, without a box, just wrapped in white, like baby Jesus in the manger. She or I wrote the address in ink onto the white cotton. I shiver when I think now how they must

have been shocked in Jelšane when the postman carried on his shoulders a light-colored little package from America, bundled up like a newborn baby from a hospital.[45]

The correspondence reflects Pepica's extreme care for her brother's family.[46] Because the packages meant survival, the correspondence became tense and anxious. The packages were proof of love and care wrapped in white. The letters became darker and darker laments that the recipients never wrote back as to whether they received the packages, that they didn't list what they did and didn't get, and that there was no word from them and that they don't understand how difficult it is to be waiting for news from the old place. The letters clearly show what the migrant experience consists of and what distances and remoteness mean. For Pepica, the departure from her native village didn't mean a final farewell but instead meant an expansion of her household to the other side of the ocean. As the researchers of female migration emphasize, the idea of a home and a household becomes far more than a permanent place of residence—it becomes a translocal and transcultural network of support. The Hrvatin-Udovič-Valencic family correspondence makes this absolutely clear.

A translocal and transcultural network of support includes an infinite number of things: the exchange of money to pay fascist taxes that threatened the existence of the farm in Jelšane before the war, the exchange of the Jelšane sausages and mother's earrings, and the exchange of food, clothes, vitamins, tools, *kafe* ("coffee"), and *bendiči* ("bandages") during the extreme shortages following World War II. What the presented exchange meant to the part of the family on the European side of the ocean, as Cilka Udovič says, "is indescribable," and what the real Kras juniper brandy from the Slovenian Karst region meant on the other side of the ocean when it came to the gravely ill Jože is best expressed in his letter of thanks from September 1957: "This is like a medicine from the Kras juniper."[47]

The expressions of love, loyalty, and devotion were exchanged, and they were sometimes more important than dollars and flour,

Figure 9. Cilka, Miran, and Rado (Ivan and Elka's children) in 1950. *Courtesy of Cilka Udovič*

as they preserved the density of the family network even in times of altercation, disagreements, resentment, hurt, and misunderstandings that were further complicated by lost letters, too-long gaps between receiving a letter and responding to it, and personal problems that correspondents had. They exchanged memories; photos; news of health, illnesses, and general state of being; plans for the future; and cares and worries. They exchanged attention, such as in the case of Jože, who cared enough to send his niece Cilka dictionaries in 1956 and wrote to his brother that "If you can, send her to school to Ljubljana, the child is talented, let her learn. I will help as much as I can."[48] Pepica sent her brother Tone in Buenos Aires a piece of *potica*,[49] about which Tone writes to Ivan in Jelšane in September 1949:

> As far as I know you're already aware that on 26 August, Merica, our sister's daughter, got married. On the same day, one of the women from Tatre who used to go there to visit her sister, but lives here near me, told me she saw our brother Jože and our sister. She brought me a few gifts. And I had the chance to taste potica that our sister Pepica made.[50]

Translocal and Transcultural Network of Support

That the idea of a home and a household becomes a network of support is the emphasis of the mostly female researchers of female migration.[51] But when reading the Hrvatin-Udovič-Valencic family correspondence, another perspective is revealed. Through the innumerable exchanges, we witness in the letters that the role of the brothers is honed and is of equal standing, as they were just as eager to care for the tight network of family ties as their sister was. When the household expands, it is not just the letters and the packages; it is also the feeling that every family member has another home on the other side of the ocean and another family.

When Jože was asking his younger brother if he cut grass and made hay on time, he seemed to be asking an earnest question because he was sincerely interested in the hay from the meadows that he hadn't seen in thirty years. Brother Tone, who lived in Argentina alone, gathered clothes and made packages with food that he wrote about in letters, such as in 1951: "Three pocket pens, one for Marijan, 1 for Radovan, and 1 for Cilka, 1 kilo of coffee, 1 kilo of rice, 1 kilo of sugar, cheese, a bit more than a kilo of shoe-soles, 8 boxes of meat, 2 soaps for the face, 1 soap for clothes and half a kilo of pasta."[52] Some weeks later he wrote:

> On 6 December I sent you some clothes weighing 5 kilos, and on 12 December 5 kilos of food. Today on 24 December I'm sending the following: 1 kilo of rice mixed with 1 kilo of beans, because we're not allowed to send rice on its own, 1 kilo of dried pancetta, one bottle of honey, 1 cheese, 4 boxes of canned meat and 2 kilos of white flour.[53]

In 1956 he wrote to his niece Cilka: "I'm pleased that you intend to be a teacher like Jelka. I'm very happy that I have diligent nieces and that they study and that they will teach for the benefit of the humankind, this is my thinking exactly."[54]

Brother Jože also sent packages with food and money and wrote letters, albeit rarely, as he was loaded with work and could only write late at night. He cared that the niece could continue schooling and that the house got fixed after the earthquake, and in 1957, some thirty-four years after he left home, he wrote to his brother Ivan: "I know that you have so much work right now, but do take care that you will cut the grass on time. Give my regards to all the friends. My warmest greetings to all your family, and especially to you, Ivan."[55] The letters clearly show that preserving the network of support, help, and commitment isn't necessarily a women's thing, as Jože and Tone, together with their brother Ivan, were equally devoted to preserving the network of family ties and support as were Pepica and Elka. And Jože wasn't worried only about the grass being cut on time, the house being fixed, and the niece attending school in Ljubljana; he also sent Ivan a Slovenian American paper so he would be informed and get educated. In a letter from 1954, Jože told Ivan:

> You mention that you again received the newspaper Prosveta [Education] from America. I'm pleased that you like it! This is a paper that opens our eyes. If you read carefully, it will become clear to you what and how is happening here and around the world. Let's hope that better and brighter days are shining on you now, too. This is my heartfelt wish. I paid your subscription for the paper for another six months. Read it, and pass it on to others to read. It won't do you any harm, and nobody will be scandalized because of that.[56]

Pepica addressed most of her letters to Elka, her brother's wife, whom Pepica trusted even though she didn't know Elka well. From the time of Ivan and Elka's wedding in 1939 Pepica wrote more confidential letters to Elka, such as the one in 1941, a year after mother Helena's death. In it, Pepica describes to Elka how difficult her life was from the time of her arrival in Cleveland and what trials she went through when she was nursing her sick husband. Pepica tells her about years-long unemployment and the difficult relationship with her mother-in-law. In this letter, Pepica congratulates Elka on the birth of her daughter Cilka, gives Elka advice on how to care for herself, and recalls her own labors:

> How many tears I shed for my mother every time when I had nobody in the hospital when I was calling her name all dizzy from the gas. And even today my tears haven't dried. I always

dream about her, but when I get home I can't find her in the house anymore, so I look for her in the graveyard. But in my dreams I quickly find my father's grave, but I cannot find mother's. So, please, write to me where Mama is buried, if she's near late father.[57]

Mostly Pepica wrote long lists of things that she was sending. For fear that a package got lost or stolen or because sometimes there was no answer from Jelšane as to whether they got a package or not, the lists of the items sent appear several times. Besides that, the letters are full of desperate pleas ("when you get it write to me if everything arrived"), restrained reproaches ("I have no sound from none of you, I don't know what the reason is that none of you can give me some delight by writing a few lines"), and happy thanks: "after a long wait I finally received your dear letter, thank you very much. I was all worried for you and waited every day when the postman will stop by with the letter. I was also worried about the packages, because we here are also happy when we hear you get them all alright."[58] Were Pepica's care and anxiety an overreaction and her wish to find out whether they received the packages slightly obsessive? Given the circumstances in the postwar Slovenian countryside, probably not. Cilka paints the following picture in her story:

> But Aunt Pepica became the most important, or we felt that she existed and that she knew us, the children, as well, when she started sending us packages after World War II. The three children of father Ivan and mother Elka were born during the war (1940, 1942, 1944) in great shortage of food, clothes, shoes, everything. Also without any kind of vitamins or supplements, without sugar. We had rickets and all the problems of the children in places where there were, or still are, wars. I still don't know how we managed to survive it all. Yes, she sent us everything, from needles and thread, to all types of clothes, cutlery, nylon stockings when there were none yet here, cushion covers, shaving kit for the father, beautiful handbags and wallets, rings and earrings for me (when I grew up). In 1949 she sent me a beautiful doll. The

head, arms, and legs were made of porcelain; the rest of cloth. She was exquisitely dressed and shod. On her back she had a button, and when you pressed it she said mama or something similar. I remember the first and other packages that Aunt Pepica sent us; they were like a miracle to us. We were just staring and ooohing and aahing! Dresses, shirts, T-shirts, trousers, some footwear, household items, special candy, and special toys that we'd never seen and nobody in the village had; that's what she sent to us. The clothes for me were particularly pretty; they must have been from her daughter Cilka. Sometimes I was really embarrassed in front of my friends who had nothing to wear.

Aunt also sent us coffee beans and sugar. Coffee was another thing that nobody had, or almost nobody could afford. It was a luxury. Our mother roasted the beans carefully so it didn't get too brown. Its heady aroma lingered in the kitchen and beyond. Mother distributed coffee between neighbors and relatives. She had a measure, a cup of about 100 grams, and she wrapped these portions in paper and distributed them. But what was worth the most was flour, white flour that the aunt, and also Uncle Jože, sent us from time to time. At the time, all of us here ate corn bread that wasn't even like bread. It was thick and so hard that you could hardly eat it. I can still see a big blue pot in which mother distributed the flour to the neighbors so they could have a taste of this delicacy. The flour was particularly welcome in times of grass cutting and harvest, when mother baked bread so good, so delicate, and risen so high that it couldn't stand in the tin in which she served it to the cutters and women who helped us harvesting. What these packages meant cannot be described![59]

In a letter from 1948, Tone wrote about the chain of middlemen he used to send some money to Jelšane. This is interesting information about the fact that after World War II, some emigrants from the Primorska region started returning home. From the letters, it is impossible to tell whether the return was forever or just for a visit. Likewise, in February 1948 Tone writes from Avellaneda: "As far as returning to the homeland I still don't know when?... When will I come! I don't know!"[60] It isn't clear whether he talks about a visit or is thinking about returning permanently. In Tone's letters, the expression "homeland" appears consistently rather than the "old place," and this is particularly obvious after the war. Considering that it is possible to discern from the letters he wrote between 1930 and 1940 that he was of a socialist persuasion, it is clear that he looked favorably on Slovenia and Yugoslavia. Besides, we must consider that the liberation of the Primorska region was extremely important to the people who had been forced to emigrate due to the Italian fascist denationalization policy. Tone wrote in 1949:

> There I read a lot about the homeland. I've never thought that your progress is so swift that soon you'll have all the roads covered with tarmac and you won't be allowed to use horsecarts on them. You'll have to use lorries, just like we do here. I got a letter from Elka and was really happy that you got the package. If you weighed it, I sent 5 kilos of coffee and 4 of sugar. I've not thought it would come so quickly. I thought you'd get it for Christmas. Well, it's better that you're this way.... But the one who loves his land must persevere in the face of bora and storm and hope for a better future![61]

Despite the fast progress that Tone read about far away in Argentina, this better future was slow in coming—too slow for the relatives in Jelšane, exhausted from the fascism and the war. Despite the packages that were coming from America and the money that was sent in many ways, sometimes through the Kollander Travel Agency from Cleveland or the bank, sometimes with the fellow Slovenians who hurried from Argentina to go home to the Slovenian Primorska, life was becoming unbearable. There was no more patience or strength.

Instead of returning from abroad to the liberated Slovenian Primorska region, the letters in 1950 show Ivan's desire to emigrate with the family from Jelšane to America. The goal was Cleveland; the method was to opt for Italy and then move from Italy to America. Jože and

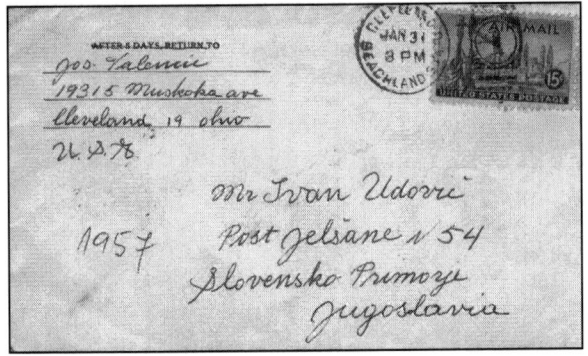

Figure 10. An envelope from 1957. *Courtesy of Cilka Udovič*

Pepica were charged with researching the possibilities to realize the plan. Jože wrote from Cleveland:

> Dear Ivan! What would you do in Italy, when there's only misery. Stay at home, where you are, and if it were true that you could come over to us in America, I'd do anything I can to help. But in this way, you're risking your life, family, and home; I do not recommend this. Pepica also told me that you wrote. She looked for information, too. Well, she will reply with what she feels. I could not give you a different answer. No offense, I'm telling you to endure a little longer; it will all turn out for the best.[62]

The final resolution is very briefly summarized in Jože's letter: "A few days ago I received a letter from our brother Tone in Argentina. He wrote me as well that he advised you to stay at home, in the homeland. As the old proverb says—home, sweet home."[63] Pepica described the investigation in more detail:

> If you come to Italy, you'll be Italian citizens and will have to wait for the Italian quota. Our Tomi went to the Italian consul and the consul asked him how old you were. He told him that maybe some grandfather or mother might make it, but the young ones would have to wait for the quota and it is so small that it would take years. Ivan, I understand how eager you are to rescue yourself and not go to Italy to live there, because the circumstances there are terrible; you want to go to have better opportunity to

come over here; many people come here from all over, those who were escaping in the times of the occupation.... Our brother Jože and I were talking that if something could be done and once you were here we'd organize life somehow just like the others do; we'd all help as much as we can. We'd be very pleased to have you and your children. I'd do anything to help your babies. Ivan, I can give you no advice. Kolander told me that you'd best go to the American consul over there and see what he has to say to you. Also, he told me he was very afraid for our people, that they will regret when they come to Italy. That they won't be able to go neither forward nor backward, and that you be careful what you do.[64]

The realization that they can only meet again in Jelšane was followed by years of planning for this meeting. The first to travel was Jožc with his family in 1955. In 1957 Pepica's daughter Cilka visited Jelšane, Novokračine, and Brgud. She brought a bottle of juniper brandy to her uncle Jože in Cleveland, and he, as he writes to his brother Ivan in September of the same year, "opened it immediately so he could taste the Divine liquid of our land, from our rocky soil. This is like a medicine from the Kras juniper. I also tasted your prosciutto to see and taste how well it is cured, so delicious that my mouth still craves for it."[65] A year later brother Jože died following a long and difficult illness. Pepica needed a long time before she could describe his last months in a letter. Then she sent an extremely long, detailed, and painful explanation of everything that was going on in the months when their brother was fighting for his life. She began with:

> I've never thought it would be so long before I write to you. Because I know you want to hear in more detail what happened with Jože's illness. For this reason, I took the pen several times, but then had to put it down. Because it starts clenching me around the heart when I start thinking and go through those sad memories again. Ivan, it's impossible to put on paper what you go through when you see one of your own suffer in agony and can do nothing to help, nothing to save.[66]

Figure 11. In front of the house in Jelšane in 1960. From the right: Ivan, Pepica, Cecilia, Joe, Cilka, Miran, and Rado. *Courtesy of Joe Valencic*

During this period, Pepica started planning her visit to the old place. When she informed her relatives in Jelšane about her plan, she wrote that she thinks she is dreaming, while a year later right before the departure she said that she was so excited that she was afraid it could be bad for her health. She didn't know how she would endure the time before the departure. In March 1960 she wrote from Cleveland: "Once I'm with you I think I will feel better, because I want to breathe your fresh air and enjoy the beautiful nature we miss so much here in the city."[67] In June 1960 Pepica stood again in front of her home in Jelšane that she had left thirty years earlier.

Cilka Udovič describes the visit of her aunt with the children Cecilia (Cilka) and Joe (Joško):

> Our family went to wait for them at the train station in Sežana. We hired the only taxi at that time from Ilirska Bistrica and took the macadam road through the Vreme Valley to Sežana. How excited we were when our beloved relatives got off the train! The aunt! It was a very heartfelt meeting. The aunt spoke beautiful Jelšane

dialect, with a Slovenian word thrown into it here and there, and rarely an English one. Cilka tried to speak Slovenian, while Joško couldn't really do it. We were looking at each other, asked questions, and soon it was like we'd always been together. The aunt found the village much changed. Where's that walnut, the mulberry, since when has there been a bridge across the stream where there used to be only a footbridge? Then she went to the graveyard and burst into tears. The aunt brought us whatever she could, as if she had a hunch what we were lacking. And not just us; she didn't forget other relatives, friends, and neighbors. Unfortunately, the circumstances, the living conditions, were very bad in our village at the time. We had no lavatory in the house, nor did other people. There was probably no running water in the house either; there was a latrine in the garden, and I don't remember where we slept, because we only had two rooms, and suddenly we were eight.... "O, my God!" Aunt would say. The food situation was no better. Simple home food. It was lucky we had prosciutto.[68]

After 1960 the number of packages slowly decreased, just like during the postwar shortage. Even five years after her visit Pepica still sent several packages a year, and she then sent one package a year until the mid-1980s or so. Joe Valencic remembers that after 1960 they no longer sent food, only coffee and aspirins, and after 1970 they no longer sent clothes. The packages were replaced with phone calls, visits, and an "extra suitcase in which we always brought an extra amount for relatives."[69] This was no longer the need for things; this was the need to keep the weaving of the translocal and transcultural network of family support and solidarity across the ocean intact—at least for as long as the memory of the family members remains.

The Routes of Passage

A passage from the rural environment under fascist occupation to a liberal state in the midst of an economic crisis posed a double problem of cultural survival for the Primorska migrants in the United

States in the mid-1930s. Their original culture was under pressure from a state that was systematically erasing it from public life and wanted to erase it from the family, too. The migrants went from the vice where the maneuvering space for expressing identity was rapidly shrinking and moving toward clandestine political work and military resistance. They arrived into a politically open space that enabled cultural autonomy, but they found themselves in economic conditions that took up most of their existence.

The outcomes of the two original situations are today clear. Cultural identity survived in both. In one hundred years one side of the Atlantic saw a new country established, and on the other a new nation was established. The migrants in the United States recomposed the elements of their transplanted identity into a new cultural identity, which—together with the elements of cultural identity from other regions and absorption of the American culture—created a new nation. This nation not only has a specific cultural identity but also has a precisely determined geographic location as well as national institutions, museums, archives, associations, and political organizations of different profiles. America also has its own history, which, like the history of the original identity, is subject to different ideological interpretations. Likewise, America has a typically heterogeneous political, class, gender, and ideological composition. This composition depends on the origins of the migrants, their ambitions and abilities, their family networks of support, political and religious convictions, and their age.

The starting point and the outcome are transparent. The question that needs to be asked is what was happening in transit. On the migrant's individual level, what was the evolution of the parallel processes of acculturation into a new environment and the preservation of those elements of identity that survived the filter of the Atlantic Ocean? The key to this is the problem of reliable documentation of the passage. That problem is solved in this chapter by the almost entirely preserved archive of the family correspondence that I have collected

Figure 12. Ivan at the train station in 1960. *Courtesy of Joe Valencic*

and reconstructed during five years of thorough research. Month after month it recounts the story of one identity that separated into two and reveals the resulting uninterrupted dialogue. Men, women, and their children participated in this process. The recomposition of identity and transfer to younger generations happened side by side like two lines that often met only with children, when the second or third generation renewed the procedure in the surprising interpretations of their identities. A question of bonds, dialogue, and simultaneous evocation of memory is posed. I analyzed this double process through the correspondence of the Valencic-Udovič-Hrvatin family from the village Jelšane in Primorska. I put a woman's story in the center, a story in letters and packages written by Pepica, Pepa, Josephine, Josie, a wife, mother, daughter-in-law, daughter, volunteer, singer, sister, Slovenian, Italian, American, a woman from Primorska. This story at the same time reveals the influence of cultural persistence and changing through the routes of passage that are a way of life and not a destination written on a ticket. What was Pepica thinking when, from her wagon, she caught on the camera for one last time the image of her brother standing on the platform?

Pepica was leaving home to go home. Pepica from Jelšane, a citizen of the United States of America, a woman of the world who spoke three languages, went by train to a French port with a ticket for a comfortable sea voyage to New York. What was she thinking in the moment into which decades of preserving ties between two increasingly defined and separated identities were bound, when she was bidding farewell to a place she would never see again?

Notes

1. Pepica Valencich to mother Helena, November 25, 1930, private collection of Cilka Udovič. Cilka (Cecilia) Udovič from Jelšane and Joe (Joško) Valencic from Cleveland allowed me to copy and use the following parts of the correspondence: the letters that Pepica kept in her home in Cleveland (private collection of Joe Valencic) and the letters that Pepica's niece Cilka keeps in the family home in Jelšane (private collection of Cilka Udovič). The correspondence begins in 1930 with Pepica's first letter from the ship *Saturnia* and other letters quoted at the beginning of the chapter. The correspondence changes with weddings and deaths of family members, which can be seen from the family tree in figure 1.1. The central part of the letters that I worked with includes some five hundred pages of material: letters, greeting cards, postcards, money orders, photos, etc. I would like to express my gratitude to Cilka Udovič and Joe Valencic for access to this correspondence, their help in understanding family relationships, and their trust.

2. The initial stage of my years of researching on this vast documentation has been presented at the conference (Post-)Yugoslav Migrations: State of Research, New Approaches, Comparative Perspectives, Berlin, December 2006 and published in Mirjam Milharčič Hladnik, "From a Dollar Bill in an Envelope to a Petition to the White House: The Significance of Slovenian Migrants for Those Back Home," in *Transnational Societies, Transterritorial Politics: Migrations in the (Post) Yugoslav Region, 19th–21st Century,* edited by Ulf Brunnbauer, 193–21 (Munich: R. Oldenbourg, 2009).

3. Throughout the chapter, the names appear as they do in the letters and may be confusing. To make it easier for the reader, here is a short explanation: Pepica is short for Jožefa (Josephine), and Josip is short for Jožef (Joseph). The name "Joseph" appears in several variations, most often as "Jože," sometimes "Joško." It is worth remembering that Jožef was the second most popular male name among the Slovenians up to the 1940s (Anton/Tone was the third most popular), so it is not surprising that Pepica's father, brother, and husband are all called Jože. Her son Joe Valencic has been called Joško among his relatives in Slovenia. Her second daughter's name is Cecilia (Cilka in Slovenian). Her niece, the daughter of her brother Ivan, is also called Cilka. They both appear in this chapter. There are three family names: Jože and Tone Hrvatin were children from Helena's first marriage; Ivan and Pepica Udovič were children from her second marriage. Pepica took the name Valencich when she got married, but in this chapter we use Valencic, the contemporary version of the name. The original name before they left for the United States was Valenčič (see the family tree in figure 1.1).

4. Avellaneda was a working-class neighborhood of Buenos Aires with a large Slovenian community.

5. Brother Tone to sister Pepica, 1930, private collection of Joe Valencic.

6. Son Josip (Jože) to mother Helena, 1930, private collection of Cilka Udovič.

7. The farm was midsized, and Jože Udovič was an educated farmer. He was the mayor of the Jelšane borough, a real estate estimator, and also a coroner. He died in 1928.

8. Mother Helena to daughter Pepica, March 4, 1931, private collection of Joe Valencic.

9. In the Slovenian territory of Primorska—which became part of Italy after World War I with the Rapallo Treaty—the Italian fascist regime prohibited use of the Slovenian language; changed all personal and family names into Italian ones; prohibited newspapers, books, and all other literature in Slovenian; banned Slovenian organizations; and introduced rigorous penalties for those who disobeyed.

10. Sister Pepica to brother Ivan, October 30, 1935, private collection of Cilka Udovič.

11. Brother Jože to brother Ivan, April 8, 1940, private collection of Cilka Udovič.

12. Brother Jože to brother Ivan, November 3, 1953, private collection of Cilka Udovič.

13. Samuel L. Bailey and Franco Ramella, eds., *One Family, Two Worlds: An Italian Family's Correspondence across the Atlantic, 1901–1922* (New Brunswick, NJ: Rutgers University Press, 1988), 2.

14. Marta Verginella, *Suha pašta, pesek in bombe: Vojni dnevnik Bruna Trampuža* [Dried Pasta, Sand and Bombs: A War Diary of Bruno Trampuž] (Koper: Univerza na Primorskem, Znanstveno-raziskovalno središče Koper, Zgodovinsko društvo za južno Primorsko, 2004), 11.

15. Some European countries, such as Germany, the Netherlands, and Norway, have gathered and organized collections of migrant correspondences that contain tens of thousands of units and are being complemented and also published. The intentional collecting, archiving, and publishing of such materials is not practiced in Slovenia.

16. Bruce S. Elliot, David A. Gerber, and Suzanne M. Sinke, eds., *Letters across Borders: The Epistolary Practices of International Migrants* (New York: Palgrave Macmillan, 2006), 3.

17. Paul Thompson, *The Voice of the Past: Oral History* (Oxford: Oxford University Press, 1988), 104.

18. John Bodnar, *The Transplanted: A History of Immigrants in Urban America* (Bloomington: Indiana University Press, 1985), xvii.

19. Samuel Baily, *Immigrants in the Lands of Promise: Italians in Buenos Aires and New York City, 1870 to 1914* (Ithaca, NY: Cornell University Press, 1999), 10–11.

20. "I have to stress that we never said Yugoslavia, or Slovenia, or Carniola. The expression was always 'the old place.'" Joe Valencic, e-mail to author, March 20, 2006, in possession of the author.

21. Thompson, *The Voice of the Past*, 103–4.

22. Solveig Zempel, *In Their Own Words: Letters from Norwegian Immigrants* (Minneapolis: University of Minnesota Press, 1991), xiii–xiv.

23. David A. Gerber, "Epistolary Masquerades: Acts of Deceiving and Withholding in Immigrant Letters," in *Letters across Borders: The Epistolary Practices of International Migrants*, edited by Bruce S. Elliot, David A. Gerber, and Suzanne M. Sinke (New York: Palgrave Macmillan, 2006), 143.

24. "America letters" is a general name for the Norwegian migrant correspondence, which is collected in the special archives in the United States and Norway and includes for our circumstances an unimaginably large number of units. The researchers started collecting early; Theodore Blegen, for example, began collecting as early as 1928. See Theodore Blegen, ed., *Land of Their Choice: The Immigrants Write Home* (Minneapolis: University of Minnesota, 1955).

25. Zempel, *In Their Own Words*, xiv.

26. "Hyphenated identity" is a term that originated in the United States at the end of the nineteenth century and is used to describe immigrants who feel

affiliation to the culture they came from as well as the country and culture they migrated to. In the beginning the term had a pejorative meaning but gained a positive connotation with the policy of multiculturalism. The term is also used metaphorically to describe the modern notion of identity as multilayered, composite, hybrid, and fluctuating.

27. Joe Valencic speaking on his mother's arrival in Cleveland, a contribution for debate at the international conference Vloga žensk v migracijskih kontekstih slovenskega etničnega prostora [The Role of Women in the Migration Contexts of the Slovenian Ethnic Territory], Ljubljana, October 17, 2004. *Nonna* is an Italian word for a "grandmother" that was and still is used in the Primorska region.

28. In 1934 Jože Hrvatin and his friends established the Sloga (Concordia) choir, named after the one in Jelšane. Pepica and Danica were also members, and the choir was active until 1941. Prosvetno društvo Sloga in Jelšane was established in 1866 and had a mandolin, a choir, and drama sections. In 1928 it was prohibited by the Italian state, like all other Slovenian organizations.

29. Cecilia (Cilka) Valencic Dolgan and Joe Valencic, interview by the author, May 17, 2002, Cleveland, Ohio, tape recording in possession of the author.

30. Joe Valencic, e-mail to author, March 17, 2006, in possession of the author.

31. From the letters and interviews, it is clear that Pepica was an excellent seamstress who made new clothes for herself and her children or altered old ones.

32. Dolgan and Valencic, interview.

33. Suzanne M. Sinke, *Dutch Immigrant Women in the United States, 1880–1920* (Urbana: University of Illinois Press, 2002), 4.

34. Daughter Pepica to mother Helena, July 28, 1934, private collection of Cilka Udovič.

35. Mother Helena to daughter Pepica, 1934, private collection of Joe Valencic.

36. Cilka Udovič received me several times at her home in Jelšane (the same house from which Pepica left for America in 1930) during 2005 and 2006 and spoke to me at length. She also compiled the family tree in figure 1.1 and clarified many things that were unclear in the intertwined network of family ties and relationships.

37. Cilka Udovič, interview by the author, September 6, 2005, Jelšane, Slovenia, written transcript in possession of the author.

38. Brother Tone to brother Ivan, July 22, 1945, private collection of Cilka Udovič.

39. Brother Jože to brother Ivan, May 26, 1947, private collection of Cilka Udovič.

40. Sister Pepica to brother Ivan and his wife Elka, May 18, 1945, private collection of Cilka Udovič.

41. Sister Pepica to brother Ivan's wife Elka, December 29, 1945, private collection of Cilka Udovič.

42. Brother Tone to brother Ivan, August 25, 1947, private collection of Cilka Udovič.

43. Brother Tone to brother Ivan, November 4, 1948, private collection of Cilka Udovič.

44. Brother Jože to brother Ivan, April 24, 1949, private collection of Cilka Udovič.

45. Joe Valencic, e-mail to author, March 7, 2006, in possession of the author.

46. Pepica sent many packages to other relatives, too: those on her mother's side in Brgud and on her husband's side in Novokračine.

47. Brother Jože to brother Ivan, September 18, 1957, private collection of Cilka Udovič.

48. Brother Jože to brother Ivan, May 30, 1956, private collection of Cilka Udovič. Jože's daughter, Jelka Hrvatin, was the first of the extended family who went to college.

49. The traditional Slovenian walnut bread is eaten at every important family occasion.

50. Brother Tone to brother Ivan, September 1, 1949, private collection of Cilka Udovič.

51. See Helma Lutz, ed., *Migration and Domestic Work: A European Perspective on a Global Theme* (Surrey, UK: Ashgate, 2008); Rhacel Salazar Parreñas, *Children of Global Migration: Transnational Families and Gendered Woes* (Stanford, CA: Stanford University Press, 2005); and Janet H. Momsen, ed., *Gender, Migration and Domestic Service* (London: Routledge, 1999).

52. Brother Tone to brother Ivan, December 6, 1951, private collection of Cilka Udovič.

53. Brother Tone to brother Ivan, December 24, 1951, private collection of Cilka Udovič.

54. Tone to his niece, brother's Ivan daughter Cilka, March 19, 1956, private collection of Cilka Udovič.

55. Brother Jože to brother Ivan, June 2, 1957, private collection of Cilka Udovič.

56. Brother Jože to Brother Ivan, March 28, 1954, private collection of Cilka Udovič.

57. Pepica to Elka, March 12, 1941, private collection of Cilka Udovič.

58. Pepica to Elka, 1946, private collection of Cilka Udovič.

59. Cilka Udovič, interview by the author, March 7, 2006, Jelšane, Slovenia, written transcript in possession of the author.

60. Brother Tone to brother Ivan, February 16, 1948, private collection of Cilka Udovič.

61. Brother Tone to brother Ivan, November 15, 1949, private collection of Cilka Udovič.

62. Brother Jože to brother Ivan, 1951, private collection of Cilka Udovič.

63. Brother Jože to brother Ivan, April 30, 1951, private collection of Cilka Udovič.

64. Sister Pepica to brother Ivan, February 10, 1951, private collection of Cilka Udovič.

65. Brother Jože to brother Ivan, September 18, 1957, private collection of Cilka Udovič.

66. Sister Pepica to brother Ivan, July 11, 1958, private collection of Cilka Udovič.

67. Sister Pepica to brother Ivan, March 20, 1960, private collection of Cilka Udovič.

68. Cilka Udovič, interview by the author, March 24, 2006, Jelšane, Slovenia, written transcript in possession of the author.

69. Joe Valencic, e-mail to the author, March 27, 2006, in possession of the author.

References

Baily, Samuel L. *Immigrants in the Lands of Promise: Italians in Buenos Aires and New York City, 1870 to 1914*. Ithaca, NY: Cornell University Press, 1999.

Baily, Samuel L., and Franco Ramella, eds. *One Family, Two Worlds: An Italian Family's Correspondence across the Atlantic, 1901–1922*. New Brunswick, NJ: Rutgers University Press, 1988.

Blegen, Theodore, ed. *Land of Their Choice: The Immigrants Write Home*. Minneapolis: University of Minnesota, 1955.

Bodnar, John. *The Transplanted: A History of Immigrants in Urban America*. Bloomington: Indiana University Press, 1985.

Elliot, Bruce S., David A. Gerber, and Suzanne M. Sinke, eds. *Letters across Borders: The Epistolary Practices of International Migrants*. New York: Palgrave Macmillan, 2006.

Gerber, David A. "Epistolary Masquerades: Acts of Deceiving and Withholding in Immigrant Letters." In *Letters across Borders: The Epistolary Practices of International Migrants*, edited by Bruce S. Elliot, David A. Gerber, Suzanne M. Sinke, 141–57. New York: Palgrave Macmillan, 2006.

Kaplan, Carla, ed. *Zora Neale Hurston: A Life in Letters*. New York: Doubleday, 2002.

Lutz, Helma, ed. *Migration and Domestic Work: A European Perspective on a Global Theme*. Surrey, UK: Ashgate, 2008.

Milharčič Hladnik, Mirjam. "From a Dollar Bill in an Envelope to a Petition to the White House: The Significance of Slovenian Migrants for Those Back Home." In *Transnational Societies, Transterritorial Politics: Migrations in the (Post)Yugoslav Region, 19th–21st Century*, edited by Ulf Brunnbauer, 193–21. Munich: R. Oldenbourg, 2009.

Momsen, Janet H., ed. *Gender, Migration and Domestic Service*. London: Routledge, 1999.

Parreñas, Rhacel S. *Children of Global Migration: Transnational Families and Gendered Woes*. Stanford, CA: Stanford University Press, 2005.

Sinke, Suzanne M. *Dutch Immigrant Women in the United States, 1880–1920*. Urbana: University of Illinois Press, 2002.

Thompson, Paul. *The Voice of the Past: Oral History*. Oxford: Oxford University Press, 1988.

Valencic-Udovič-Hrvatin family correspondence. Private collection of Cilka Udovič and Joe Valencic.

Verginella, Marta. *Suha pašta, pesek in bombe: Vojni dnevnik Bruna Trampuža* [Dried Pasta, Sand and Bombs: A War Diary of Bruno Trampuž]. Koper: Univerza na Primorskem, Znanstveno-raziskovalno središče Koper, Zgodovinsko društvo za južno Primorsko, 2004.

Zempel, Solveig. *In Their Own Words: Letters from Norwegian Immigrants*. Minneapolis: University of Minnesota Press, 1991.

Chapter 2

A Wife at Home
Longing and Writing

Marjan Drnovšek

The weather is always nice, a little bit of rain and then again the warm sun. The time is flying by, soon it will be winter again. We're not ready to come to Holland, because the little one is not yet fit to be in company much. Oh, I wish so much to talk to you already, but I don't know when the time will come to do so. Come home, I'd like it if you came home. I still miss you so much, I dreamt about you last night; you came home without writing first, you simply stepped into the house and I was changing Lojzek's[1] nappies and the first words you said were: where were you that you look so tubby? I didn't know what you meant; I laughed a little at your words and woke up. Now, I greet you heartily one more time and send you a warm kiss. Your little children, the old father and especially I, your always loving and faithful wife Francka, greet you.[2]

The period of the Yugoslav monarchy (1918–41) was short but very dynamic when it came to migration. The golden gates of the United States were by now barely ajar; Europe, however, became livelier migration-wise. The migration currents prior to World War I were incomparable to those in the period after the war, especially in the number of migrants. In the period that this chapter deals with, the conditionally free migration across the Atlantic was tightened, and control over the movement of people in Europe was strengthened. One of the consequences of World War I was the deficit in the male population, as many men had not returned from the battlefields. The war also triggered the needs of national economies for new pairs of diligent working hands. For this reason, soon after the war new migration waves started in the direction from the European east to the west, particularly to France, Belgium, Luxemburg, and the Netherlands. The Soviet Union was a closed system, although it beckoned ideologically suitable workers to work in that country. During the first decade after the war, France was considered to be the new America because it opened its doors wide to the workforce, including Yugoslav workers. However, the great economic crisis that began in 1929 stopped this growth. Working conditions were constricted, xenophobia increased, and forced returns of workers to their countries of origin occurred. Two totalitarian regimes, the fascist regime in Italy and the Nazi regime in Germany, were gaining strength, and the Spanish Civil War was a harbinger for the misery that lay ahead for people in both their country of origin and their country of migration.

During the period of this great economic crisis, the story of a small family living near Ljubljana took place. Maks, the father, who had been a migrant worker before the war in the coal mines in the United States, decided to go to the Netherlands in the year when the Great Depression began, thus leaving behind his wife Francka with a small child, a new child on the way, and his aged father-in-law. The departure of the husband and the father cut deep into the lives of both spouses and their children, too. Despite the correspondence, a huge gap was created as they distanced themselves from each other, especially the husband who was not particularly happy with his life abroad. The most heartbreaking was Francka's reaction to his cold attitude toward her, which was probably the result of him not wanting to have another baby.

Here I must draw attention to the importance of the archive materials and especially the correspondence of migrants, which reveals something that only the eyes of the addressees were supposed to see: the intimate and deeply personal portrait of how the main actors—the person who remained at home and the migrant—perceived their fate. It is only these stories that open the depth of the not known, the rarely heard, and the seldom seen, of something that gives a researcher the possibility of analyzing less known data, which must of course be handled and presented sensitively and ethically.

The preservation of sixty-one letters that Francka wrote to her husband Maks in the Netherlands in just under a year, from March 1, 1929, to January 26, 1930, affords us insight into their lives on the microspatial and temporal level. From these letters, we learn a lot about Francka's life in the relatively small area of Gorenjska near Ljubljana and about her husband's stay in Heerlerheide in the Netherlands. Francka's letters are very personal: they require sensitive handling, because they disclose personal and sometimes intimate details that were in no way intended for a third pair of eyes to read. For this reason, the place-name is not mentioned in this chapter. As often happens in such cases, fate intervened, and the letters fell into the hands of strangers and finally into the hands of a migration researcher. How? They were purchased at a Ljubljana flea market.[3] When I was leafing through Francka's letters a panoply of themes opened in front of me, not unlike those observed in similar migrant correspondence. In this case, however, those themes are observed through the eyes of a wife who stayed at home, a wife who gives us a glimpse of the husband's thoughts and state of mind through the questions she poses and the answers she gives in the letters to him. As a researcher and an archivist, I asked myself about the ethical aspect of browsing through their written conversations. My dilemma was how to analyze the letters, since an analysis that didn't take into consideration the intimate and personal part of the correspondence would be somehow depleted. According to the current archive legislation in the Republic of Slovenia, materials that include sensitive personal data (i.e., data on racial, national, or ethnic origin; political, religious, or philosophical persuasion; party and union membership; state of health; sexual practices; and criminal records or removal from criminal records) pass into the public domain and are available to researchers seventy-five years after they were created or ten years after a person's death.[4] The letters date from 1929 and the beginning of 1930, and Francka was born at the end of the nineteenth century: both requirements are undoubtedly met. But more than by legislation, I am led by the conviction that intimate personal correspondence is a valuable piece in the mosaic of migrants' correspondence.[5] The frequency and frankness of writing, the verbosity, and the repetition of personal topics allow us to monitor numerous oscillations in decisions and doubts, while the sincerity and some other issues give Francka's letters an added research value. Her letters don't tell us about great national, cultural, and political acts but instead tell us about the life choices and dilemmas that the separated family had to face during the period studied. In short, it is a story of seemingly insignificant people and their personal and everyday problems.

The letters are particularly marked by Francka giving birth while her husband is absent, taking care of a family, and finally deliberating her dilemma: to follow her husband or to stay at home. Mindful of these details, I have decided not to list the basic and identifying characteristics, specifically last names, or will use only the initial. I use the same criterion for Slovenian towns: with this I somewhat protect identities and free myself from self-censorship. I have aimed to be respectful to both accidental protagonists in this story while analyzing it. I wanted to get to know them and present them in light of the migration activities on the brink of the great economic crisis at the end of the 1920s. The story of their written correspondence is only eleven months long. Short? Yes, but very rich in contents.

From an American to a Holender

Maks set off to the Netherlands as an experienced migrant with acquired mining skills. There, he became one of the "Holenders," as they were known as at home.[6] (By the way, one of the letters mentions that Maks's mother received his mail from Germany, where he had probably been working before leaving for the Netherlands.)[7] We don't know if he was a member of a Slovenian association, nor do we know his possible political and ideological persuasion, which in the Netherlands at that time would have been either Catholic or communist. We also don't know whether he read the Catholic newspaper *Rafael*[8] or the leftist (communist) newspaper *Slovensko delavsko—Kmečka republika*,[9] both of which were published in Heerlen.[10] After nearly a year of correspondence, Francka asked her husband if he subscribed to any newspapers and if so which. Maks was not a great reader; we can deduce that much from Francka's warning that he must not lie about it. She read *Domoljub*,[11] as we can understand from her letters. And without waiting for her husband's reply, she decided to buy him a three-month subscription to the Saturday newspaper *Slovenec*.[12] With the next letter, she also sends him *Slovenčev koledar*.[13]

For a peasant wife, the role of mother and housewife was not only self-evident but was also an inseparable part of the workforce on the farm.[14] Traditionally, the man (i.e., the husband and the master of the farm) assumed the leading role. However, things changed when the husband/master went overseas or abroad to work, as was the case with Maks. Francka had to take the burden of the work on the farm, although her letters show that she tried to shift the important decisions to her husband, in line with the common practice in farming families. She turned out to be a heedful head of the farm, which wasn't a big one, but she did need hired help at peak times—in the spring and during harvest. The same was true for the winter work in the forest. In short, Francka was a "cultivator," as the statistics of the time stated, and she busied herself with farming activities. She was a farmer by heart as well. This is why she told her husband the details about the weather, planting and mowing, the prices of the produce, the pay for the workers in the field or in the woods, etc. She also told him in detail what produce and wood she sold and what she purchased for the farm. She didn't have a cow, and when her husband left for the Netherlands she also sold the horse; some villagers doubted the correctness of her decision. Because of this, she was even more dependent on other people. In short, Francka was tied to the farm.

Maks was registered in the borough of Heerlen from March 6, 1929, to March 1931, when he moved to the borough of Geleen some eleven miles north. Probably at that time he took employment in the Maurits mine and lived in a place called Lutterade, a part of the Geleen borough. When he was registered in Heerlen in the town Heerlerheide, he lived at different addresses. Migrants moved a lot. There were several Slovenian immigrants living on Kampstraat Street, which shows the tendency of compatriots to settle close to each other. This was a true Slovenian street where a lot of people from the Primorska region lived. Like the majority of miners living there, Maks first worked in a private mine, Oranje Nassau III, where he was employed as an apprentice as a *leerlinghouwer* ("digger"). Skilled miners usually started off as leerlinghouwers or *houwers* ("hewers"). Maks had mining experience from his time in the United States, so he could skip the level of an unskilled worker. The Oranje Nassau III mine preferred to employ a foreign workforce. Despite Maks thinking of going to work in a factory or somewhere where the work was easier and circumstances were better, this didn't happen, at least not during the time covered by Francka's letters. He also thought about going to Belgium or France because the work in Dutch mines was so hard but never followed through, at least not during the period of the existing correspondence with his wife.

Please, Write Back Soon

There is not a single letter that Francka doesn't end with a plea for her husband's reply. During the separation of two people who are close, letters assume the role of daily conversations about personal, family, and economic matters and other topics of interest for both correspondents. Unfortunately, we are dealing here with one-sided issues and questions and only learn about the husband's reactions indirectly. Francka and Maks carried on a dialogue similar to the one they might have at the dinner table at home on a Sunday afternoon. Writing was the only possible way to continue exchanging information, because the correspondents were physically separated. Letters are a limited form of communication, as they can never replace personal contact or a discussion, especially if neither party is a skilled writer. Francka's writing was on the level of primary education: she had problems with punctuation, capital letters, and word order. However, in our story we are more interested in the content of their discourse than its linguistic and grammar characteristics. As far as writing, Francka was a lot more actively and systematically committed to written communication than her husband Maks, if we judge from her efforts and pleas to him to write her back regularly. She wanted to receive her husband's letters at least once a week and tried to establish a pattern whereby every letter was answered immediately, which would feel more like a dialogue. She became cross several times because she had to pose him the same questions more than once, which she felt was an extra burden for her and also a waste of paper. The impression we get is that the husband was less inclined to talk or write, and although we don't have his letters to his wife, he clearly didn't respond enough to hers.

Francka often mentions in her letters that she is writing in the evening or at night, which is not surprising because daytime was dedicated to farmwork, raising her daughter, and later caring for the newborn. So, she writes that it took her a full two hours to write a letter that was a sheet and a half long.[15] The time aspect of writing as well as reading letters is interesting. I don't think she made drafts, as she was economizing with the paper. Her letters were clean copies with only a small number of corrections. Therefore, I presume that she wrote directly but slowly and with consideration. We can

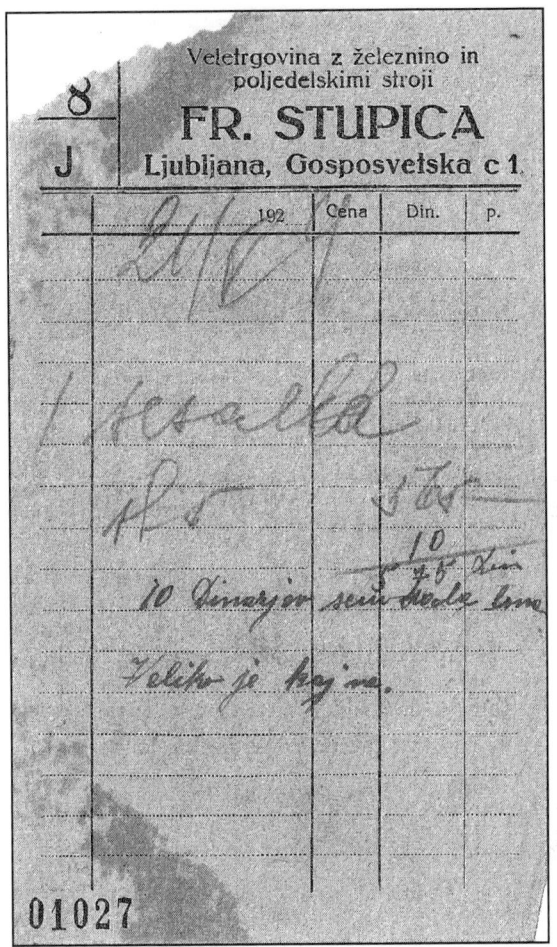

Figure 2.1. An invoice for a water pump, which made carrying water from the well to the house easier (Francka to Maks, May 22, 1929). *Courtesy of Marjan Drnovšek*

often notice that she has lost the stream of thought, which brings unexpected leaps in contents to her writing. As for the length of her letters, she pointed out several times that she wrote a lot so that Maks could take several hours to read.[16] She often asked him not to hold it against her because she writes so badly and too fast, which was supposed to be her habit. But if she stops writing, he will get a letter one day later. She closes with a tender "goodnight, sweetheart." She often asks if he is also eager to get her letters.[17]

Francka dated her first letter March 1, 1929. The postal stamp from March 2 tells us that it was posted from the local post office. By then, she had received two postcards from her husband, which were not preserved, the first from Ljubljana dated February 26 and the second from Munich dated February 28. Maks sent them en route to the Netherlands. The last preserved letter was dated January 26, 1930. While Maks often interrupted the continuity of their correspondence, the last letter obviously doesn't signify the end of their long-distance communications. The collection of Francka's sixty-one letters is not complete. As they were bought at the flea market and a few postcards are missing, it is probable that a third person meddled with them, especially because some of the envelopes in the collection are empty.

As if following a pattern, in the beginning of Francka's letter she thanks her husband for his letter with an oft-repeated phrase: "I received your letter, so dear to me, which I'd been expecting so eagerly, thank you so very much."[18] At the end of the letter we can often see her plea for him to answer her, as she is eagerly awaiting his letter.[19] She often complains: "Please, dear Maks, write back soon."[20] As a reaction to the probably short letters from Maks, she asks him to write her not only soon but often. She often chides him that he doesn't write enough and that he's not interested in anything.[21] In mid-May 1929 she got angry with him because he hadn't written or responded to her letters. She wondered if he took offense or if she had insulted him, and as the last possibility she mentioned that the expected letter must have gotten lost in the mail. From her letter, written on May 12, 1929, we can feel that she was craving for his response. And even though the response often didn't come—as in this particular case—she still decided to write to him, albeit with a bit of indignation. She was eager to get her husband's letters, and this eagerness is proved in the last sentence in one of them: "please, please, write back soon, respond immediately."[22] Although I don't know the husband's letters, I can presume that it was easier for her to write in response to them. In short, she insisted on a written dialogue. That the expected answer didn't come became clear when she received Maks's letter claiming that he never got her letter from April 28.[23] She was surprised that it would get lost, as she posted it personally when she took the bus to a nearby city, and the postman brought it on the bus together with the rest of the mail. So, she blames the foreign postal service for the loss.[24] A different situation occurred at the end of May 1929, when she even claimed: "I know you've received it, but Lord knows, I expect your response every day and it doesn't come." So she would have to write again, because she didn't know if he had already written back or if the letter got lost again. Francka asks Maks to send a registered letter when he writes something important and scolds him because he hasn't yet come up with this idea himself. She doesn't know whether to respond to him or if the letter got lost en route again. She's consumed by doubt and hence demands that he send her a registered letter. She asks him to remember how worried he was when he was posting a letter to the Netherlands before leaving. She asks him to write more often, but her plea remains unsuccessful, and she continues: "if I had as much time as you do, I'd write more often." She is, however, afraid that he'll think she's nagging if she does. But she also knows that he wouldn't like if she didn't write to him. She needs the contact with him, which is why she asks his advice on how to do everything she does. But she still entertains the possibility that the letters get lost (which she doesn't like) and the thought that other people might read them, and ends with "please, my dear Maks, please do as I asked you to," that is, to use registered letters. This is one of Francka's letters that is full of despair because her husband hasn't answered her questions, and the despair was undoubtedly a consequence of her advanced pregnancy.[25] (In the next letter she apologizes for her sharp tone.) The demand for registered letters and the fear that the letter might end up in someone else's hands repeats several times in Francka's letters.

This went on from June 30, 1929, when Maks wrote to Francka for the last time, until July 26, when she finally received a response. In the meantime, on July 3 she gave birth to a baby boy. She sent Maks a notification of his son's birth from the delivery bed.[26] Two days later on July 5, she described the event a bit more in detail.[27] After a week, on July 12, she got cross again. While still in bed after childbirth, she dedicated a whole letter to the uncertainty, because there was no written response from her husband. She started off very politely ("My dearest, most beloved husband Maks!") but then mentioned the possibility of his ill health and in the same breath reproached him because she had not received a single letter from him when she was in bed after labor. She dedicated her letter to the question of his silence and again voiced her fear that he might be sick or that the letters were lost. She reproached him again for not sending her registered letters. She has reconciled with the fact that he writes less, but his letters should at least reach her: if he finds spending money for a registered letter extravagant, he can write less often. She voiced her indignation that he hasn't supported her with his letters in this time and continued:

> I'm asking you today and if you don't listen to me now I will never again ask for anything in this respect. If I get it I get it, and if not, I'll keep quiet. Please receive from all of us the kindest greetings and kisses, especially from your forever loyal and loving Francka. Please, reply![28]

Her next letter was calmer, but she reiterated her ideas of letter sending and expresses sadness because she hasn't received any answers. She emphasized again her state after childbirth.[29] Finally, she'd received his letter. She almost apologized to him for not having left him in peace but at the same time complained once more that he didn't send any greetings after she had given birth and that it felt strange and boring to be in an empty home. The days seemed long. Because she didn't get his letter she would wake up in the middle of the night, afraid that something had happened to him. As she stated finally, she got his letter because it was registered.[30] At the end of another letter she again shows her discontent and reproaches Maks that he no longer feels like writing, not even once every week, despite the fact that she's so glad to receive every single one of his letters.[31] To make even more certain that he received her previous letter, she sent it by express registered mail with a return receipt, which she received with his signature. She is asking him not to take offense that she sent it this way. She had to pay nine dinars for it. It was more expensive, which she tried to smooth over with Maks in the next letter: "as you tell me you now earn well already."[32] In one of the letters Francka connects Maks's delay in replying to the fact that he has to write in the kitchen and reconcilably adds that "it is truly not easy to write in the kitchen, because I know there are other people present who are nosy about what you're writing! What about when you receive the letter, do they ever comment on how often you get them? Please write and tell me!!!"[33]

By Francka's last known letter from January 26, 1930, there was more satisfaction expressed about their correspondence than not, although several times critical words were expressed on account of her husband's irresponsiveness. And a mild clash occurred in the final letter when Francka reproaches him that he loves receiving letters but not so much responding to them. She concludes that he prefers to answer when he has received one or two letters, adding "isn't that so?" And she continues that she always writes to him if she possibly can, but she always loves receiving letters from him.[34] Because her letters contain information of an intimate nature, Francka often cautions her husband to never tell anyone what she writes to him.[35] At times she is dissatisfied because she hears pieces of information from the Netherlands from the neighbors rather than from him. It looks like the local shop is the hub for news and gossip. She stresses that she could write to him a lot about what is going on or being heard of at home, but she isn't sure if he would like it or not. And as often occurs, she indicates that she would like to have a written conversation with him, although mail isn't cheap. She eagerly awaits his letters, as they give her pleasure and fill her spare time.[36]

Abroad You Suffer in Those Dangerous Mines

Francka wants to know what things are like in the mine. Are the caves wet or dry? Do they mine for coal or some other ore? What is the language there like; is it more like German? And then she flips over to gossip from the village. There have been claims that Maks has had to pay a deposit to travel to the Netherlands, which Francka has dismissed as a lie. The first steps in the new environment were difficult. In the middle of March 1929 Francka consoled her husband, who wrote to her about (presumably difficult) work in the mine and difficulties in understanding the language. She tried to convince him to be a little more patient, despite the fact that he was constantly in danger; she was afraid of what people might say if he returned home too soon. (Later she found out that he wanted to come home immediately upon arrival. She had learned from A., a woman from the village, who received a letter from Franc P., that Maks wanted to return home after five days in the Netherlands. Francka got quite angry that she found out via this route and advised him not to associate with Franc P. much and tell him as little as possible, because this Franc P. wrote his wife about everything. But the news about this went around, and Francka didn't like it.) Francka concluded her letter by saying that many at home were happy when they felt he was none too boasting about his life in Holland. We encounter typical enviousness and the glee over the trouble of someone else. She hopes that he will get used to it and that things will get easier.[37]

For Francka, the good side of Maks's work abroad was his salary. She makes a comparison with the Trbovlje mine in Slovenia, where he would have earned very little. Trbovlje miners are poor, "everybody says so," emphasizes Francka, "because their salaries are too low." And as her final point in her advice to her husband, she adds that they are "quite a bit in debt," although she is economizing. Francka asks how they will pay it off if he doesn't earn more.

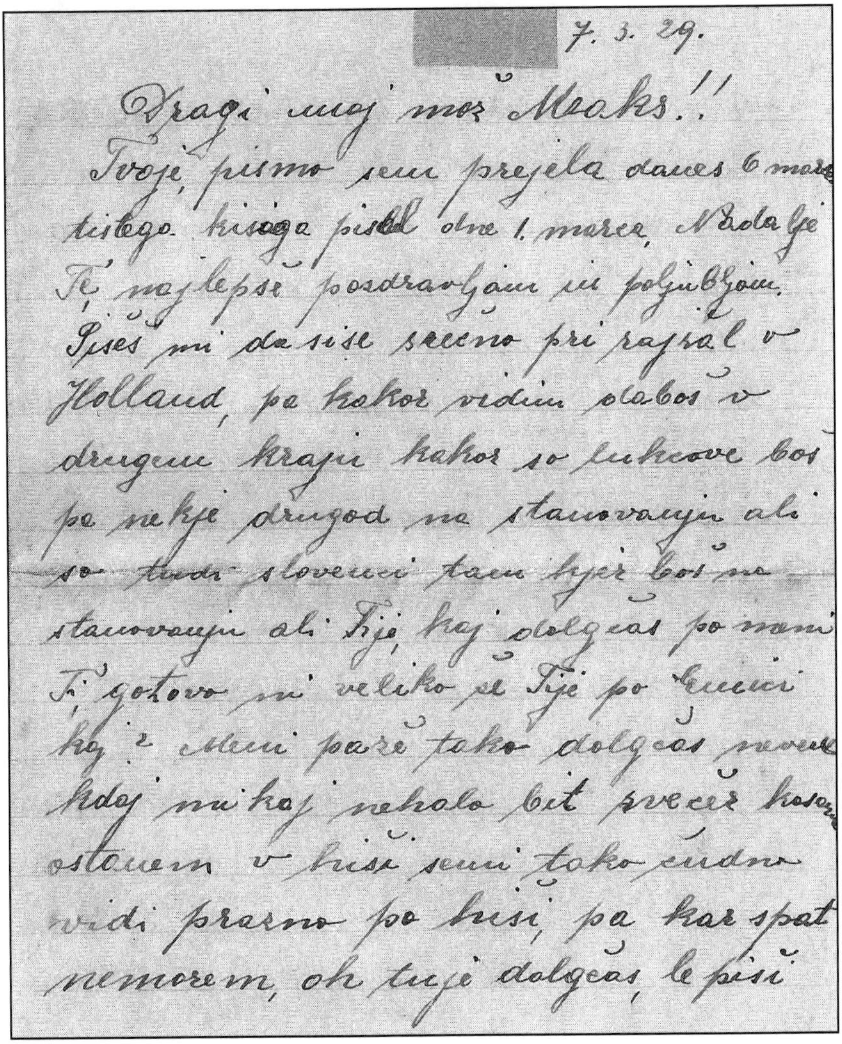

7. 3. 29.

Dragi moj mož Maks!!
Tvoje pismo sem prejela danes 6 marca
tistega kisega pisal dne 1. marca. Na dalje
Te najlepše pozdravljam in poljubljam.
Pišeš mi da si se srečno pripeljal v
Holland, pa kakor vidim slabos v
drugem kraju kakor so lukcove bos
pa nekje drugod na stanovanju ali
so tudi slovenci tam tyer boš na
stanovanju ali Tije kaj dolgčas po mani
Ti gotovo mi veliko se Tije po ...
kaj z mani paže tako dolgčas nevem
kdaj mi kaj nehalo bit zvečer ko se
ostanem v hiši sem tako čudno
vidi pravno po hiši, pa kar spat
nemorem, oh tuje dolgčas, le piši

Figure 2.2. The first page of Francka's letter to her husband Maks, dated March 7, 1929. *Courtesy of Marjan Drnovšek*

And Francka's thoughts flip again: if only it isn't too dangerous. She suggests to Maks that he stay long enough to earn money for the ticket and that if he still doesn't feel any better then, he should come home and they can again work on the land. She was content at home but knew that he hadn't been. She hoped he would be happier abroad but realized that he wasn't. She advises him to stay for a while to earn some money and then return home to her. She knows that he's bored, as she is, but tells him to be patient, that all of this shall pass and maybe soon.[38]

It is clear from the letters that Francka is afraid for Maks. She is also overwhelmed by the feeling that her husband wasn't content and happy at home—this makes her sad, and she returns to the previous thought: "now you're there abroad, toiling in those caves, I'm worried, whenever I think of you, what kind of danger you're in; we thought it would be a lot better, than it really is."[39] She's afraid that something would happen to him in the mine, and it tortures her even at night. She advises him to say an "Our Father" or "Hail Mary" or two, although she knows that he doesn't attend church on Sunday in the Netherlands. She is interested in what he does on Sundays, what religion they have in the Netherlands, and if people there are of a better class generally.[40] When she is telling him about the work on the land, she mentions in passing that she will work all of it and plant corn in addition to oats in the hope that he might come home that year. What is she in fact saying? The crisis that her husband felt was not over. Again, he wrote to her about the dangers due to gas and low ceilings in the mine shafts. Just like before, she again advises that he earn something and come home. She only wishes to pay off the debts and buy a cow.[41] She is afraid because he works in deep pits and links this to her fear of not knowing what would happen to the children if he had an accident; she can't ever shake off this fear. In the beginning of April he wrote that he would come home that year. She leaves the decision to him if he believed that he was in danger there. Slightly disappointed, she responds "so you'll leave work, you have a home after all," and concludes that "if you come it's better than to risk your life in those dangerous pits." In the same letter she vaguely expresses her hope that he might come after all, and if he doesn't, she'll manage on the farm by herself. At the same time, Francka emphasizes the lack of money and the constant expenses at home.[42]

Maks wrote to Francka about the explosion in one of the mines in Belgium, where three Slovenians were killed. Francka responded that she had read about it in *Domoljub*. She is terrified whenever she reads something like that. Francka is worried; she thinks about Maks night and day and is afraid that he will have an accident.[43] At the same time, she repeats several times that he wouldn't earn anything at home. Behind all that, we can sense her desire that he stay in the Netherlands as long as he is healthy and other circumstances don't aggravate. She asks him to write her about it because she is eager for news, especially on Sundays and holidays.[44] When receiving the message that his leg hurts, she gets frightened that it is the result of an injury in the mine. She fears for him and worries about what she would do at home with the children if they had no father. At that, she is again oscillating between the decisions of whether he should stay or return home. But in the same breath she mentions that they have debts. She advises him to be careful and writes that "it is true, though, that everything can't be helped; over there, the wages are good, but it's dangerous," and she expresses her hope: "you won't stay long right?"[45]

Maks wrote to Francka that in the Netherlands not only is the work hard, but it is also difficult to earn money. Francka responded that farmwork is also extensive and that he is better off over there, because, unlike her, he clocks off his hours and is then free. She can't afford that.[46] This is about comparing the hardness of the work on one side and the other. At the end of July he writes to her that the income is a lot better than at home. He also writes that he would go to Belgium if he spoke French; it would be better there, because the food is cheaper and it would be easier to live. Because he doesn't speak the language, Francka advises him to stay where he is.[47] He writes again that he will try to go elsewhere. Francka tells him to decide by himself. She suggests trying to find work in the state-owned mines if they are better organized there and if he doesn't like the private ones.[48] In the beginning of August he again writes that he is suffering. He is planning to find employment in a factory in the spring: the work is easier than in the very dangerous mine. Francka believes that by then he will also understand the language better.[49] At the end of August, Maks wrote to her about protection in the Netherlands for miners in

A WIFE AT HOME   83

cases of death or injury, writing that the mine administration pays for the expenses and in case of injury takes care of the wife and the children. But he believes that she is not indifferent and is afraid for him, although everything is taken care of. And she concludes that if she lost her husband, she wouldn't find a better one than her Maks.[50]

Marital Fidelity and Missing Her Husband

Immediately upon Maks's departure, Francka described the feeling of emptiness in the house and her insomnia because of his absence, which she expresses in a number of letters with "Oh, it's so boring here." She links her loneliness to the wintery conditions, snow, and the bora winds. (The weather was an important issue in debates with her husband, because it was important for farming.) So she often asks him about the weather in the Netherlands and hopes that it is better than at home. Then she asks him to write her often so she will feel better.[51] Francka uses the word "boredom" to mean different things: actual boredom, the fact that she misses having her husband near, and the negative reaction to their situation, such as "I know you don't miss me, maybe you only miss your daughter."[52] She starts all the letters with warm greetings, also on behalf of their daughter Emica and occasionally her own father as well. The expressions of warmth can be seen in her wishes for this letter to find him in the best mood and health, in her wishing him luck at work, and often in sending him kisses. At the same time she thanks him for his letters and kisses and greetings received. The words that she has been eagerly awaiting his dear and beloved letter always appear early on in her writing, undoubtedly the consequence of his already mentioned irresponsiveness to her letters. She also reminds him of the one-month anniversary of his departure from home, so she decided she would write a few lines. Deep love and vivaciousness can often be observed in her letters, such as when she writes that she is sending him nice and cordial greetings. Mostly, she begins each new section of the letter with "My dear, beloved husband Maks!" The farewell in the letter is also full of warmth, candid greetings, hot kisses, expressions of her love, and also greetings from their daughter Emica who can't forget him. After Lojzek's birth she includes him in the greeting.

Francka felt emptiness especially during holidays, such as around St. Joseph's Day and Easter.[53] In the second half of April she repeated her question about how Maks passes his Sundays, because she finds the house on Sundays and holidays very dull, and tears often come to her eyes when she is listening to her daughter asking after her father.[54] When Maks didn't send Francka a letter for Christmas 1929, she got angry:

> My dear, beloved husband Maks. Before I write any further, I would like to kindly greet and kiss you, as would both children and the grandfather. Then, I ask you why is it that you're not responding to my letters? I don't understand, are you maybe angry with me and this is why you don't write to me? Maks, write to me about what's going on. I was very sad when I got no greetings for the holidays, not even for New Year.[55]

Francka spent the Christmas holidays by the tiled stove (*kmečka peč*), and they seemed extremely long to her.[56] After the usual greetings she asks Maks again to respond to her immediately. Most of the letters express her longing for him: she lives for herself and her children but mostly remains at home all day long. At that time, she is left with nothing but the feeling of missing her husband, which she expresses with words: "many pass by, but mine doesn't come." She feels lonely and hopes that eventually it will be better.[57] She often complains about the children and loneliness at home and says that Maks is better off because he has work and company over there.[58]

When she was still a young mother and not yet showing, men must have been swarming around her house. She doesn't write about this but merely hints about it at times. Because she bought firewood from a different seller than usual, her old provider must have become a little angry: Francka claims that she prefers to see him slightly angry than to see him come to her house while her husband is absent. People would immediately think that they have a thing going. When the seller was approaching the house she moved away or firmly closed the main door, and she added that "he's full of tricks."[59] In short, Francka's loneliness in the gossipy and smug village environment, in a house where she lived with her children and her father who had a drinking problem, had an influence on her physical and emotional state and safety.

Francka keeps repeating her plea that Maks should stay faithful to her and continues that because in a foreign place even husbands are more like boys, she hopes that "you're not one of them, right."[60] All of Francka's letters are full of expressions of loyalty and love for her husband. She often talks about herself, especially in the time of childbirth and after:

> Yes, my dear Maks! I have no peace, neither during the day, nor at night, I am always worried sick about something. This is why I find it hard to go through life, which is not, after all, a simple song.[61]

Occasionally Francka expresses jealousy, because the village environment is rife with accounts of infidelities on both sides, at home and among the emigrants. She is critical of husbands and boyfriends in Maks's circle in the Netherlands. About A. from his circle she claims that he is a slob and a womanizer and that she is afraid he will corrupt Maks. A. was a womanizer at home, which Francka was told by the midwife, who had heard it from the doctor, and also that A. was anxious to go out into the world in order to have other women. But he won't stay young and handsome forever, writes Francka, and concludes that "oh, what has the world come to, no more true love and fidelity in marriages, what will become of this."[62]

Write to Me and Tell Me If You're Pleased: Emica, Childbirth, and Lojzek

Daughter Emica features prominently in Francka's letters. In one of them Francka describes Emica as similar to her father and his family in appearance and character. She is a girl one has to like, with round, rosy cheeks and bright eyes who prefers eating meat and drinking tea if it has wine in it and always asks for bread and coffee. Francka believes she has an excellent memory. Emica still remembers the time when her father Maks was at home.[63] And there was a new baby on the way.

Francka became pregnant in the autumn of 1928. Even then she was worried how she would bear the pregnancy.[64] In the letter of March 25 she complained of pains in her legs and growths on her skin, which she connected to the pregnancy. The fetus wore her down. She wrote that she felt it like a heavy rock, as if it were dead. As for the pregnancy, she was not sure if the villagers knew anything about it, because she hadn't told anyone about her condition yet.[65] By the end of April her predictions from the autumn of 1928 about the difficult pregnancy have turned out to be true. Now, she consoles herself with folk complacency: "whatever will happen will happen, there's nothing to be done."[66] At the end of May 1929, about a month before her due date, she mentions that she often remembers Maks's anger when she became pregnant again.[67] (We must consider at least two more children she had before, Maks Jr., who probably died, and the lively Emica.) The household also included Francka's aged father, who lived with Francka and occasionally helped with work and played with Emica. Francka was looking for help at the farm as well as for the time of the birth, but in her opinion help didn't come cheap. The relationship with her husband's family who lived nearby was cold.[68] She was also saddened by the news of difficult childbirths and stillborn children in the neighborhood. Francka was shattered by the deaths of the children who succumbed to the contagious scarlet fever: she writes in detail about three sisters aged ten, fifteen, and seventeen who died of it within a week.[69] She voices her fear that Maks will forget her. In the letters, she complains that she has nobody to help her, that she works hard, and that she needs to pay for what she needs. Above all she is bored; in other words, she misses her husband. There is no one she can talk to about her problems, and she only waits for the end of the pregnancy, whatever that will be.[70] When Maks asked when the baby was due, she responded that at the time they had calculated together, sometime by the June 20. She often complains that she is lonely, that she can't sleep, and that she can't work alone the way she would want to. She would have complained to her husband more often about the pregnancy problems, but she didn't dare: "men don't know what this is like, and if you don't experience it yourselves, then you don't like to believe it."[71]

Francka loved planning for the future, so she asked her husband how she should notify him about the birth of the child: with a letter or a telegram. She believes that she won't be able to write at least for a week. She wished that the husband pick the child's name, whether a boy or a girl. She's afraid of dying in childbirth and consequently fears for the fate of her own children, who would pass into the hands of other people and wouldn't be privy to a mother's love, which she can give them. The fear of death is expressed several times. As for her husband, she knows that he wouldn't be able to raise them, as they are still too small. She is also afraid that she will carry the child past term. At the end of May she complains that she is afraid of the end of the pregnancy and the delivery itself, because there are many cases when a doctor is called to the labor because of complications. She is scared because she is on her own and mentions in passing that she is sorry to have let her husband go in such a time. She is sad because they don't live together, she is bored, and she is missing something because he is not at home.[72] But it upsets her to get no response or commentary on her detailed account of her trouble from his letters, and she wants to know why. She wants to be prepared just in case something happens to her. She links Maks's lukewarm response to his displeasure when she got pregnant. Francka says that he told her he wouldn't care for the baby when she got pregnant. Maks didn't want this baby, which he further confirms in his response to Francka's question as to whether she should send him a telegram when the baby is born.[73] On June 1 she received her husband's letter with his photo and calmly repeated her question from the previous letter. As for the pregnancy, she calmly wrote that they're both responsible for it. She insisted that he should

Figure 2.3. When Francka was visiting a nearby town, she sent her husband a postcard featuring a group of children (Francka to Maks, October 23, 1929). *Courtesy of Marjan Drnovšek*

choose the name. Because of the fetus's position, the midwife predicted a complicated delivery; Francka wrote that the delivery was normal for the first son and daughter. Her husband hinted that maybe she should give birth in a hospital, but she found this too wasteful, and in addition it would be the beginning of the grass-cutting season. During the couple of days before the delivery they were cutting and drying hay and clover. Her anxiety about everything is sometimes replaced by her optimism because of the new family member within a week. The letter was written on June 16. In the next letter Francka informs Maks that she hasn't yet given birth. She knows that Maks would prefer a boy.[74] She still hopes that the date of delivery will be around June 20. Then she slips into depression again and shows it with the expressions of fear that everything will go wrong and because everything is dragging along while the child is getting bigger and bigger, and she is worried what will happen to her. Francka doesn't know when she can send Maks news of the birth. She decides to dismiss the maid who helped her because she doesn't know when she will give birth, and she wrote that she wished her state would be over, "but only God knows when the time will come!"[75]

In the last part of the letter written three days before the delivery, Francka expressed some dark thoughts regarding the farm, which we could place within the framework of the prepartum depressive state. She writes to Maks that she has no intention of working the fields if he doesn't come back, because she couldn't do it on her own while taking care of the children. She draws a question mark beside this, as it is more intended as a question to her husband. This year they won't have a cow and certainly no pig. Francka has enough lard and doesn't care about the meat. She will only plant potatoes and some oats, nothing else. Working the land with strangers is worth nothing, she adds. Their own experience with the land has shown them that they had a lot of work and no money. They were always without money. She is concerned that Maks was annoyed and angry with her, even though none of it was her fault. She won't keep hens either, just a few for their own needs. She would rather sell all the oats: without livestock, the sty will remain so empty and cold that hens won't even lay eggs.[76]

On the afternoon of July 3, Francka gave birth to son Alojz. The same day she sent a letter to her husband about the event.

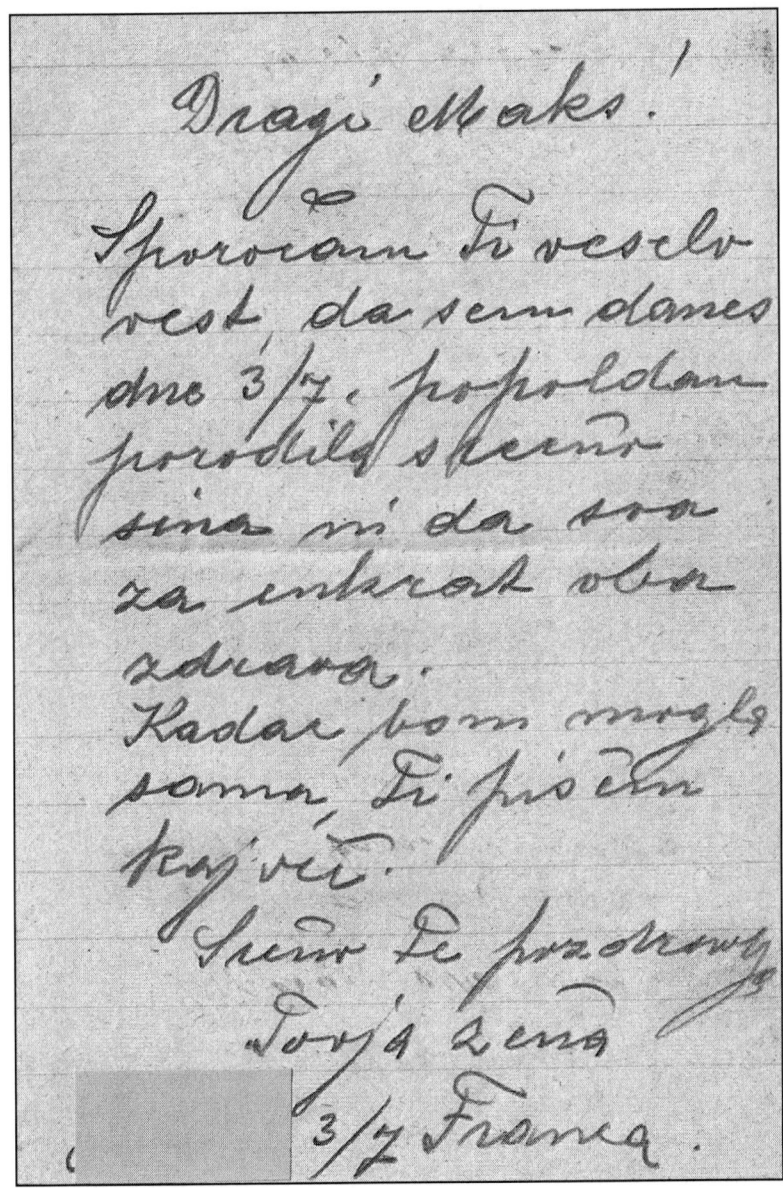

Figure 2.4. The letter about childbirth from the delivery bed (Francka to Maks, July 3, 1929). *Courtesy of Marjan Drnovšek*

On that day she was drying hay until three in the afternoon and was in the hay barn an hour later when the contractions started. She gave birth at a quarter to six in the evening.[77] On July 5 Francka sent Maks a letter with an optimistic note: "please receive my regards from Rome,"[78] and she thanked him for the letter he sent her on June 30. She writes that she and the baby are healthy, that the boy is beautiful and looks like him, and that all three of them are his. Francka says that Emica looked at the baby in awe, especially because he was crying.[79] After ten days when Francka got out of bed, she had received no letter from Maks. She expresses indignation. That she asks him today for the last time, and if he doesn't listen regarding his answers to her letters, she will never ask him again.[80] The first letter after childbirth came to her address between July 17 and 27. It is difficult to say why the letter came so late. (Based on my present knowledge about their relationship, I can conclude that his silence wasn't accidental and was probably a consequence of his rejection of the baby.)

Francka went to a healer because of the postpartum difficulties, and the healer told her that she was probably pregnant again. Francka denied this, explaining that her husband wasn't at home, to which the healer retorted that she might be honest, but there were a lot of women who gave in to sexual life while their husbands were away.[81] By the way, Francka's letters contain a lot of village gossip, and much of it has to do with adultery, which was commonplace among the villagers and also among the husbands working abroad. Francka fills her letters to Maks with a good number of these stories and often adds her hope and at the same time expresses her trust that he is faithful to her in the Netherlands.

Presumably because of the rumors and insinuations, Francka discusses sex with Maks, or lack thereof, which she describes with the word "boredom." Despite occasional misunderstandings and gripes, the longing for her husband is always present. And when she was dreaming about her visit to the Netherlands, she quickly regains composure more than once and writes that she doesn't want to visit him because of sex; Maks knows her well and knows that she can be celibate.

Until the birth of their son Alojz, or Lojzek, she often informs her husband in the introduction or the conclusion—or sometimes in the middle—of the letters about their daughter's development, illnesses, and image of her father abroad. When the son arrived, she expanded her information to him as well. Her letters follow a regular pattern: first she greets Maks in her own name, then in her daughter's, and only then in the name of her aged father. Immediately after Maks's departure she asked him if he missed his daughter. The girl mentions him every day: she no longer says that papa went away to work but that he should write home.[82] Francka reiterates often that Emica hasn't forgotten him, that she has grown, and that she can open the door by herself and can speak fairly well already.[83] Francka says that Emica is becoming more and more like her father, that she's healthy, and that the little one will be just like him as well.[84] The daughter misses him, remembers him every day, and likes looking at his photo. She is constantly asking where father is and hasn't yet forgotten how mummy slept next to him, because the child knows very well, remembers very well, and has an excellent memory.[85] Francka conveys Emica's words and sentences in child's language and tries to emulate her chatter and thoughts for Maks. Emica plays in the courtyard with cats and chickens. Her grandfather keeps her company, and they get along really well. She stated that she would go to her father in the Netherlands by herself; she would sleep at his house and get some money from him.[86] She helps her bring firewood into the kitchen, she talks a lot, she's tall and slight, and takes after her father.[87] When Francka received her husband's letter, the daughter just knew that it was from her father. Francka stresses what a good girl Emica is and the grandfather is in awe. Francka writes that Emica is just like him because she likes eating eggs and other finer things: "she's so much your daughter!"[88] After the childbirth in the beginning of July, in the time of Maks's silence and her and Lojzek's health problems, Emica takes backstage in her letters for a while. At first she was surprised because of the newborn, but later she accepted him. Francka writes that Emica keeps asking why her father is not there and why he doesn't come to see the baby sleeping in the crib.[89]

Just over three weeks after childbirth, Francka writes to her husband that they are all in good health. She complains about tiredness and the lack of rest. Lojzek is constantly sick. There are the children, she's alone for all the work in the house, but she can't yet work outside. The son was getting stronger. She complains to Maks several times that she has a lot of work with the children, laundry, and especially the newborn boy who doesn't sleep enough during the day. Francka is asking herself if the children will love their father as much as she does. Distressed because of the boy's insomnia, she envies her husband who can spend at least the nights undisturbed, unlike herself. And Emica? If anybody asks her about her father, she retorts immediately that he is digging coal in the Netherlands, that she will go to him, and that he will buy her cakes.[90]

Here, Francka mentions St. Nicholas (Sv. Miklavž), whose feast on December 6 was still many months away, and hints to her husband that she set out the basket for him last year and he brought her Lojzek. Somewhat jokingly she wrote that she doesn't care for these kinds of presents, because they're nothing but trouble. She says to her husband: "if it's possible, we've had enough of those, right?"[91] The problems with the son's health continued. Francka is still breast-feeding; she's healthy and can still breast-feed. At the same time, she mentions that she now lives better and more easily than she used to. When she was in labor with Emica she was afraid that she would die, which did her great harm; pregnancy also changed her figure. Francka now is only worried about Lojzek, who is still ill. She doesn't know what would happen to him if she died. The husband and Emica could do without her, but it would be harder for Lojzek, because he's so small. She supposes that Maks would find another woman and then skips to another topic. In the end, she returns to Emica and chides her a little bit, that she has become naughty and would need her father to bring her up because she's not afraid enough of her mother. When Francka was still in bed after childbirth, Emica was being naughty and was jumping around the house so much that everything was shaking. Emica was curious when Francka was writing to her husband and kept asking what she was writing, so she added to the letter that Emica greeted him specially.[92] In the letter that she wrote at four o'clock on a Saturday morning she conveyed to him Emica's desire to go to the Netherlands to see her father and also see a Dutch Christmas Nativity scene.[93] Francka also sent him the children's New Year's greetings on behalf of Emica:

> Dearest papa! We wish you (happy New Year) both, Lojzek and I. I got your postcard; thank you very much. We're also sending you many warm greetings and kisses for the New Year. I am well; mummy baked me a big potica which I am eating and I'm waving and sitting on the tiled stove. Many greetings from your Emica and Lojzek.[94]

Francka also added that she had received his letter and would write back soon.[95] In the beginning of January 1930 she wrote to her husband that she was still breast-feeding her son and didn't know how to wean him, because he won't drink anything else. He still had a skin disease.[96] But she still had no answer as to whether Maks was happy that a son was born.

In Spring We Shall Come to Holland

In the middle of April 1929 Francka tells Maks about painting the cot and the door and that she is planning to have a new table made for the house this year. As for the Netherlands, "I know we won't travel to the Netherlands, you'd rather come back home to me, wouldn't you?"[97] In the letter that Francka received on June 1, 1929, Maks hinted that she should come to the Netherlands in the autumn. She would, she responded, if she is well but continues that there are also Emica and another baby on the way. Then Francka writes extensively about the issue of breast-feeding and boiling milk. (Milk has a special place in Francka's story. From the first to the last letter she occasionally touches upon the topic of milk, which she bought from the cheapest source. She cut off all ties to her previous supplier, who was insulted because of that and was also probably a relative. Her previous supplier never forgave her for that. Even when she was breast-feeding and was writing to her husband in the Netherlands, she emphasized the question of milk and what the situation might be like there. I have to stress that despite having two children, the house did not have its own cow; however, milk was their basic food.) Maks puzzled her with this invitation, and she said that she would have to think about it. She would like to come, but she has some obvious obstacles. In this letter, she discusses sex as well:

> You know, my beloved Maks! I should love to come to you, if only I didn't have circumstances that keep me here; I'm so bored at home and miss my Maks. I know I can't get used to this, but don't think I'm so needy in that other respect—for that only I could be alone for years and years, you know me, Maks, don't you! Those kinds of worries you just don't need to have; well, I know that you don't and that I have more about you, how will you put up with it: do write me about that as well![98]

At that, Francka mentions the departure of the wife of one of Maks's colleague's: "she's happy to be reunited with her husband, I know what it's like, and she has no farm, so she could leave everything behind and go."[99] Francka's hesitation to leave for Holland was understandable because of the farm and the children. She oscillated between enthusiasm about leaving and anxiety. To only go for a visit or to settle there were the dilemmas. She was afraid of the foreign language. Maks was also not very convincing in this regard. In short, all we know is that in 1931 he was still abroad while Francka was at home with both children.

Conclusion

I can write that the story of Francka's family—which is marginally also a story of the rest of the relatives and other villagers, both at home and in the Netherlands—is only a fleeting impression that introduces us to a segment of the life and fate of a separated family. More than the beginning, we miss the end of the story. I have not dealt with all the questions that arise from reading the letters; I have focused on those connected to the personal and migration issues. While we do not have

Maks's letters, we can see Francka's sincerity in a large number of her letters written in a relatively short time span. Their careful construction, reiterated questions, and information—especially their human warmth, the expressions of joy and even more so of disappointment, and the inclusion of the children, particularly Emica whose words reveal a child who longs for her father and expects him to return or keep in touch—give the story a personal and affected touch. Through Francka's letters we see the everyday life of a woman, a wife, and a mother whose husband works abroad. In short, I can define this story as Francka's story, a story of a woman who must take care of a farm surrounded by neighbors, some kind, some less so, and some downright hostile, and also goes through pregnancy and childbirth. The most surprising aspect is the husband's attitude in the times immediately before, at, and after the birth. The letter silence on the side of the husband is more or less obvious; Francka's fear and despair are clearly stated. Nevertheless, the last preserved letter, from January 26, 1930, begins and ends with the following words:

> My dear, beloved husband Maks! I cordially greet and kiss you, as do your two small children.... So from all of us, a warm greeting and a kiss, especially from myself, your loyal and loving Francka.[100]

Notes

1. The child's given name was Alojz. Lojzek is a diminutive form and a common nickname for Alojz, especially for young boys.

2. Francka to Maks, August 10, 1929, private collection of Marjan Drnovšek. All letters in this chapter are from the private collection of Marjan Drnovšek unless otherwise noted.

3. I received the letters from Zmago Tančič, a collector and an expert in antique postcards.

4. Vladimir Žumer, ed., *Arhivski predpisi v Republiki Sloveniji* [Archival Regulations in the Republic of Slovenia] (Ljubljana: Arhiv Republike Slovenije, 2007).

5. Marjan Drnovšek, "Osebno in javno v izseljenski korespondenci" [The Personal and the Public in Emigrant Correspondence], *Dve domovini/Two Homelands*, no. 20 (2004): 113–51.

6. A popular name for the Slovenian migrants in the Netherlands.

7. Francka to Maks, May 4, 1929. Maks had a very distant relationship with his mother. Was this the consequence of the fact that she disliked Francka? Maks's mother was angry with him because he went to work abroad; he should have stayed at home and worked, for he had a horse and could drive, or transport, and make his money that way (Francka to Maks, May 4, 1929).

8. The Catholic Slovenian newspaper *Rafael* for migrants was published in the Netherlands between 1931 and 1935. In 1931 it had as many as 1,500 subscribers.

9. The communist *Slovensko delavsko—Kmečka republika* [Slovenian Worker—Peasant Republic] was occasionally published in the beginning of the 1930s. It is a newspaper for Slovenian workers and peasants abroad.

10. Marjan Drnovšek, "Izseljensko in drugo časopisje med Slovenci v zahodni Evropi do leta 1940" [Emigrant and Other Newspapers among Slovenians in Western Europe before 1940], *Dve domovini/Two Homelands*, nos. 2–3 (1992): 287–88, 298–99.

11. *Domoljub* [Patriot] was a conservative middle-brow paper for rural areas. It was published during 1888–1944.

12. Francka to Maks, December 27, 1929. *Slovenec* (1873–1941) is a Catholic paper. Under the editor Dr. Ivan Ahčin (1929–1941) it became one of the leading Yugoslav papers, thanks to editorials and commentaries of international events.

13. Francka to Maks, January 5, 1930.

14. Ana Barbič, "Kmetica in kmečka družina v tranziciji: Teoretična razmišljanja in empirične ugotovitve" [The Female Farmer and the Farm Family in the Time of Transition: Theoretical Considerations and Empirical Findings], *Družboslovne razprave* 16, nos. 34–35 (2000): 97–125.

15. Francka to Maks, March 31, 1929.

16. Francka to Maks, March 12, 1929.

17. Francka to Maks, March 16, 1929.

18. Ibid.

19. Francka to Maks, March 7, 1929.

20. Francka to Maks, March 21, 1929.

21. Francka to Maks, April 19, 1929.
22. Francka to Maks, May 12, 1929.
23. Francka to Maks, April 28, 1929.
24. Francka to Maks, May 15, 1929.
25. Francka to Maks, May 31, 1929.
26. Francka to Maks, July 3, 1929.
27. Francka to Maks, July 5, 1929.
28. Francka to Maks, July 12, 1929.
29. Francka to Maks, July 16, 1929.
30. Francka to Maks, 1929.
31. Francka to Maks, July 19, 1929.
32. Francka to Maks, July 27, 1929.
33. Francka to Maks, November 26, 1929.
34. Francka to Maks, January 26, 1930.
35. Francka to Maks, September 23, 1929.
36. Francka to Maks, March 31, 1929.
37. Francka to Maks, March 7, 1929.
38. Francka to Maks, March 12, 1929.
39. Francka to Maks, March 31, 1929.
40. Francka to Maks, March 16, 1929.
41. Francka to Maks, March 21, 1929.
42. Francka to Maks, April 4, 1929.
43. Francka to Maks, April 8, 1929. In an accident on Easter Saturday, April 2, at Zwartberg-Vaterschei mine, eight Slovenian miners were killed; six of them were married. Approximately ten thousand people attended the funeral, while the Queen of Belgium visited the families of the injured miners (Hrvatski državni arhiv [Croatian State Archives], Zagreb, Izseljenski komitarijat, Box 566).
44. Francka to Maks, April 19, 1929.
45. Francka to Maks, April 22, 1929.
46. Francka to Maks, June 16, 1929.
47. Francka to Maks, June 27, 1929.
48. Francka to Maks, June 31, 1929.
49. Francka to Maks, August 5, 1929.

50. Francka to Maks, August 29, 1929.
51. Francka to Maks, March 7, 1929.
52. Ibid.
53. Francka to Maks, March 25, 1929.
54. Francka to Maks, April 19, 1929.
55. Francka to Maks, January 5, 1930.
56. Francka to Maks, December 27, 1929.
57. Francka to Maks, September 2, 1929.
58. Francka to Maks, 1929.
59. Francka to Maks, May 18, 1929.
60. Francka to Maks, July 2, 1929.
61. Francka to Maks, 1929.
62. Ibid.
63. Francka to Maks, April 22, 1929.
64. Francka to Maks, April 28, 1929.
65. Francka to Maks, March 25, 1929.
66. Francka to Maks, April 28, 1929.
67. Francka to Maks, May 31, 1929.
68. Francka to Maks, April 8 and 13, 1929.
69. Francka to Maks, March 16 and 21, 1929.
70. Francka to Maks, May 12, 1929.
71. Francka to Maks, May 15, 1929.
72. Francka to Maks, May 26, 1929.
73. Francka to Maks, May 31, 1929.
74. Francka to Maks, June 21, 1929.
75. Francka to Maks, June 25, 1929.
76. Francka to Maks, June 30, 1929.
77. Francka to Maks, 1929.
78. The Slovenian phrase "Pozdrav iz Rima!" ("Greetings from Rome!") is an old-fashioned and discreet way for a woman to announce that she has given birth.
79. Francka to Maks, June 5, 1929.
80. Francka to Maks, July 12, 1929.
81. Francka to Maks, November 26, 1929.

82. Francka to Maks, March 7, 1929.
83. Francka to Maks, May 4, 1929.
84. Francka to Maks, May 15, 1929.
85. Francka to Maks, May 18, 1929.
86. Francka to Maks, May 22, 1929.
87. Francka to Maks, June 25, 1929.
88. Francka to Maks, June 30, 1929.
89. Francka to Maks, 1929.
90. Francka to Maks, August 5, 1929.
91. Francka to Maks, October 29, 1929.
92. Francka to Maks, December 12, 1929.
93. Francka to Maks, December 21, 1929.
94. Francka to Maks, December 26, 1929.
95. Ibid.
96. Francka to Maks, January 5, 1930.
97. Francka to Maks, April 13, 1929.
98. Francka to Maks, June 2, 1929.
99. Ibid.
100. Francka to Maks, January 26, 1929.

References

Barbič, Ana. "Kmetica in kmečka družina v tranziciji: Teoretična razmišljanja in empirične ugotovitve" [The Female Farmer and the Farm Family in the Time of Transition: Theoretical Considerations and Empirical Findings]. *Družboslovne razprave* 16, no. 34–35 (2000): 97–125.

Drnovšek, Marjan. "Izseljensko in drugo časopisje med Slovenci v zahodni Evropi do leta 1940" [Emigrant and Other Newspapers among Slovenians in Western Europe before 1940]. *Dve domovini/Two Homelands*, nos. 2–3 (1992): 265–316.

Drnovšek, Marjan. "Osebno in javno v izseljenski korespondenci" [The Personal and the Public in Emigrant Correspondence]. *Dve domovini/ Two Homelands*, no. 20 (2004): 113–51.

Hrvatski državni arhiv [Croatian State Archives], Zagreb, Croatia.

Letters of Francka and Maks. Private collection of Marjan Drnovšek.

Zgodovinski arhiv Ljubljana, Enota za Gorenjsko [Historical Archives of Ljubljana, Unit for Gorenjska], Kranj, Slovenia.

Žumer, Vladimir, ed. *Arhivski predpisi v Republiki Sloveniji* [Archival Regulations in the Republic of Slovenia]. Ljubljana: Arhiv Republike Slovenije, 2007.

II Silenced Stories
Emancipatory Experiences

Chapter 3

Aleksandrinke in Egypt
Between Condemnation and Adoration

Daša Koprivec

> I was working for a family of Copts in Cairo. I took care of two girls. They were a nice family, they were very kind. But here's what it was: we weren't so free. I couldn't go out. I missed that a lot. Only on Sundays they somehow let me out. But I got used to that, too. I had a wonderful job, I sometimes think, why did I get married![1]

This is what Mrs. Karmen Žuljan told us during our research. She was one of the many young girls who traveled from Europe to Egypt in the 1920s because they knew they would be able to get work as housemaids, chambermaids, or nannies. This chapter will discuss the life stories of the female migrant workforce from the western part of the Slovenian ethnic territory to Egypt. In Slovenia we call them *aleksandrinke* [sing. *aleksandrinka*], after the Egyptian port of Alexandria where most of them found employment. Some authors state that as early as the beginning of the twentieth century, there were forty-five hundred aleksandrinke living in Alexandria and more than a thousand in Cairo. In this chapter we will use the results of a research project of aleksandrinke and their descendants currently being conducted by the Slovene Ethnographic Museum in Ljubljana.

The research project is multilayered because it includes fieldwork and the use and study of other relevant materials. Fieldwork in Slovenia is mostly carried out in the Goriška region. Fieldwork in Egypt has so far taken place in Cairo and Alexandria in 2007 and 2010. The study includes members of four generations: the aleksandrinke themselves and their children, grandchildren, and great-grandchildren. We have also established contacts with descendants of the aleksandrinke abroad. We have the most contact with those in Australia, Canada, Switzerland, Denmark, and also Egypt.[2]

The migration of Slovenians to Egypt started soon after the construction of the Suez Canal, which opened the route for European migration into Egypt. Egypt saw the influx of cotton merchants, architects, traders, doctors, clerks, and others. For Slovenian women this was important as early as the 1870s, particularly the migration of Italian and Austrian families to Egypt. During the first phase of migration, which lasted until the end of World War I, Slovenian women from the Goriška region lived within the Austro-Hungarian Empire, and many were employed as housemaids in its cities, such as in Trieste, Milan, and Gorizia. In fact, the first Slovenian women arrived in Egypt with Italian families from Milan and Trieste and with Austrian families from Vienna and continued to work for the families in Cairo or Alexandria.

The migration of European families to Egypt grew more intensive from the 1890s onward. The Suez Canal had a central role in the economic progress of Egypt. Meanwhile, Egypt was more and more dominated by foreign forces. In addition to the Ottoman authorities, the English and the French increased their presence in the economy and in politics. After the dissolution of the Ottoman Empire, Great Britain, France, and Italy affirmed their political and economic supremacy in the area: Great Britain in Egypt, Sudan, Jordan, Iraq, and then Palestine; France in Syria, Algeria, Morocco, and Tunisia; and Italy in Libya.[3] The political and economic power of the European countries in the Middle East enabled migration for many European individuals and families because they got the chance to earn money.

Figure 3.1. Aleksandrinke in working clothes, Alexandria, 1930s. *Courtesy of the Slovene Ethnographic Museum*

In this period, people of many nationalities lived in Egypt, including French, Germans, English, Italians, Jews, Egyptians, Copts, Greeks, Armenians, Syrians, Turks, Lebanese, Maltese, and Sudanese.[4]

Even after World War I, the migration of the Slovenian population to Egypt was characteristic for the western part of the ethnic territory, the part that was annexed to Italy after the war and the dissolution of the Austro-Hungarian Empire. The tradition of migration to Egypt continued because it was still possible to get work there, and sea travel between Trieste and Alexandria was easy.[5] Slovenian women left for Egypt mostly from the rural hinterlands of the cities of Trieste and Gorizia. The two Slovenian regions from which the most people migrated were Goriška and Karst. The available data shows that the vast majority of the migrants were women, but there were also some men and children.[6] In the museum research, we paid more attention to female migration to Egypt. It was very intensive for more than sixty-five years, from 1870 to 1935, and was only interrupted in the turbulent times for the Mediterranean as World War II loomed.

Migration to Egypt

After World War I, the western part of the Slovenian ethnic territory was in great economic and social distress. The migration of women and girls to Egypt afforded the possibility of improving family economic and social status. There was a possibility of choice but more so for women than for men. The men who stayed at home were on the one hand dependent on the income of their wives or daughters in Egypt, and on the other hand they existed in some sort of a lethargic state. They were casually employed or decided to immigrate to Argentina, which was an extreme choice because there was fear that men would never return—something that indeed did happen and not only rarely.[7] The husbands of aleksandrinke who decided against migrating to Argentina or Egypt mostly stayed on with their parents or in-laws, depending on where they started a family. The functioning of their families in such cases differed from the established perceptions of labor division between husband and wife, as the wife was the breadwinner and the husband the primary caretaker of the children. The society often stigmatized them, and some men eased their distress with alcohol. From a time distance, a granddaughter of two aleksandrinke, on both her mother's and her father's sides, told us:

> These men stayed alone at home; the women worked and earned money for the land and other things. And these men, they had

nobody, just the tavern, children, and those wives who stayed at home. And then they went to the tavern, a glass here and there; one can imagine the stories they were told. This is where that voice came from that the women who came from Egypt, one would think they would tell them thank you so much for everything, but in fact they were somehow pushed aside. And from the mothers-in-law, the husbands, and the children who'd forgotten them. They were, so to say, the ones who were the most estranged. That was the pity. There was nothing to make that money worthwhile then, one would say.[8]

Migrations to Egypt significantly influenced family life, because for the women who stayed in Egypt for ten, fifteen, or even twenty years this was not just about the departure to Egypt but was also about the accepted way of life, accepted in one way or another by all adult family members.

The variegated social circumstances, numerous economic reasons, and different emotional impulses were all reasons for departure to Egypt. However, aleksandrinke were individuals. The economic status of the family could therefore either be the reason or merely a trigger for departure—a possibility to leave the situation that caused distress to a particular woman in her home environment. The economic situation was thus a welcome trigger to leave for Egypt, where it was easier for them to live. The distinction between the trigger and the cause for departure has not been sufficiently emphasized in the existing studies or the cause and the trigger were considered the same, because the division line between them is subtle and only very few women would admit that upon leaving home they also felt relief.

Young girls went to Egypt, married there, and started families. Daughters went to help their father's family. Young wives went to help their in-laws, and young widowed mothers went because they had no other solution but to earn money in Egypt. They left their children with their parents, with their in-laws, or in foster care with another family from the village. I was surprised by the number of young widows in these parts, ages twenty-two to twenty-five, usually with a child

Figure 3.2. Husband and daughter sending a photo to mother in Egypt, 1930s. *Courtesy of the Slovene Ethnographic Museum*

or two, who had lost their husbands, usually a couple of years their senior, to pneumonia, tuberculosis, or general exhaustion after World War I. Numerous young widows decided to leave for Egypt, and when they returned home their children were adults. Thus, girls and women over several generations left. About the history of female migration in her family, the daughter of one aleksandrinka said that "Mother was also in Egypt. And her sister. Four aunts, my father's sisters, were also in Egypt. And grandmother also; don't worry, grandmother also went. She went to be a wet nurse, came back, had a baby, and went to Egypt to breast-feed. So they could buy some land."[9]

Figure 3.3. Aleksandrinke on the beach with the children they take care of, Alexandria, 1930s. *Courtesy of the Slovene Ethnographic Museum*

One aleksandrinka from the village of Bilje who was born in 1912 left for economic reasons. She said the following about her departure and the circumstances:

> We bought a house and father couldn't pay it off, so he took a loan from a bank. Father was a carpenter, but he earned badly; he worked but had losses. Therefore, he decided to go to Argentina in 1926. To leave, he also had to take a loan. At first he wasn't doing so poorly in Argentina. But in 1929 the Great Depression came there, and father lost his job in Buenos Aires. In 1931 I went to Alexandria. Every month I sent money home, and I was only paying for the interest on my father's loan. In 1936 I returned home for a visit for the first time; at the time I was twenty-four years old. I didn't intend to return to Egypt, but the interest on the house wasn't paid off yet, and father promised me a half of the house if I continued to work in Egypt and pay the interest. So I went back and paid for nine years—until 1939 when the war started and the lira was devaluated. Then father asked me to stay

in Egypt so they could buy a cow, so they could survive. I stayed and worked in Egypt for thirty-five years.[10]

An aleksandrinka born in 1916 remembers her departure differently: "I was so happy to go. And my mother, she told me all about life there because she had spent five years in Egypt. And I was happy that I'd see all the places where my mother was. And then my aunt took me where my mother worked; she took me to see that lady as well."[11] She said that she was pleased to leave because she was interested in everything new, and her mother's narration was an important emotional impulse for departure. Although her reasons were mostly economic, because the parents had lost a part of their estate due to debts and sent their daughter to Egypt for this reason, I do believe that the narration of mothers, aunts, and other female relatives who experienced Egypt from a positive side influenced girls' decision to leave.

An aleksandrinka's son, born in 1922, born in 1922, remembers family circumstances that took his mother to Egypt:

> Mama helped here at home, but my father was not for work. My grandparents, with whom we lived, were very strict and always wanted to "*work, work, work.*" My parents also had a vineyard that my father worked.... Then, slowly, he abandoned everything. They lost a lot; there was a plot of land left here, a patch there. Then mother decided to go to Egypt, when she saw there was no solution at home. I was three when she left me. When I was ten, she sent for me.[12]

Another aleksandrinka's daughter, born in 1928, told us that the economic reason wasn't the only one for the departure of her mother to Egypt, because they had a big farm at home and lacked nothing:

> Father said, why did mother go to Egypt, when they could otherwise have another baby, because we had a large estate at home. In the end, there were just my brother and I. Such was fate.[13]

A granddaughter of yet another aleksandrinka pointed out the subtle nuances of interpersonal relationships in families that could lead to young wives' departures to Egypt, even when economic circumstances weren't so dire:

> You have to also look at what families were like. A bride married into a family, and there was a mother-in-law who wanted to *eat her alive*. It often started from there. The bride had nowhere to go. The mother-in-law had children, and sometimes there was twenty years' difference between the eldest and the youngest, so they were like grandchildren. And she wouldn't let go. And then the bride went to Egypt.[14]

At Work in Egypt

Slovenian women in Egypt, mostly in Cairo and Alexandria, were employed with families or in hotels or worked independently. In families, they did different jobs: some took care of the children, some took care of the elderly, and some managed the actual households. For all of them, it is characteristic that they lived with the families they worked for. Nannies took care of toddlers, wet nurses took care of infants, and nannies and governesses took care of older children. Slovenians did all of these different jobs. Chambermaids, cooks, and housekeepers took care of households and houses. Some were employed as ladies' maids and took care of their mistresses' clothes.

Slovenian women also worked in hotels as chambermaids. The rare ones did other work too. For example, they were seamstresses and worked and lived in their own homes and not with their masters' families.

Slovenian Wet Nurses in Egypt

Slovenian researchers find that our collective memory of aleksandrinke is imbued with the memories of wet nurses, although in the entire period of migration to Egypt fewer than one-quarter sought such employment.[15] This text is linked to a number of life stories also collected during our research, particularly testimonies of the children of those wet nurses who left for Egypt in the 1920s and 1930s.

Figure 3.4. An aleksandrinka with her daughter and a friend in Alexandria, Egypt, 1930s.
Courtesy of the Slovene Ethnographic Museum

A daughter of a wet nurse told us that her mother left in 1922, when the daughter herself was seven months old. Her mother and father were both widowed and on their second marriage. By 1922 they had five children altogether, and the money was scarce. After going to Egypt the mother didn't return except for occasional visits and died in Cairo in 1959. Then the narrator added: "We got nothing from our mothers, nothing at all. They left us and went away."[16]

The daughter of another aleksandrinka told us that her mother went to Egypt for the first time in 1930, when the narrator was two years old. After a couple of years the mother returned and then went back to Egypt as a wet nurse after the narrator's brother was born.

Figure 3.5. An aleksandrinka nanny with the children she takes care of in Cairo, Egypt, 1920s.
Courtesy of the Slovene Ethnographic Museum

Mama went down there as a wet nurse, she had a baby here and then went to Egypt to breast-feed. To prepare so they could buy some land. In 1935 she gave birth to my brother and left him with grandmother, her mother, and my brother and I lived there until 1947, until she returned from Egypt. But then we were more attached to grandmother, not mother, because it was grandmother who took care of us.[17]

A granddaughter of a wet nurse who left in 1925 told us that her grandmother had gone to Egypt after her husband's death. The grandmother had married onto her husband's farm but was not particularly welcome. She had two children. After the birth of the second child, her husband, who was a railway worker, fell ill and died of pneumonia. "With the death of her husband, her status in the family went down to zero," said the narrator. What to do? She decided to go to Egypt as a wet nurse. Her daughter was nine months old at the time.[18]

A daughter, born in 1941 after her mother's return, told us that her mother went to Egypt after the birth of her first child, the narrator's brother: "Mother went down there in 1930 and returned in December 1939. She went to be a wet nurse for a two-month-old baby girl. Her goal was to buy property."[19]

In the museum research we wanted to know a bit more about how the babies of those aleksandrinke who left as wet nurses were taken care of at home. We found out that mothers organized care for their children, mostly by hiring another wet nurse for them at home. The departing woman found a wet nurse for her baby among women close to her, maybe a sister, an aunt, or a neighbor with whom she could leave the baby. Women at home helped aleksandrinke, who paid them to breast-feed their children with the money they earned in Egypt. The wet nurses at home breast-fed two infants, their own and another one. I believe that this was a form of help among women, those who were leaving for Egypt and those who stayed at home. As Ellis Douek states,

> We know very little about the families in Egypt who decided to hire a wet nurse, because thus far we haven't carried out any studies. Did they decide to do so when the mother in Egypt didn't have enough milk to feed the newborn or did they hire a wet nurse as help, since the mothers in the higher echelons of society were busy participating in social life?[20]

Douek also questioned the reasons why the families in Egypt hired wet nurses. As a child he was taken care of by Maria Koron, from the village of Batuje. Douek was distressed when he learned about the death of Koron's mother, a wet nurse in Alexandria at the turn of the century who died there of typhoid fever. He was looking for the reasons to hire wet nurses and also for reasons that made women

Figure 3.6. Children of an aleksandrinka together with the child their mother takes care of in Egypt during her visit to the aleksandrinka's home, Prvačina, 1930s.
Courtesy of Slovene Ethnographic Museum

from certain environments choose emigration and accept work as paid wet nurses. Douek emphasized that it is only relatively recently that milk replacements and formula have been available, and before this if a mother had no milk or had died in childbirth, the infant would be lost too unless another woman was found to breast-feed it. When asking why women from Goriška—where his nanny's mother came from—emigrated to Egypt to take up paid positions as wet nurses, he particularly stressed the economic necessity of the time before World War I. He wrote that farming families from the village of Batuje, where his nanny (and her mother before her) came from, were faced with hunger before World War I and had only one resource still available, but it was one that had saved them from destitution or famine many times before, and they knew what they had to do. All they had to offer the outside world was their lactating mothers.[21]

In this sense, the migration of Slovenian women to Egypt is a topic closely linked to emotions—the emotions of migrants themselves and the emotions of their descendants. The emotional impulses are even more intensive when we think of an alekasandrinka as an absent mother or as a wet nurse. In such cases emotions can be tied to censure, incomprehension, and a feeling of shame. Although the aleksandrinke did take care of their own children as much as they could, researchers find that wet nurses were pelted with accusations of cruelty and negligence, because they were, after all, sentenced to leave their babies at home and go away to feed other women's infants.[22] As Inga Miklavčič-Brezigar wrote, the relatives of the aleksandrinke at home accepted the help of mothers and wives but at the same time resented them for leaving. The resentment and forgiveness are even today intertwined with understanding and misunderstanding of those times.[23]

Slovenian Nannies in Egypt

Slovenian nannies in Egypt were mostly young girls, but there were also married women who were already mothers and had left their children in the care of others at home and returned home after working in Egypt for years. Young girls often got married in Egypt, but some remained single all their lives and worked for the same families for more than twenty years. For a nanny, the work for the family was not simply employment in the traditional sense of the word; it was also a lifestyle. A time dimension played an important role there: for some, their stay extended to several years. We know of examples of aleksandrinke who stayed in Egypt for thirty, forty, or more years and only left there after the Suez Crisis in 1956 and returned to Goriška.

Figure 3.7. Slovenian nanny with the child she takes care of in Alexandria, Egypt, 1920s. *Courtesy of the Slovene Ethnographic Museum*

The nannies were closely tied to the families of the children they took care of. The nannies lived with the families, ate with them, raised their children, and were present all the time. They shared every hour of the day with the children and often shared a bedroom with the girls. In the morning, the nannies were the ones who woke up the children, prepared their breakfast, took them to school if they were of school age, waited for them after school, fixed them lunch, studied with them in the afternoon, took them to a park so they could play, made their dinner, washed them, and put them to bed.

As Ellis Douek says:

> Mothers, some distance away, were associated only with the better and more important things. They did not deal with cleanli-

ness or toilet or even daily meals. They were not involved with tantrums or the irritations of everyday life and some, I gathered from other children, were hardly ever there.[24]

The nanny brought her own character to the family, her habits and values, so her influence over the children she took care of was more long term than at first it may have seemed that it would be. They became new family members for ten, fifteen, and even more than twenty years. Hence, the testimonies of these children are of particular importance for Slovenian researchers, because they are a valuable source of information from the other side. Their testimonies are important for shedding light on what our nannies took out into the world when they went to work.

Slovenian nannies introduced new foods to the families that employed them, the taste and smell of which the children remember to this day. Some of the nannies taught the children a couple of Slovenian words or short ditties. The nannies were there when their children were growing up, so the importance of the nannies was not only in fulfilling the household chores; the upbringing by the nannies was etched into the psychological base of the growing children. Claudia Roden, Ellis Douek's sister, was also cared for by Maria Koron:

> Maria provided emotional and physical security for us children. Our nanny was like a rock on which the family stood. She was always there; we could always trust her, tell her everything, ask her things. Maria always gave me the feeling that I must do what I feel and believe. So she supported me; she supported me in a way to not accept things which I don't believe in.[25]

In the research, we most often encountered children from Jewish families who were brought up by Slovenian nannies; however, the nannies also took care of children in Greek, Armenian, and other families. Claudia Roden and Ellis Douek come from a family of Cairene Jews, and Maria lived with them in the quarter of Zamalek from 1934 to 1956. Unlike most of the other aleksandrinke who went to Egypt when they were younger, Maria was thirty-two years old when she arrived in Egypt, single and childless. She dedicated twenty-two years of her life to the three children of the Douek family. The name of Maria Koron became familiar to readers of Roden's and Douek's books.[26]

The testimonies of the children, whether oral or written, make the entire story of aleksandrinke somehow more real. When we hear similar stories from them as we did from aleksandrinke, the narratives of both join into a harmonious whole. This is why I asked Claudia about a typical day from her childhood, one that she would have spent in the care of her nanny Maria.

> First of all, there was a school. I went to the English school in Heliopolis, which at the time was still in the desert. The bus used to come and catch us from the bus stop near our house. It was a school bus, and Maria would come down with our school bags and waited for the bus with us. And then we went off. When we came back, it was usually around one, she was waiting for us at the bus stop. And then in the afternoon she would make a tea; she would make us food, and we would play. Our parents were usually not at home. Father was out at work, and my mother was with her friends or at the club. And there were always some activities. When we were very young we were quite wild, and I think Maria got into trouble. I was sorry about that, because I didn't want it. We used to hang from stuff; we were throwing things from the balcony; we were fighting against other people from the building. It was a special building with balconies. We used to spend all our time on the balcony, playing. We had many cousins who lived nearby and would all visit. Maria was a part of a huge—we were a big extended family. I think we kept her very busy.[27]

The children can thus testify not only about their own everyday experiences of life with their nannies but also about other dimensions of communal living. They talk about family relationships, the relationship between the mother and the nanny, and also about their own emotional division between their mother on one side and their nanny on the other.

Figure 3.8. Two children taken care of by a Slovenian nanny, Alexandria, 1920s. *Courtesy of the Slovene Ethnographic Museum*

Sometimes I felt torn between these two women, my mother and my nanny Maria, as I loved them both and in my mind I tried to avoid betraying the one to the other. Even now, in thoughts and memories, I feel the need to maintain a balance in what was truly a surfeit of love.[28]

Strong emotional ties were sometimes established between the children and the nannies, and the children still remember the nannies today.

Departure from Egypt

The migrations of Slovenian women and their families back home that began after World War II were numerous. In the postwar period, Egypt went through quick changes in its political system. The important years were 1948, 1952, and 1956. After the Egyptian political revolution that occurred from 1952 to 1956, the property of the families

Figure 3.9. A 1932 ticket for the ship *Esperia*, which brought an aleksandrinka back home. *Courtesy of the Slovene Ethnographic Museum*

without Egyptian nationality was seized. The English, French, and Jewish families that employed Slovenian women left Egypt by the end of the 1950s, and with their departure the economic basis that gave our people work and wages departed with them.

Narrators say that the political change in Egypt in the beginning of the 1950s came quickly and unexpectedly, and the people there weren't prepared for such a monumental life change. The harbinger of the change was also the foundation of Israel in 1948, with which Egypt immediately entered a war. The conflict between the two countries was most acutely felt by families of the Egyptian Jews, who were the first to leave. As a consequence, the Slovenian migrants who worked for them left as well. The political change in Egypt in the period 1952–56 established an independent Egyptian state with President Gamel Abdel Nasser as its head. In 1956 this was followed by a tripartite military attack by Israel, Britain, and France against Egypt over the nationalization of the Suez Canal. Because of the war, the foreigners mostly decided to leave Egypt, especially those holding a British or French citizenship; among them were also many Jewish families with foreign citizenship. In most cases, this was the end of the communal living of Slovenian women and their employers' families. Slovenian women and their families moved all over the world, to Australia, Canada, Brazil, Argentina, the United States but also to European countries such as Italy, France, Switzerland, and Belgium. Some Slovenian families came to what was then Yugoslavia, particularly to the Goriška region. Aleksandrinke who had married Jewish men mostly left Egypt soon after 1948. Most other nationally mixed marriages left in gradual waves. The first group left between 1946 and 1948, the second group left between 1952 and 1958, and the last group left between 1960 and 1962.[29] Among other locations, their descendants now live in Melbourne and Sydney in Australia, Montreal and Calgary in Canada, São Paulo in Brazil, and Rome, Turin, Bologna, Trieste, Gorizia, and Milan in Italy. "Only the graves remained in Egypt," said the son of an aleksandrinka who lived in Egypt for twenty years.[30]

Goriška after the Return

The aleksandrinke who returned to the Goriška region had to readjust to their home environment after being in Egypt. This was particularly difficult for mothers and those wives whose marital relationships had grown cold over the years. The relationships between spouses are well illustrated in the following statement: "Some wouldn't even come home while their husbands were alive."[31]

Mothers had a hard time establishing a relationship with their children after having been absent for ten or even more than twenty years. One daughter remembers her mother's arrival:

> She came during vintage. I happened to be at the door; we had a lot of work that day. She came and said, "Good afternoon, who are you? *Who are you!?* You're so dirty!" That was the greeting! You know what, mother was distanced from us. We had our grandmother for our mother. She took care of us. My brother and I never got along with Mother, because we weren't used to her. And Mother as well; she was used to over there and those children.[32]

The daughter still wishes today that her mother at least had not left for such a long time. Her mother left for the first time when the narrator was two years and stayed for four years (from 1930 to 1934). She returned, gave birth to the narrator's brother in 1935, and soon left again, for a long twelve years (1935 to 1947). The daughter was almost

Figure 3.10. Passport of an aleksandrinka and her daughter who was born in Egypt, issued upon their transfer from Egypt to Goriška, end of the 1950s. *Courtesy of the Slovene Ethnographic Museum*

twenty years old when she saw her mother again after spending her childhood and youth in the care of her grandparents.

> And then, when they came back, they were shocked. Even so, if you're with children every day, there are problems. Think now if you come home like that and you get a boy or a girl, fully formed. It also depended what words the husband used. You know, they were used to manners, breeding, there in Egypt.[33]

The knowledge that aleksandrinke had received in Egypt (for example, of foreign languages) had no value and could not be used constructively. Their relationships with their own children were distant. The material standard upon returning to Goriška was very poor compared to Egypt. They had to take to farmwork that they had become unused to in Egypt. If they were lucky, their families had used the money they sent from Egypt constructively, to renovate the house or to buy a vineyard, land, or cattle. In less fortunate cases, the families had lost everything during

World War II or the husband had given into drinking, and there was nothing left to show for the years of hard work. Many circumstances had a negative impact on the economic contribution that aleksandrinke gave to their home environment. World War I canceled out their contribution from the last quarter of the nineteenth century and the first decade and a half of the twentieth century, because the Goriška region was heavily involved in World War I as part of the Isonzo (Soča) Front. Everything was destroyed, and the exchange rate of the Austro-Hungarian currency decimated their savings. Interests for loans that state banks and building societies gave to families for postwar reconstruction gobbled up money that came from Egypt. And when the people of Goriška had finally recuperated a little bit there came a new war, World War II, and afterward a new country and a new devaluation.

> The home village was in ruins. They had nothing, not even a cauldron to cook. Banks pressured the debtors who'd borrowed money to renovate their homesteads, but were not able to return it on time. It was the same after World War I and World War II, when the lower end of the village Marija married into, was burned down. Two times nothing and starting anew from nothing![34]

So remembers a migrant who left for Egypt after World War I and returned after World War II. She worked in Egypt for twenty years, from 1926 to 1947, as a wet nurse and a nanny, and when she returned home there was precious little left of her savings. Likewise, political changes after World War II in the Goriška region caused the contributions of the aleksandrinke to be diminished; this was especially caused by socialism in regard to agricultural land, when many of the plots and houses that aleksandrinke had paid for with their work in Egypt were nationalized. At the same time, farmland became less and less valuable because of the rapid industrialization in the 1960s, and as young people found employment outside the villages, fewer worked on family farms. The land paid for by aleksandrinke continues even today to be overgrown and neglected because there is no one to work on it. "You can see that it was a farm, but today it's all overgrown," said a daughter of an aleksandrinka whose mother and grandmother worked in Egypt.[35] On the other hand, the material standard in Goriška after World War II grew rapidly, and a lot of what aleksandrinke had saved or brought with them no longer had the same economic value in the new circumstances.

> My mother went to Egypt as a girl; she worked there. She was there for four years; she prepared her entire trousseau there by herself. She had so much lace, crocheted lace. And there's none of it left; everything got lost.[36]

Thus, in the forefront of the memories of aleksandrinke remains an emotional evaluation that can either be negative and linked to the memory of an absent mother or positive when the descendants remember how their mothers brought home a cosmopolitan challenge. They brought the broadness of the world, tales of Paris, Nice, and Switzerland where they had spent summers with the children they took care of because the hot summers in Alexandria were unbearable for the rich foreigners from Europe. The aleksandrinke brought the European fashion in clothes, knowledge of foreign languages, and new dishes such as *kek, molokhiyah, hummus, tabbouleh,* and *foul*.[37] They brought home otherness that showed itself as an essential characteristic of their identity after their return to Goriška.

Evaluation of the Aleksandrinke Today

In recent years the aleksandrinke have come to Slovenian consciousness as so-called women with a wound on their soul, divided between home and Egypt, between life in the rural environment and the cosmopolitan city. Specifically, their image was one of women split between children by blood and children by milk. But we must consider how much courage was needed to take the fate of the family on their shoulders and leave to work in a foreign country with an entirely different culture, language, and living conditions. The legacy that aleksandrinke have left is not just the houses, fields, and entire estates that they bought with the money they earned, not just

Figure 3.11. Combination of an old postcard and a new photograph. Guided by the postcard, in 2006 the granddaughter of an aleksandrinka found the house where her grandmother had been employed in Alexandria. *Courtesy of the Slovene Ethnographic Museum*

yellowed photographs and various objects from Egypt. Rather, their legacy is in their stories, their wisdom, and their courage that can be our ideal and our pride even today.

In the text that accompanied the exhibition prepared in 2006 in Goriška, in places from which the most girls and women and in some cases entire families left for Egypt, the descendants of aleksandrinke described their experiences.[38] Over the last decade, the interest in aleksandrinke has grown a lot, not only for the economic benefit they brought to the modest rural environment in the first half of

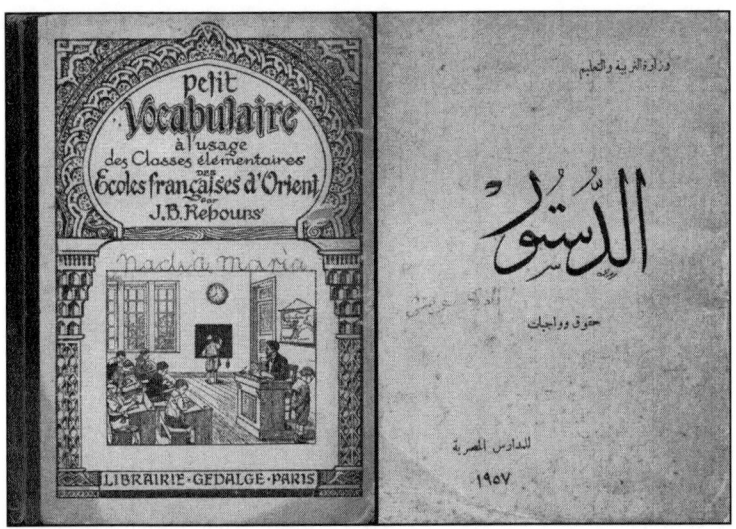

Figures 3.12a and 3.12b. Textbooks in French and Arabic. The daughter of an aleksandrinka brought them from Egypt, where she attended primary school in the 1950s. *Courtesy of the Slovene Ethnographic Museum*

the twentieth century but also for their life stories. Who were these women? What were they like? How did they manage in a new cultural and ethnic environment? How are they remembered by the children they took care of? Why were the aleksandrinke so special that everybody still remembers them today, after all these decades? These and a series of other questions encourage the research of this migration process to go further and deeper. I find that the wider interest for aleksandrinke was first encouraged by their granddaughters and great-granddaughters, who approached the project of revitalization and reevaluation of the memory of aleksandrinke. These descendants conveyed the insight into the lives of their grandmothers and great-grandmothers to the public through different media, including a theater performance,[39] a documentary,[40] exhibitions,[41] lectures,[42] and a series of academic papers and articles.[43] Between 2006 and 2011, aleksandrinke were presented at seven different exhibitions, shown in places where they came from and also at the regional Goriška Museum in Nova Gorica and the Slovene Ethnographic Museum in Ljubljana.[44] Some of these exhibitions have also been taken to other places in Slovenia and Italy. Exhibitions, documentaries, and academic debates are in fact a material manifestation of a new attitude toward female migration processes from the Slovenian ethnic territory that took place in the first half of the twentieth century. We should also newly and positively evaluate the participation of the female population in the development of the individual Slovenian provinces. Aleksandrinke are so much more interesting, because there is a veil of secrecy wrapped around them still, as their migration process to Egypt was suddenly interrupted. Thus, we cannot observe the continuity of their lives there as we can, for example, within the Slovenian migrant communities in Australia or Argentina. In the local environment, aleksandrinke were considered for a couple of decades after the war to be a hushed topic, but today their descendants want to actively bridge this gap. Their life stories are collected by different generations and students in local primary schools and high school. There have been several bachelor's theses written on this topic, and granddaughters have collected the stories, as have historians and others. It is thus not only the process of migration that is interesting but also the modern evaluation of aleksandrinke, which remains our current research challenge.

Notes

1. Karmen Žuljan, interview by author, January 18, 2010, Domžale, Slovenia, tape recording in possession of the author.

2. "Daša Koprivec: Aleksandrinke and Their Descendants." A research project of the Slovene Ethnographic Museum (2005–11). The testimonies are kept at the Slovene Ethnographic Museum in the form of tape recordings and field notes.

3. Elizabeth Warnock Fernea, ed., *Remembering Childhood in the Middle East* (Austin: University of Texas Press, 2002), 67.

4. Michael Haag, *Alexandria City of Memory* (New Haven, CT: Yale University Press, 2004), 10–17.

5. Marjan Drnovšek, "History and Concealment," in *Go Girls: When Slovenian Women Left Home*, edited by Marina Lukšič-Hacin and Jernej Mlekuž (Ljubljana: Založba ZRC, 2009), 37–39.

6. Andrej Gaberšček, *Goriški Slovenci, 1901–1923* [Slovenians of Goriška, 1901–1923] (Ljubljana: Printed by the author, 1934), 256–58.

7. Marko Sjekloča, *Čez morje v pozabo: Argentinci slovenskih korenin in rezultati argentinske asimilacijske politike* [Across the Sea to Oblivion: Argentines of Slovenian Descent and the Results of the Argentine Assimilation Policy] (Celje: Fit media, 2004), 95–108.

8. Boženka Jelerčič, interview by author, November 13, 2005, Prvačina, Slovenia, tape recording in possession of the author.

9. Violetka Stubelj, interview by author, November 3, 2005, Gradišče nad Prvačino, Slovenia, tape recording in possession of the author.

10. Marija Černe, interview by author, October 28, 2005, Bilje, Slovenia, tape recording in possession of the author.

11. Lidija Susič, interview by author, November 25, 2005, Bukovica, Slovenia, tape recording in possession of the author.

12. Dragotin Volk, interview by author, June 28, 2005, Gradišče nad Prvačino, Slovenia, tape recording in possession of the author.

13. Violetka Stubelj, interview by author, November 3, 2005, Gradišče nad Prvačino, Slovenia, tape recording in possession of the author.

14. Boženka Jelarčič, interview by author, November 3, 2005, Prvačina, Slovenia, tape recording in possession of the author.

15. Katja Škrlj, "Komaj sem čakala, da zrastem in postanem aleksandrinka: Demitizacija aleksandrink" [I Could Hardly Wait to Grow Up and Become an Aleksandrinka: The Demythization of Aleksandrinke], in *Krila migracij: Po meri življenjskih zgodb* [Dressed to Go: Slovenian Women's Stories on Migration], edited by Mirjam Milharčič Hladnik and Jernej Mlekuž (Ljubljana: Založba ZRC, ZRC SAZU, 2009), 164, 185.

16. Marija Černe, interview by author, April 23, 2007, Prvačina, Slovenia, tape recording in possession of the author.

17. Violetka Stubelj, interview by author, November 3, 2005, Gradišče nad Prvačino, Slovenia, tape recording in possession of the author.

18. Ada Mihelj, interview by author, September 22, 2008, Prvačina, Slovenia, field notes in possession of the author.

19. Lucija Martinuč, interview by author, May 16, 2007, Renče, Slovenia, tape recording in possession of the author.

20. Ellis Douek, *A Middle Eastern Affair* (London: Peter Halban, 2004), 39.

21. Ibid., 115–16.

22. Škrlj, "Komaj sem čakala, da zrastem in postanem aleksandrinka," 150.

23. Inga Miklavčič-Brezigar, "Aleksandrija: Po poteh in sledeh žena, deklet in šolskih sester na začasnem delu v Egiptu" [Alexandria: Following the Trail of Slovene Women, Unmarried Girls, and School Sisters Working in Egypt], *Glasnik SED* 49, nos. 1–2 (2009): 91.

24. Douek, *A Middle Eastern Affair*, 39.

25. Claudia Roden, interview by author, March 3, 2008, Ljubljana, Slovenia, tape recording in possession of the author.

26. Ibid.

27. Ibid.

28. Douek, *A Middle Eastern Affair*, 39.

29. Zvone Žigon, *Izzivi drugačnosti: Slovenci v Afriki in na Arabskem polotoku* [The Challenges of Diversity: Slovenians in Africa and on the Arabian Peninsula] (Ljubljana: Založba ZRC, ZRC SAZU, 2003), 12–21.

30. Viljem Sulič, interview by author, July 27, 2007, Logatec, Slovenia, tape recording in possession of the author.

31. Vidojka Vecciet, interview by author, May 19, 2005, Prvačina, Slovenia, field notes in possession of the author.

32. Violetka Stubelj, interview by author, November 3, 2005, Gradišče nad Prvačino, Slovenia, tape recording in possession of the author.

33. Boženka Jelerčič, interview by author, November 3, 2005, Prvačina, Slovenia, field notes in possession of the author.

34. Dorica Makuc, *Aleksandrinke* (Gorica: Goriška Mohorjeva družba, 1993), 118.

35. Violetka Stubelj, interview by author, November 3, 2005, Gradišče nad Prvačino, Slovenia, tape recording in possession of the author.

36. Alojzija Gregorič, interview by author, April 25, 2005, Zalošče, Slovenia, field notes in possession of the author.

37. Barbara Gregorc, Ema Šen, and Jure Bizjak, *Med burjo in puščavskim peskom: Vpliv aleksandrink na prehranjevalne navade svojcev* [Between the Bora and the Desert Wind: The Influence of Aleksandrinke on the Nutritional Habits of Their Relatives] (Šempeter pri Novi Gorici: Biotehniška šola, 2008).

38. *V spomin aleksandrinkam* [In Memory of Aleksandrinke], exhibition by Tina Mihelj et al., organized by the Društvo za ohranjanje kulturne dediščine aleksandrink, held at the House on the Square, Prvačina, 2006.

39. *Trieste-Alessandria EMBARKED: Štorja od lešandrink* [Trieste-Alexandria EMBARKED: The Stories of Aleksandrinke], play by Draga Potočnjak; directed by Neda Bric Rusjan; produced by Maska, Institute for Publishing, Production and Education, Ljubljana; premiered at Dance Theatre, Ljubljana, September 11, 2005.

40. *Aleksandrija, ki odhaja* [Departing Alexandria], documentary by Vesna Humar and Ivo Saksida (Nova Gorica: Produkcija Vitel, 2009), DVD.

41. *Skoraj pozabljene* [Almost Forgotten], exhibition by Dejana Baša et al., organized by the Društvo za ohranjanje kulturne dediščine aleksandrink at House on the Square, Prvačina, 2010; *Aleksandrinke z Gradišča nad Prvačino* [Aleksandrinke from Gradišče nad Prvačino], exhibition by Sonja Gabrijelčič, organized by the Društvo za ohranjanje kulturne dediščine aleksandrink at Gradišče nad Prvačino, 2008; *V spomin aleksandrinkam*, exhibition by Tina Mihelj et al.; *Aleksandrinke z Vogrskega* [Aleksandrinke from Vogrsko], exhibition by Ana Marija Prijatelj, organized by the Društvo za ohranjanje kulturne dediščine aleksandrink, at the House on the Square, Prvačina, 2010; *Aleksandrinke iz Renč* [Aleksandrinke from Renče], exhibition by Stazica Zorn, at the Društvo za kulturo, turizem in razvoj Renče, Renče, 2011.

42. Barbara Skubic, "Od gradnje do krize: Sueški prekop, oblikovanje egipčanske države in kaj so tam čez počele Slovenke" [From Building to Crisis: The Suez Canal, the Forming of Egypt and What Slovene Women Did There], lecture, Cankarjev dom, Ljubljana, March 5, 2008.

43. Katja Škrlj, "Komaj sem čakala, da zrastem in postanem aleksandrinka," 143–89.

44. *Skriti obrazi Aleksandrije: Slovenske šolske sestre in aleksandrinke* [Hidden Faces of Alexandria: Slovenian School Sisters and Aleksandrinke], exhibition by Inga Miklavčič-Brezigar, held at the Goriški muzej, Nova Gorica, 2009; *Jaz, mi in drugi: Podobe mojega sveta* [I, We and Others: Images of My World], exhibition by Daša Koprivec et al. held at the Slovene Ethnographic Museum, Ljubljana, 2009.

References

Douek, Ellis. *A Middle Eastern Affair.* London: Peter Halban, 2004.

Drnovšek, Marjan. "History and Concealment." In *Go Girls: When Slovenian Women Left Home,* edited by Marina Lukšič-Hacin and Jernej Mlekuž, 17–59. Ljubljana: Založba ZRC, 2009.

Gaberšček, Andrej. *Goriški Slovenci, 1901–1923* [Slovenians from Goriška, 1901–1923]. Ljubljana: Printed by the author, 1934.

Gabrijelčič, Sonja. *Aleksandrinke z Gradišča nad Prvačino* [Aleksandrinke from Gradišče nad Prvačino]. Exhibition, Društvo za ohranjanje kulturne dediščine aleksandrink, Gradišče nad Prvačino, 2008.

Gregorc, Barbara, Ema Šen, Jure Bizjak. *Med burjo in puščavskim peskom: Vpliv aleksandrink na prehranjevalne navade svojcev* [Between the Bora and the Desert Wind: The Influence of Aleksandrinke on the Nutritional Habits of Their Relatives]. Šempeter pri Novi Gorici: Biotehniška šola, 2008.

Haag, Michael. *Alexandria: City of Memory*. New Haven, CT: Yale University Press, 2004.

Humar, Vesna, and Ivo Saksida. *Aleksandrija, ki odhaja* [Departing Alexandria]. DVD. Nova Gorica: Produkcija Vitel, 2009.

Koprivec, Daša. "Migrations of the Children of the Alexandrian Women from the 1930s to the 1960s." *Dve domovini/Two Homelands* 32 (2010): 93–104, http://twohomelands.zrc-sazu.si/onlinejournal/DD_TH_32.pdf.

Koprivec, Daša, et al. *Jaz, mi in drugi: Podobe mojega sveta*[I, We, and Others: Images of My World]. Exhibition, Slovenski etnografski muzej, Ljubljana, 2009.

Makuc, Dorica. *Aleksandrinke*. Gorica: Goriška Mohorjeva družba, 1993.

Mihelj, Tina, et al. *Skriti obrazi Aleksandrije: Slovenske šolske sestre in aleksandrinke* [Hidden Faces of Alexandria: Slovenian School Sisters and Aleksandrinke]. Exhibition, Goriški muzej, Nova Gorica, 2009.

———. *V spomin aleksandrinkam* [In Memory of the Aleksandrinke]. Exhibition, Društvo za ohranjanje kulturne dediščine aleksandrink, Prvačina, 2006.

Miklavčič-Brezigar, Inga. "Aleksandrija: Po poteh in sledeh žena, deklet in šolskih sester na začasnem delu v Egiptu." *Glasnik SED* 49, nos. 1–2 (2009): 89–91.

Milharčič Hladnik, Mirjam. "Historical and Narrative Perspective of Slovenian Women Migrants' Experiences: Social Networking, Gender Priorities, and Questions of Identity." In *Historical and Cultural Perspectives on Slovenian Migration*, edited by Marjan Drnovšek, 113–36. Ljubljana: Založba ZRC, ZRC SAZU, 2007.

Prijatelj, Ana Marija. *Aleksandrinke z Vogrskega* [Aleksandrinke from Vogrsko]. Exhibition, Društvo za ohranjanje kulturne dediščine aleksandrink, Prvačina, 2010.

Sjekloča, Marko. *Čez morje v pozabo: Argentinci slovenskih korenin in rezultati argentinske asimilacijske politike* [Across the Sea to Oblivion: Argentines of Slovenian Descent and the Results of the Argentine Assimilation Policy]. Celje: Fit media, 2004.

Škrlj, Katja. "Komaj sem čakala, da zrastem in postanem aleksandrinka: Demitizacija aleksandrink" [I Could Hardly Wait to Grow Up and Become an Aleksandrinka: The Demythization of Aleksandrinke]. In *Krila migracij: Po meri življenjskih zgodb* [Dressed to Go: Slovenian Women's Stories on Migration], edited by Mirjam Milharčič Hladnik and Jernej Mlekuž, 143–89. Ljubljana: Založba ZRC, ZRC SAZU, 2009.

Skubic, Barbara. "Od gradnje do krize: Sueški prekop, oblikovanje egipčanske države in kaj so tam čez počele Slovenke" [From Building to Crisis: the Suez Canal, the Forming of Egypt and What Slovene Women Did There]. Lecture, Cankarjev dom, Ljubljana, March 5, 2008.

Trieste-Alessandria EMBARKED: Štorja od lešandrink. [Trieste-Alexandria EMBARKED: The Stories of Aleksandrinke]. Play by Draga Potočnjak. Directed by Neda Bric Rusjan. Produced by Maska, Institute for Publishing, Production and Education, Ljubljana. Premiered at Dance Theatre, Ljubljana, September 11, 2005.

Warnock Fernea, Elizabeth, ed. *Remembering Childhood in the Middle East.* Austin: University of Texas Press, 2002.

Žigon, Zvone. *Izzivi drugačnosti: Slovenci v Afriki in na Arabskem polotoku* [The Challenges of Diversity: Slovenians in Africa and in the Arabic Peninsula]. Ljubljana: Založba ZRC, ZRC SAZU, 2003.

Zorn, Stazica. *Aleksandrinke iz Renč* [Aleksandrinke from Renče]. Exhibition, Društvo za kulturo, turizem in razvoj Renče, Renče, 2011.

Chapter 4

Dikle in Italian Cities
Personal Experiences, Public Interpretations
Jernej Mlekuž

What Does the Voice of Authority Say?

The greatest and most revered of the Slovenian poets, France Prešeren, finishes his poem *The Beautiful Vida* with

> Daily Vida stood at window sill,
> For son, father, husband weeping still.[1]

Most Slovenians will be familiar with the poem from school: a woman tempted by travel and foreign lands falls for the words of a Moor and, after leaving her husband and a child, now feels remorseful, regretful, and traumatized. The voice of Slovenia's greatest poet hasn't gotten lost through time and space. The Beautiful Vida is probably among the most used and adapted motifs in Slovenian art. In addition to almost a hundred poems, plays, novels, and short stories that are linked to either Prešeren's version or the traditional original, Beautiful Vida has inspired many music, theater, and fine arts variations that feed on the topic of longing for the remote, the new, and the different and also on the regret because of emigration, separation, and submission to the foreign.

Beautiful Vidas—women who went abroad to work—were very often the object of pity and, not infrequently, of blame. Ana Barbič and Inga Miklavčič-Brezigar find that the attitude among Slovenians toward female labor migration from the mid-nineteenth century to the mid-twentieth century—mostly expressed through the writings of men in newspaper articles, official correspondence, and popular nonfiction—is often one of blame and remorse because the women were victims of "the moral and physical ruination," but this is swiftly followed by the desire for "deserved sentence" and the remorse women themselves should feel.[2] Marta Verginella finds that the same is true for the ethnically mixed Trieste where, as she indicates, the Slovenian liberal bourgeois circles were far more interested in the women from the hinterlands and their work for profit than they were in the urban female population. In the perspective of these "men who were emotionally invested in the nation," as the author graphically depicts them, "particularly washerwomen and maids who came in contact with the foreign national milieu, with its most intimate and therefore most dangerous part, the 'dirty laundry,' were the source of shame."[3]

The voice of authority has always been and continues to be the voice of contempt. Female labor migration met with the sage-and-blaming voice of the Catholic Church, the voice of "science,"[4] and the voice of the self-righteous grandeur of omnipotent individuals and groups. The string of texts representing the church's point of view seems to go on endlessly. Just to show that this authoritative voice doesn't only materialize in male bodies, let's give the podium to Miss Antonija Stupca from the 1913 Slovenian-Croatian Catholic Jamboree in Ljubljana:

> Many girls, and women as well, are also driven by their desire for freedom abroad, the wish for easier work, a more comfortable life. They strive for something higher; they want to try something, become distinguished, but often they wade into a swamp. Many dangers are out there preying on our inexperienced maidens. They can become miserable for time and eternity; they may

forever lose their happiness, in the shortest time possible, even without it being their own fault.[5]

Such was also the voice—the authoritative voice—present in the pages of the *Matajur* newspaper, the gazette of a small community of ethnic Slovenians from the region of Slavia Veneta, a community of Slovenian-speaking population in the Friuli-Venezia Giulia region[6] that witnessed sustained pressure and violence from the Fatherland of Italy, mass emigration, and employment of girls as housemaids—the so-called *dikle*—in Italian cities:

> We, Slovenians from Friuli, know that the work of dikle is hard, humiliating, and dangerous for any woman, especially a young one. We would not like to see hundreds and hundreds more of our women and girls become destitute or morally corrupted or lose their health, as is still happening. No law, no matter how good, can prevent that. But the *meštir* [profession] is *maledet* [cursed], and a woman only takes it up when she can't find another job; this meštir is slavelike, a remnant of the old days.... Our women and girls who work as dikle must fight against it, too. They must fight so that this shame stops once and for all, that this slavery of ours, this true *schiavitu* [slavery] will be gone.[7]

But here we will not give the floor to this self-righteous, vehement, authoritative voice[8] that so firmly claims that females cannot represent themselves, so they must be represented—to paraphrase Karl Marx.[9] We shall instead pull from the dusty past craving for oblivion the proverbially unimportant, empty, chattering voices of those women of whom the authoritative voice speaks and, of course, forbids them to speak for themselves. What shall we thus ask the voice of the Beautiful Vidas? We shall (only) ask about the things that the authoritative voice speaks about so zealously, so earnestly, with so much conviction. Was this profession really cursed, really schiavitu? But before we give a word to the voice of the Beautiful Vidas, let us ask ourselves what this voice hides, forgets, and adds.

A Thing or Two on the Voice of the Beautiful Vidas

The curse and conversely the fascination, the richness, and the power of personal narratives, stories, and testimonies[10] reside in their subjectivity. Personal stories are understood as an individual's narration, talking, and chattering and hence are utterly subjective. Therefore, they seem to be a useless tool when searching for great truths, theories, models of society, culture, and other things noble and important. However, the stories are never empty and fleeting words; they are never words spoken in a vacuum. The world is not conveyed to us directly and mechanically, as something existing independently from us that we can comprehend objectively. This world is only existent insofar as our everyday perception can grasp it, make sense of it, give meaning to it, interpret it, and then convey it to others—in other words, turn it into a narrative.

The narrative, the story, and the testimony are therefore constructs—as it is fashionable to call them today—built from this thing that exists independently and the meaning ascribed to it, the interpretation. Thus, the distinction that the anthropologist Edward M. Bruner makes between reality (what is really out there, whatever that may be), experience (how that reality presents itself to consciousness), and expressions (how individual experience is framed and articulated) refers—in a life history, biography, narrative, or story—to the distinction between life as lived (reality), life as experienced (experience), and life as told (expression). Only a naive positivist would believe, says Bruner, that expressions are equivalent to reality.[11]

The question of this chapter must be posed here more clearly, more scientifically: What did migration mean to the women, the house servants? More than the questions surrounding the event itself, the phenomenon, we are interested in the question of its meaning, its experience. The narratives, stories, and testimonies will tell us more about the meaning and experience of the events and phenomena than they will about the events and phenomena themselves. Therefore, farewell ontology, hello phenomenology.

But let us stay with the verb form "did mean" for a while: "did mean," or "meant," not "means." Is there a problem with the past tense? Yes! Telling a story isn't just speaking and remembering but is also reconstructing the meaning of the past from the position of the present and ascribing the meaning to the past in a way that it has meaning for the present. As Bruner says, the meaning is always in the present, in the here and now.[12] We are therefore dealing with expression, the meaning of past events, phenomena that have not been preserved untouched until now. (They are not, so to speak, frozen tears that can be thawed on demand and be the same and flow down the exact same face, making the exact same expression as at the moment of freezing.) We are dealing with the expression and the meaning subjugated to the changes conditioned by the subsequently altered norms and values and finally packaged and sent to market by the present. (We are thus given the original tears, mixed with at least some of the later tears, and of course the more or less calculating expression of the present that is not indifferent toward today's form of the thawed tears.) The problem with this act is that we are probing the meaning of experience in the time when they occurred.[13] Some Beautiful Vidas, regardless of the original meaning of the experiences, look back with remorse and pain; some look back with joy; and some look back with indifference.

We are thus placed in front of a serious methodological-theoretical problem: Is it even possible to oppose this vehement other voice armed with a weapon that can be considered seriously flawed? All we have at our disposal is a reconstructed meaning produced and marketed by a temperamental enterprise from the present; we do not have the untouchable, original, relict meaning from the past. The answer must of course be positive, because in the opposite case our work is meaningless. This cannot mean that we are supposed to close our eyes to the temper of this present enterprise. Quite the opposite. Our eyes and ears must pay particular attention to it.

One other thing pushes us to oppose, despite any methodological scruples we might have: this vehement voice must be answered to with another voice that is less calculating and authoritative, even though it comes dusty decades too late. In the opposite case, the authoritative voice lives on as the only and eternal truth.

What Does the Voice of the Beautiful Vidas Talk About?

The voice talks about the migration of girls from Slavia Veneta, the so-called dikle who found employment in Italian cities. The very name of the region reminds us of its particularities. It was ruled by the Venetian Republic, and after its demise in 1797 it came under Austrian governance and briefly French administration until 1866, when it became a part of the Italian state to which, as a part of the Friuli-Venezia Giulia, it continues to belong. With the exception of a relatively brief period when the Slovenians from Slavia Veneta were joined with other Slovenians, their historic paths were separate; this shaped their culture and identity in a very particular way. Slavia Veneta felt only echoes of the nationalist movement that took hold of the Slovenian nation in the second half of the nineteenth century; it also never had Slovenian schools that played a key role in establishing the unified standard language and national consciousness. Among the region's many distinctive traits is undoubtedly the occurrence of very strong emigration that did not spare women.[14]

According to the data of different authors, the emigration of girls from Slavia Veneta and Friuli as a whole to take employment in households increased after World War I.[15] This emigration was caused by similar or even the same factors (so-called push factors) that caused all other types of emigration from the region: the structure of agrarian society not ready to accept the innovations of a capitalist nature, while on the other hand being more and more dependent on the outside market and socioeconomic influences. The key characteristics of the region that contributed to the emigration in the second half of the nineteenth century and the first half of the twentieth century were a distinct partition of the lands and the smallness of the farms, management methods based on the patriarchal family (the biggest part of the farm and other property went to the firstborn son), farms that were more or less geared toward being self-sufficient, rapid demographic growth and the crisis of the patriarchal family linked to it, and high tax burdens.[16]

Emigration that continued soon after the World War II—and I will primarily focus on it because personal testimonies are more readily available—must on the one hand be understood as the continuation of tendencies that caused the emigration processes before the war. As has already been said, these are linked to the difficult socioeconomic situation in Slavia Veneta and Friuli in general, which some authors refer to as a "crisis." The newspaper *Messaggero Veneto,* which long after World War II was considered the mouthpiece of the then-ruling Christian Democratic Party and as such presumably was not interested in raising problems that the state apparatus was supposed to take care of (among others), wrote that "the inhabitants of the Natisone Valley were living in distinctly unfavorable circumstances."[17] The economy, based almost exclusively on working very fragmented pieces of land (57.6 percent of the landowners owned less than two and a half acres of arable land), allowed for very little income.

On the other hand, two types of state measures or interventions were of key importance for the strength and courses of migration from Slavia Veneta. The first direct state migration policy measure is from 1947, when the Italian government devaluated its currency, which caused the national economy to wade into a long depression that the government then tried to solve with the programmed outflow of the workforce to seek work abroad. The emigration was also, albeit indirectly, influenced by the legislation aimed at the development of mountain areas that caused a more or less planned emptying of Slavia Veneta.

Of course, there were many reasons for or factors that prompted emigration. After the significant emigration era between the two world wars, emigration became a part of the economic logic for at least a part of the population. In addition, the authority of the patriarchal family began to crumble, which had a great influence on abandoning the central economic activity of Slovenians in the region (agriculture) and indirectly again on emigration. There were also the sociocultural influences of the factors of modernization. Another factor was the creation of a new state border (which at least in the first couple of decades after World War II was tightly sealed and carried great ideological and symbolic weight), which in addition to difficult socioeconomic circumstances heightened the feeling of being on the periphery. This grew into a political and nationalist pressure that was expressed most clearly in the intimidation of the tricolorists and later the so-called patriots.[18]

There is no detailed and thorough study[19] about the employment of women from Slavia Veneta in the households in Italian cities, although it was undoubtedly a very common occurrence.[20] In the numerous articles about this phenomenon in the newspaper *Matajur* (for many years the only newspaper for Slovenians in the region), from 1961 we find an estimate that in addition to the 806 women from the seven municipalities in the Natisone/Nadiža Valley who officially lived abroad, there were at least as many girls who were employed in households in northern Italian cities.[21] No statistics are available to allow us to discern the number of migrant employed as household help in Italian cities due to the very nature of both the censuses and the undocumented employment. The majority, according to the statistics, was listed as part of the nonactive population. Elsewhere we find information that among approximately fifty thousand housemaids in Rome, there were several hundred girls from Slavia Veneta.[22] The extent and importance of this phenomenon—we must know that the majority of housemaids were sending most of their money home to their families or to common household trust funds—can also be observed in the following text from *Matajur*: "The dikle are one of the most important social layers of our nation. If they're doing poorly, we're all doing poorly, if they're weak, we're all weak. So let's help our dikle, and thus help ourselves."[23]

The phenomenon became less and less widespread in the second half of the 1960s. There are several reasons for this, and we have to look for them in the social, economic, and administrative changes in both Slavia Veneta and Italy. The differences were also noticeable between different areas and places in Slavia Veneta. It seems that in the valleys of Natisone, the phenomenon died out quickly with the flourishing of industry in the flat parts of the Friuli (the industrial triangle around Manzano). Thus, for example, Luisa[24] from Mersino di Sotto/Dolenji Marsin, who served with a family in Udine/Videm from the time she was twelve years old in 1964, left domestic service after nine years and went to work on an assembly line in a wood-processing plant in Manzano. As there was no public transportation to work from her home village (as there was from some other villages in Slavia Veneta), she bought a car with her uncle's help because she had to commute thirty-three miles one way to get to work each day.[25]

The girls mostly found employment through relatives, friends, or other women from their village who were already employed in the cities. The most important sources in searching for a job were family, friendship, and village networks. For example, Teresa, who was working for a family in Naples, found a similar job there for her sister.[26] Maria from the same village found the third sister a place with a family in Milan. As the second sister wanted to be closer to home, the third sister found her a new family in Milan.[27] We could find many similar combinations of intertwined family, friendship, and village networks. In certain cases, the same family serially employed (exchanged) relatives or friends. When one woman left the employer's family, another one replaced her. For example, Giulia from Rodda/Ronac went to serve in Rome in the early 1960s with a family her mother had served before World War II; when the mother left after six years, her sister had taken her place.[28] At times, the employers or masters themselves came to look for girls, either directly or through municipal employment offices (in the postwar period only), where the latter directed them toward girls or their families. In certain cases, village priests and nuns acted as finders of respectable families. We can read the following on this topic in *Matajur*:

Our girls have to go to serve as dikle, because they have no choice. We have no factories, and there's nothing else for them but the *bitter* [again the authoritative voice] job of dikle. Once they stay with families for a while, some can help themselves to find a good job or get married. Our girls have mostly found the work as dikle by themselves, mostly through friends or acquaintances who have already worked. At times, families have turned to local priests to find them good dikle they could rely on.[29]

This points to another important trait of the studied phenomenon. Girls worked as maids for a shorter period, in most cases from a number of months to ten years. Girls who decided to go into service were very young, mostly ages twelve to twenty-two. Women usually stopped working as maids after marriage, so we can find few married ones (narrators believe that married women were more frequently found working as maids before World War II). This employment almost always meant some kind of transitory beginning phase: before marriage or other employment. As one of the women says, "It was to begin with, then the world opened more."[30]

However, there are exceptions. A nineteen-year-old, Luigia, from Cepletischis/Čeplečišče went to Naples in 1956 or 1957 and has lived with the same family ever since (today, she only cares for the elderly lady of the house). Very soon, she says, she became "a part of the family."[31] And with this testimony we have now reached the next topic.

Maledet, Schiavitu? When the Voice of the Beautiful Vidas Is Finally Heard

We shall thus finally ask the Beautiful Vidas if this meštir, this profession, was really maledet and schiavitu. In other words, was the profession of dikle really cursed and slavery? But wait, we shall not ask them directly!

The material on the basis of which I formed the answers to this question was mostly collected in 2003 for the project *Dikle—Tiha zgodba* [Dikle—A Silent Story].[32] The goal of the project was to publish a more general text on housemaids—about the causes of the phenomenon, its extent and importance for the community of origin, the working and living conditions of the housemaids, etc.[33]

The original goal of the present text was to enrich, improve, and expand the material by going to the field once more. But this would mean that I would have to go to the field with a clear motive and goal, as I had already started the text as an answer and, even more problematic, also as a rebellion against the authoritative voice from the beginning of the text. It would probably also mean that the voice of the questioner would be heard in the answers and even more so in the voice of the questioner, who leads respondents toward the desired answers. I thus chose a less workaholic, enthusiastic, and rebellious way. I decided to stay with the old—less (or at least differently)—motivated material and to once more read it, hear it, and thoroughly mull it over.[34]

Maledet?

True, this profession was sometimes considered maledet. Many housemaids in their stories emphasize, or at least mention, difficult situations at home without any perspective. Michela from the village of Polava, who left to be a housemaid in Gorizia/Gorica in 1951 at age thirteen, tells us such a story. At home, the means of survival was almost exclusively agriculture: two cows, a calf, two pigs, and nine children: "But we understood. They [the parents] never told you to go. We understood ourselves that we had to go. Because here, there was nothing. They didn't force us, but we knew ourselves that we had to go."[35]

Michela remembers her first separation from home and family very well, and her story could be one that nods to the maledet story, a script of damnation:

> When I saw that all my sisters (seven out of eight sisters went to serve as dikle), I was not afraid to go; it was a great psychological strain; it took a toll. I kept throwing up. It was a psychological thing, the separation, going away from home. I had no idea why I kept vomiting, but this was the reason. Going away from home, a young person. It wasn't easy.[36]

But on the other hand, a number of narrators emphasize that they could have stayed at home and worked on farms. Girls from well-off farms and families who could have worked and lived at home on the farm also chose to take this kind of employment. Bruna, another woman who moved from Cepletischis/Čeplečišče in 1957, remembers that her father bought a cow—and thus increased the workload on the farm—to discourage his daughter from the planned move to Naples, where her sister had found her a job as a maid: "Father said, 'Why are you going?' There was always enough food and clothes at home. I'm not exactly sure; why did we go? Probably because all the girls from the village went. Truth is, we lacked nothing."[37]

Aldina, who left in 1952 at age sixteen to go to Rome as a maid for two years and then to Switzerland for a year and returned to Rome for another year, emphasizes that they lived well at home and had no financial or economic problems. She decided to migrate because "One liked to go away. To see the world. One went to see things. To make an experience." She kept the money exclusively for herself, since her parents had no financial problems. Her sister went as a maid to Belgium, where she stayed for a year, and then went briefly to England and ended up in Canada: "If she hadn't wanted to go, she wouldn't have gone. But everybody went, so she went, too."[38]

Bruna, obviously not deterred from leaving by her father's purchase of a cow, says that "Of course we were happy to go, because we expected to get a miracle. When one leaves, she always leaves happy. When she decides to leave on her own, she always leaves satisfied." Or, as she says later in her story when she comments on her move from Naples, where she worked as a housemaid for just under four years, to Milan in 1960, where her sister found her a job and where she stayed as a maid until 1967 and has been ever since, "I liked seeing new things, changing places. I was also the youngest, the most vivacious."[39]

Those girls who were forced to leave because of difficult, dead-end, and impossible economic circumstances weave golden threads of expectations, longing, and desire for the new. Or, as one of them says,

"*La partenza* [departure, emigration] was a little bit happy, because we didn't know where we were going."[40]

As a number of narrators say, the attraction of adventure and/or escape from the pangs of poverty were not the only impetuses for migration to and employment in Italian cities; economic independence was also an incentive. The desire for economic independence or simply a couple of lira that the girls could spend on their needs seems to be the central force that triggered the departure in many stories. As Bruna says, "[Parents] were not happy. But, you know what it's like when one goes. They were not opposed, either. But at eighteen, at home you worked for the parents. It felt good to earn your own money."[41]

Marina, who in 1954 at age eighteen left Clodig/Hlodič to work for a family in Milan, was from a family whose father had been trying to solve its financial problems with his work in Belgian mines since 1946. As she says, she could have worked at home on the farm that her mother headed, but "Yes, I was working, I was working at the farm, helping at home, but then there was no salary. If I needed a pair of shoes or a dress, where would I go for money? There wasn't any."[42]

Many women tell us similar stories. They could have stayed and worked at home, but they wanted their own money. However, many still didn't have money for themselves: "Not that my parents pushed me, it was I who wanted to go, to have my own money. But I ended up never having [money], because I had to send [it] home."[43] But this financing of the families is another story that we will touch on again in the next section.

A departure into a new and completely different urban environment meant a specific professional, linguistic, and life education for many young women, although upon leaving they didn't understand this schooling as a challenge but instead understood it more as a problem, as an inconvenience. The girls thus list a number of difficulties, including knowledge and understanding of the Italian language, of which some of them knew very little, and proficiency in completely new housework and cooking. Sonia from Topolò/Topolovo, who at age fourteen went to serve in Turin in 1947, first got work with the family of a doctor, where among other responsibilities she had to speak to the doctor's patients on the phone. Because, as she stresses, she didn't speak good Italian and couldn't answer the phone (it was the first time in her life that she'd even seen one), she had to leave and go to new employers. And she had problems with the second family, too: "I knew neither Italian nor the work, because at home we didn't have an electric iron; we had the one that used coal. There was no phone, and I didn't know how to set the table.... How could we know how to iron shirts back then? Ours didn't have such collars."[44]

Sonia's case is far from isolated. Many housemaids faced similar problems. As one of the respondents succinctly stated, "it wasn't a problem to find work, the problem was knowing how to do it."[45]

But a large majority of narrators, both those who were forced to leave because of the economic circumstances at home and those who saw migration as all sorts of other things, emphasized that working inside a house was much nicer than working at home on the farm. As Marina, born in 1936, explains, "Well, it was nicer to work in houses than on a farm. That is for certain. But the best would be if...here at home...there were some kind of work, like now when there are factories, and you just have to go early and come home in the evening. But back then, there were no such possibilities."[46]

Many who left as Marina did agree: "For us, who used to work on farms, housework was more compelling; laundry, cleaning, ironing. You worked in a warm place."[47] Often girls were not spared hard farmwork, especially in the families where there were no sons, the sons were too young, or, as was very commonplace, the sons were working abroad. And although the girls were leaving for work, they didn't leave for just anywhere. They went to work in the city, which was, as they tell us, valued higher than the village and the fields. The city was where a woman's wishes could be realized.

The departure and living in the city were also connected to different habits than the girls were used to at home. Staying in the city, despite very limited spare hours (mostly Sunday afternoons), did not only mean a workplace; it also meant contact with the environment that was as a rule more esteemed and had different habits and a different way of life. Mario, a young man from the village of Bardo in the Alta Val Torre/Ter Valley, remembers that the girls who worked as housemaids were prettily dressed, in city fashion, when they came to the city during the leave time away and that they wore makeup. This, he says, was not a custom among the village girls at that time. The girls from the city also, in Mario's opinion, had "more refined manners."[48]

Serving in Italian cities was not only prized among the girls. Parents apparently also held the work that the girls did as housemaids in high esteem, as many narrators tell us: "Ours is a lady there; she doesn't lack food."[49]

We must not neglect the fact that not only did the city offer the inaccessible and the possibility of fulfilling dreams, such as glamour, but it also opened new life perspectives. To be a housemaid most often meant, as life stories tell us, only the first step in the social and/or professional mobility of the women. As one of them says, "That was to begin with and then the world opened more."[50] But most likely the majority did not perceive or set this employment as the starting point of their professional and social path when they were leaving. Let us also add that for girls, this was the easiest and often the only acceptable way of getting into town and living there. Staying with families, no matter what it was like, meant a level of security, especially for younger girls, a security that was desired not only by the girls but also by their parents.

And yet the profession of housemaid became less desirable over the years. In the 1960s when girls had other, albeit very limited, work options, it already seemed that the popularity of being a housemaid was declining. Andreina, who was born in 1945 and at the age of seventeen went to Milan to work in a factory, where her aunt found her a job, says that she "was glad I didn't have to work as a domestic."[51] And her story is far from exceptional.

Schiavitu?

Yes, this profession was also schiavitu. Lara, who left from the village of Bardo in 1941 or 1942 at barely age eleven to go to her first employers in Prato Carnico, vividly remembers how many times she had to work until midnight and get up at six every morning. The family didn't call her by her name but instead caled her "serva," which at the time was indeed the most established expression for a housemaid, or female servant, but was often pejorative. There were many bitter, sad, miserable stories about exclusion, humiliation, etc.[52]

After a "season," as she calls the period from autumn to spring, in Turin, Sonia from Topolò/Topolovo, who saw the telephone for the first time at her employers' home, left for another season in Milan (emphasizing that she knew upon leaving that she was only going for a season, as parents counted on her help with summer farmwork). Then she went to England for three years, where she was supposed to work as a housemaid, but she ended up as a hospital attendant, and then she went to Switzerland for another three-year stint as a *dikla*. She describes her Italian episode: "I found the work in Italy harder. Well, maybe the culture was such, a dikla was scorned." Or, as she also says, "They did have a need, but they only ever took local people."[53]

From the literature we also know that servants, especially housemaids, are vulnerable to sexual exploitation by their employers.[54] While this topic was never exposed in the interviews, it does not mean that abuse never occurred. In conducting interviews with the majority of the female narrators, I did not attempt to establish the level of trust that would enable such a topic, which is already sensitive and delicate, to emerge, especially with narrators who were brought up in a strict Catholic environment, where the subject is all the more taboo.

Servants and housemaids were not subjected to just the authoritative eye of their employers but were also under pressure from their families and parents. During her season in Milan, Sonia was accused by her employer of stealing money. The woman had found money among Sonia's things that her parents had given her to write them letters, and prior to this Sonia had mentioned to the woman that she had no money of her own. Sonia stresses that after this unpleasant event she really wanted to go home but was afraid of what her family would say. The parents probably wouldn't be indifferent to her departure, as obedience and humility were the norm for the girls back then: "I couldn't wait to go home.... I was afraid what they would say at home, that I complain, and the neighbor doesn't."[55]

Family control was often carried out through older sisters or female relatives. The fourteen-year-old Lidia, who went to serve in Rome in 1944, returned home after a mere three months of work. When her aunt (who had originally found her the job) returned to Slavia Veneta, Lidia also went back home because her parents didn't want her to stay in the "Eternal City" alone.[56] Another example addresses the topic that we have already touched on: sending money home, which shows a more indirect control of the family. In the *Fotoalbum izseljencev iz Benečije* [Photo Album of the Emigrants from Slavia Veneta], we can read the story of a maid who never had possession of the money she earned. Her salary was given to a relative who lived in the same town where the girl worked. The girl's bitter surprise came later at home, when she realized that the relative used her earnings to buy linen for her trousseau: "In that pile of tablecloths and bed sheets were all my pains, all the years of suffering far from home."[57]

But this is only one side of the story. Many girls didn't necessarily perceive their work as unpleasant, unjust, or slavelike.[58] The working and living conditions of housemaids obviously varied regarding the treatment they received from individual families. While some girls had to cope with exclusion and neglect, some emphasized that they felt better than at home. Undoubtedly over time there were certain changes in the attitude of masters toward servants, or employers toward employees. Housemaids who served in the 1960s mention fewer bitter experiences, humiliating attitudes, neglect, exclusion, etc. Despite that, we cannot say that with the passing years the majority acquired a greater level of personal freedom, at least not when it comes to leisure time. Just like in the prewar period, after the war the majority of housemaids had only a couple of hours a week, mostly only once a week or even only once every fortnight (most commonly on Sunday afternoon). Unlike their earlier counterparts, the girls who became maids later in the century visited their homes and families more often because they were employed in larger numbers in the nearby cities (Cividale/Čedad, Udine/Videm, etc.). If many of them at least up to the 1950s and later only visited their families every couple of years (or even five or more years), they visited them much more often later. For example, in 1964 a barely twelve-year-old girl who went to serve a family in Udine/Videm (where she stayed for eight or nine years) after completing the five grades of compulsory education came home to Mersino di Sotto/Dolenji Marsin every Saturday afternoon and returned to work every Monday morning.

Marina says about her two years in Milan that the employers

> didn't treat us poorly.... Well, I was happy, because I was with a family. and they were working. They had a tavern, and the wife and the husband were in the tavern, and I was upstairs in the apartment where they came to eat and sleep. In short, I was treated well enough, well enough.[59]

Numerous indirect testimonies talk about being treated well by employers. Michelina from Masseris/Mašera (b. 1934), who left for Milan at the age of fifteen on the recommendation of her sister (who had gone to Milan as a maid the year before), says this: "My sister got on well down there and told me to come. So I went."[60] And as Michelina explains in her story, she had no problems either and got along well with her employers. There is also the testimony of Luigia, the narrator with whose voice we closed the section "What Does the Voice of Beautiful Vidas Talk About?" In 1956 or 1957 she left Cepletischis/Čeplešišče to work in Naples and has since then lived with and worked for the same family. Since the very beginning she has had work papers in order, insurance, etc., which was not exactly common among maids in that time.[61] She stresses that she has always gotten along with her employers and very soon became a "part of the family."[62] Likewise, not a single bad word about her longtime employers was uttered by Silvana from Mersino Alto/Gorenji Marsin, who worked for a general and his wife from 1960 to 1991. Due to the nature of the head of the household's work they moved several times but lived mostly in Bologna. The master came to find a maid at the Pulfero/Podbonesec municipality, at the employment office, and spoke to her at length before the employment. When she took the train to her new workplace near Rome he arranged for someone to accompany her, because, as she says, she had never been that far away from home before and was afraid to encounter potential troubles and problems on the way. In 1991 when her mother was ninety years old and needed care and help, Silvana returned to Mersino Alto/Gorenji Marsin, where she lives today with the pension she earned during thirty-one years of housework.[63]

The housemaids did not all feel the pressure of the control of their families in the same way. For some housemaids, such as those who kept for themselves all or at least a part of the money they earned, the paid housework represented a sphere of autonomous activity or economic independence.[64] They perceived the work that they did at home for free as the traditional role of an economically and socially subjugated female. As the testimony of Marina told us, she could have worked at home on her mother's farm, but "there was no salary. If I needed a pair of shoes or a dress, where would I go for money? There wasn't any."[65]

The Voice of Knowledge and Authority

We have let the voice of the Beautiful Vidas speak out. This we have done in part to respond to the authoritative voice from the beginning of the text.

The notion of voice was not chosen for only that purpose, by the way. In the very nature of voice and listening is something, says Mladen Dolar in *A Voice and Nothing More,* that bestows the voice with authority and offers itself for direct political use.[66] In listening to, reviving, and disseminating the testimonies, the voice of the Beautiful Vidas is thus inevitably also an emancipatory, political activity. Listening to different unheard, silenced stories keeps opening the questions of a certain field of knowledge. Knowledge is power.[67]

The girls who went to Italian cities in many cases did not understand their departure as maledet and schiavitu, as cursed and slavery. At least this is what they tell us today, many decades after the experience, meanings, and testimonies have been covered by a lot of ubiquitous dust, which we cannot completely blow away, clean off, or remove in order to come to the sparkle of the original experience. And yet this is the only voice—no matter how muted—that can stand up against the voice of authority that has resounded for half a century.

Some girls, as personal testimonies tell us, were also looking for an adventure, a change in life, or at least partial financial and economic independence. They wanted (at least partly) to shake off the shackles of a patriarchal family, to replace hard farmwork with the more attractive duties of an urban household. They wanted to get to the city, where they could admire and desire shiny shoes in shop windows, although they usually couldn't afford them. And it is from here that it would be a good idea to continue the text, but we will have to finish due to the agreed-upon constraints. We will thus end this fleeting glance at the epic proportions of an individual woman's wish.

However, in accordance with the title and ethics of this text, the final word must go to a former dikla, because she didn't miss out on what the readers and even the authors of such texts necessarily do: "One made an experience."[68]

Notes

1. France Prešeren, *Poezije doktorja Francéta Prešérna: Z dodatkom* [The Poetry of Dr. France Prešeren: With Supplement] (Ljubljana: Cankarjeva založba, 1982), 55.

2. Ana Barbič and Inga Miklavčič-Brezigar, "Občasne migracije podeželskih žena na Goriškem: Gospodinjsko delo v tujini—nuja in priložnost nekoč in danes"

[Occasional Migrations of Rural Women in Goriška: Domestic Work Abroad—Necessity and Chance, Past and Present], *Glasnik Slovenskega etnološkega društva* 39, nos. 3–4 (1999): 39–47.

3. Marta Verginella, *Ženska obrobja: Vpis žensk v zgodovino Slovencev* [Women on the Margins: The Inscription of Women in the History of Slovenians] (Ljubljana: Delta, 2006), 143.

4. For example, Martina Orehovec, "Ženske in delo v Istri v 20. stoletju" [Women and Work in Istria in the Twentieth Century] (master's thesis, University of Ljubljana, 2001), 158, found that the Istrian maids strived for "new, existentially unnecessary earnings" to fulfill their desire for status symbols. This is therefore the voice that reserves for itself the right to decide what is important, what is (un)necessary for existence. Housemaids obviously don't know that or are not entitled to decide on that.

5. Antonija Stupca, "O oskrbi za posle in kolodvorskih misijonih" [On the Care for Servants and Railway Station Missions], in *Slovensko-hrvaški katoliški shod v Ljubljani, 1913* [Slovenian-Croatian Catholic Jamboree in Ljubljana, 1913] (Ljubljana: Katoliška bukvarna, 1913), 183.

6. Slavia Veneta (also Venetian Slovenia and sometimes Julian Slovenia, and in Slovenian Benečija or Beneška Slovenija) is the name given to the part of the province of Udine/Videm/Udin where the Slovenian-speaking community lives in the region of Friuli-Venezia Giulia; see note 18 for more historic information on the region.

7. Anonymous, in "Dikle so postale osigurani delavci," *Matajur* 9, no. 9/174 (1958): 2. Although the original texts and interviews were in dialect, a mixture of Slovenian and dialect, or a mixture of Slovenian, Italian, and dialect, translations have always been made into standard English with certain preserved dialect words (such as "dikla" for a maid of a female servant).

8. It goes without saying that we must understand this authoritative voice as well and understand within the framework of some other authoritative relationship. A community that because of its ethnicity was subjected to all sorts of maltreatment, pressure, and malice from patriarchal Italy had a hard time looking at this phenomenon impartially, as the phenomenon is never impartial when it comes to affecting discrimination and ostracization based on ethnicity, class, and education.

9. Karl Marx, *The Eighteenth Brumaire of Louis Bonaparte* (Moscow: Progress Publishers, 1979), 63.

10. Personal narratives, life histories, testimonies, memoirs, oral biographies, life histories, and many other similar expressions can be best described with the expression "oral history," which does have—and that is not unimportant—a certain institutional and disciplinary weight.

11. Edward M. Bruner, "Introduction," in *The Anthropology of Experience*, edited by Victor W. Turner and Edward M. Bruner (Urbana and Chicago: University of Illinois Press, 1986), 6. However, there are many ways in which to understand and analyze this undoubtedly complicated, complex relationship between reality and expression.

12. Edward M. Bruner, "Introduction," 11.

13. Peacock L. James and Holland C. Dorothy, "The Narrated Self: Life Stories in Process," *Ethos* 21, no. 4 (1993): 367–83, distinguish between the life-focused and the story-focused approach, that is, between the two approaches that understand narrative as a mirror of reality and the approach that believes that the narrative is reality. The first approach, which is interested in life and life history and cares very little about the story or the act of narration can be divided into two subtypes. The so-called factual approach considers the spoken life as a presentation or reflection of objective facts of historic or ethnographic events, and the subjective approach is considered to be an expression of an individual's subjective inclinations and mood—the story in this case is thus a reflection of a psyche. The former emphasizes historic or objective facts, while the latter emphasizes subjective experiences and psychological events.

14. Bianca Maria Pagani, *L'emigrazione friulana dalla metà del secolo XIX al 1940* [Friulian Emigration from the Mid-Nineteenth Century to 1940] (Udine: Arti Grafiche Friulane, 1968), 161–78; Aleksej Kalc, "Selitvena gibanja ob zahodnih mejah slovenskega etničnega prostora: Teme in problemi" [Migratory Movements along the Western Borders of the Slovenian Ethnic Territory: Issues and Problems], *Annales* 7, no. 10 (1997): 194.

15. Aleksej Kalc and Majda Kodrič, "Izseljevanje iz Beneške Slovenije v kontekstu furlanske migracije s posebnim ozirom na obdobje 19. stoletja in do prve svetovne vojne" [Emigration from Slavia Veneta in the Context of Friulian Migration, with Particular Attention to the Period of the Nineteenth Century until the First World War], *Zgodovinski časopis* 46, no. 2 (1992): 206.

16. Ibid., 199.

17. Anonymous, "Prebivalstvo Nadiških dolin živi v skrajno težki mizeriji" [The Population of the Natisone Valley Lives in Great Misery], *Matajur* 7, no. 19/141 (1956): 1.

18. The pressure exercised over the renaissance and expression of ethnic consciousness of the Slovenians from Slavia Veneta, which is even more pronounced after 1945, actually goes back to 1866, when Slavia Veneta became a part of the newly formed Kingdom of Italy. Within the framework of the historic typology of the nation's formation, Italians can be classified as those who became a nation before they established their statehood or had their statehood

only as historic memory. Unlike the Germans, who also insisted on their historic statehood (the Holy Roman Empire of the German nation), the Italians had to content themselves with Italy as it was represented as a state in various historic periods. In relation to the attitude of Italy toward other (non-Italian) ethnicities, we must also mention the relative instability of its borders with its northern neighbors (France, Austria, and Yugoslavia) that continued until 1947 or 1954 and its striving to level the ethnicity and the state and the resulting desire of leveling without remains. The Italian state was formed through the unification of many elements of different populations, and for this reason the belief that ethnic-linguistic differences are not at the same time ethnic minority problems prevailed for a long time. In particular, Italian politicians firmly believed that various spoken languages were merely dialects of the same language. Between 1861 and 1918, the legal execution of this thesis led to strict unified legislation that stipulated Italian as the sole official state language. The program of Italianization and thus assimilation of the Slovenian-speaking population in Italy went in different directions. It began with the erasing of all signs of Slovenianhood (for example, the name of the village S. Pietro degli Slavi [Špeter Slovenov, St. Peter of the Slavs/Slovenians] was renamed as S. Pietro al Natisone in 1867), with the ban of speaking local non-Italian languages in public, and with the construction of the education system. See Miran Komac, "Politična kultura, narodnostna identiteta, migracijski procesi in etnorazvoj: Protislovja narodnostnega razvoja Slovencev v Videmski pokrajini" [Political Culture, National Identity, Migration Processes and Ethnic Development: Contradictions of the National Development of Slovenians in the Province of Udine] (PhD dissertation, University of Ljubljana, 1990), 104–6.

In addition to the tried and true methods from the past eras, the first decade after World War II saw the use of the most brutal forms of repression of any attempts of the renaissance national or ethnic consciousness, which included physical torture of people and murders. The first form of a military organization that was later called the tricolorists was established in the first half of 1944 as the Difesa popolare territorial, and its activities were directed against all forms of antifascist activity. From the second half of 1945 to the first half of 1947, the organization carried out hundreds of terrorist acts (beating people, breaking into flats, committing arson and plundering houses, arrests of people who participated in the resistance movement and their illegal detention, with the latter sometimes done with support of the Guardia di Finanza and the Carabinieri), so that a significant number of people were forced to flee Slavia Veneta. The terror of the tricolorists became so extensive by mid-1947 that even the foreign press wrote about this paramilitary organization. With the goal of erasing the traces of its activity, the organization moved its headquarters to Udine/Videm, renamed itself Patriots, and continued with violent acts that culminated in the murders of two representatives of the Slovenians from Slavia Veneta in 1947 and 1949. See Miran Komac, "Politična kultura, narodnostna identiteta, migracijski procesi in etnorazvoj," 115–18.

19. A partial exception to that is Jernej Mlekuž's study "Izbrani vidiki zaposlovanja beneških deklet v gospodinjstvih italijanskih mest: Tiha, grenko-sladka, nikoli povsem slišana zgodba" [Selected Aspects of the Employment of Girls from Slavia Veneta in Households of Italian Cities: Quiet, Bittersweet, a Story Never Completely Heard], *Dve domovini/Two Homelands* 19 (2004): 141–64, which is largely the basis for the present text. Mostly we can find this phenomenon mentioned or presented with more or less depth in some studies dealing with emigration from Slavia Veneta, such as Anonymous, *Fotoalbum izseljencev iz Benečije/Fotoalbum degli emigranti della Benecia* [Photo Album of the Emigrants from Slavia Veneta] (Trieste: Založništvo tržaškega tiska, 1986), 157–71; Aleksej Kalc and Majda Kodrič, "Izseljevanje iz Beneške Slovenije v kontekstu furlanske migracije s posebnim ozirom na obdobje 19. stoletja in do prve svetovne vojne," 206; and Aleksej Kalc et al., *Poti in usode: Selitvene izkušnje Slovencev z zahodne meje* [Paths and Destinies: The Migration Experiences of Slovenians from the Western Border] (Koper and Trieste: Zgodovinsko društvo za južno Primorsko, Znanstveno-raziskovalno središče Republike Slovenije and Narodna in študijska knjižnica, 2002), 62–65. In the Friuli, the phenomenon is also mentioned by Bianca Maria Pagani, *L'emigrazione friulana dalla metà del secolo XIX al 1940*, 173, and Ornorato Lorenzon and Pietro Mattioni, *L'emigrazione in Friuli* [Emigration in Friuli] (Udine: Pellegrini, 1962), 38–40, 62–63. There are also some published personal testimonies of the housemaids. For example, Majda Kodrič, "Življenjska zgodba izseljenke varuške" [The Life Story of an Emigrant Nanny], *Jadranski koledar 1991* (1990): 99–102, gives the personal testimony of a maid and nanny from Resia.

20. Janet Henshall Momsen, "Maids on the Move," in *Gender, Migration and Domestic Service*, edited by Janet Henshall Momsen (London and New York: Routledge, 1999), 1, establishes that despite deep historical roots, the migrants employed in households—who are prevalently women—are among the most silent ones. As the author establishes further, up until today the housemaids were mostly invisible in migration data, unmarked in censuses, and usually out of reach of workers' unions and nongovernmental organizations. On the other hand, in today's globalizing world there is more and more of a need to hear these marginalized, invisible, subjugated voices. But this is another story.

21. Anonymous, "Emigracija v Nadiški dolini" [Emigration in the Natisone Valley], *Matajur* 12, no. 8/238 (1961): 1.

Domestic workers from Slavia Veneta didn't go only to northern Italian cities. Particularly after World War II they found employment abroad, especially in Belgium, Great Britain, and Switzerland. Between 1950 and 1960, women employed in households represented one-third of all Italian migrants in Switzerland. Anonymous, *Fotoalbum izseljencev iz Benečije*, 93–96.

22. Anonymous, "Dikle—Domestiche" [Maids], *Matajur* 8, no. 8/150 (1957): 1.

23. Ibid.

24. The interviews were essentially set up as anonymous, and this was made clear to narrators before we started. The names of the narrators have been changed.

25. Luisa, interview by the author, January 13, 2002, Mersino di Sotto/Dolenji Marsin, Italy, written transcript in possession of the author.

26. Teresa, interview by the author, September 10, 2001, Cepletischis/Čeplečišče, Italy, written transcript in possession of the author.

27. Maria, interview by the author, November 27, 2001, Cepletischis/Čeplečišče, Italy, written transcript in possession of the author.

28. Giulia, interview by the author, December 3, 2001, Rodda/Ronac, Italy, written transcript in possession of the author.

29. Anonymous, "Dikle so postale osigurani delavci" [Dikle Have Become Insured Workers], *Matajur* 9, no. 9/174 (1958): 2, my emphasis.

30. Teresa, interview by the author, September 10, 2001, Cepletischis/Čeplečišče, Italy, written transcript in possession of the author.

31. Luigia, interview by the author, September 19, 2001, Cepletischis/Čeplečišče, Italy, written transcript in possession of the author.

32. A lot of the material had also already been collected before the mentioned project, in 2000 and 2001, as the material for my master's thesis, "Proučevanje učinkov migracij na vrednotenje prostora med izseljenci iz Nadiške Beneške Slovenije" [Examining the Effects of Migration on the Evaluation of the Space among the Emigrants of the Natisone Valley in Slavia Veneta] (University of Ljubljana, 2002).

33. Jernej Mlekuž, "Izbrani vidiki zaposlovanja beneških deklet v gospodinjstvih italijanskih mest," 141–64. The gathered material can be found in the archive box "Beneška Slovenija" at the Slovenian Migration Institute SRC SASA, Ljubljana.

34. Because the material was qualitatively so different—from recordings (several hours in length) of life stories that I have put together on the basis of several visits to the narrators as well as mere fragments from the lives or memories of lives of individuals written in the field journal—I decided that I would not burden this text with data about the number of narrators used.

35. Michela, interview by the author, August 21, 2001, Polava, Italy, tape recording in possession of the author. Female emigration to work in the household service sector was often understood as a so-called push factor of the poverty at home. The girls who emigrated and accepted the work were most often presented as victims. They were forced to take the job because they were poor. See Janet Henshall Momsen, "Maids on the Move," in *Gender, Migration and Domestic Service*, edited by Janet Henshall Momsen (London: Routledge, 1999), 10.

36. Michela, interview by the author, August 21, 2001, Polava, Italy, tape recording in possession of the author. Of course the single status was not a necessary trait of the migrants employed in the service sector. Among the so-called *aleksandrinke*—the female population from the countryside of the Goriška region who immigrated to Egypt in the second half of the nineteenth century and the first half of the twentieth century to work as nannies, wet nurses, and maids, as described by Daša Koprivec in chapter 3 of this book and other authors, including Dorica Makuc, *Aleksandrinke* (Gorizia: Mohorjeva družba, 1993)—Barbič and Brezigar, "Občasne migracije podeželskih žena na Goriškem," 39–38, mention that those who emigrated were mostly married women and mothers. The best-known housemaids of today, the Filipinas—the "servants of globalization," as Rhacel Salazar Parreñas, *Servants of Globalization: Women, Migration and Domestic Work* (Stanford, CA: Stanford University Press, 2001), calls them—who seek employment in big cities of the First World are in large part married women and mothers.

37. Bruna, interview by the author, November 3, 2001, Cepletischis/Čeplešišče, Italy, written transcript in possession of the author.

38. Aldina, interview by the author, February 2, 2002, Montemaggiore/Matajur, Italy, written transcript in possession of the author.

39. Bruna, interview by the author, November 3, 2001, Cepletischis/Čeplešišče, Italy, written transcript in possession of the author.

40. Teresa, interview by the author, September 10, 2001, Cepletischis/Čeplešišče, Italy, written transcript in possession of the author.

41. Bruna, interview by the author, November 3, 2001, Cepletischis/Čeplešišče, Italy, written transcript in possession of the author.

42. Marina, interview by the author, February 16, 2002, Clodig/Hlodič, Italy, written transcript in possession of the author.

43. Ibid.

44. Sonia, interview by the author, October 21, 2001, Topolò/Topolovo, Italy, written transcript in possession of the author.

45. Ibid.

46. Marina, interview by the author, February 16, 2002, Clodig/Hlodič, Italy, written transcript in possession of the author.

47. Ibid.

48. Mario, interview by the author, March 4, 2002, Bardo, Italy, written transcript in possession of the author.

49. Aldina, interview by the author, February 2, 2002, Montemaggiore/Matajur, Italy, written transcript in possession of the author.

50. Marina, interview by the author, February 16, 2002, Clodig/Hlodič, Italy, written transcript in possession of the author.

51. Andreina, interview by the author, November 23, 2001, Topolò/Topolovo, Italy, written transcript in possession of the author.

52. Lara, interview by the author, January 20, 2002, Bardo, Italy, written transcript in possession of the author.

53. Sonia, interview by the author, October 21, 2001, Topolò/Topolovo, Italy, written transcript in possession of the author.

54. See Ehrenreich, Barbara, and Arlie Russell Hochschild, eds., *Global Woman: Nannies, Maids and Sex Workers in the New Economy* (New York: Metropolitan Books, 2003).

55. Sonia, interview by the author, October 21, 2001, Topolò/Topolovo, Italy, written transcript in possession of the author.

56. Lidia, interview by the author, December 23, 2001, Topolò/Topolovo, Italy, written transcript in possession of the author.

57. Housemaids mostly saved up their earnings for dowries or trousseaus (the property that the wife brings into the marriage). Some bought their trousseaus on their own, and sometimes the mother prepared the trousseau for the daughters (possibly because the daughter was too young).

58. Anonymous, *Fotoalbum izseljencev iz Benečije*, 158.

59. Marina, interview by the author, February 16, 2002, Clodig/Hlodič, Italy, written transcript in possession of the author.

60. Michelina, interview by the author, February 21, 2002, Masseris/Mašera, Italy, written transcript in possession of the author.

61. Most maids were not registered, had no work papers, and had no insurance or other bonuses afforded by regulated employment. The first law that regulated the employment, payment, insurance, annual leave, accommodation, and parental permission for housemaids who were minors was enacted in 1958. However,

the interviews with former maids show that for a long while after the law was passed, they were employed without the prescribed documents, insurance, etc. As stated in an article in *Matajur* published a couple of months after the law was passed, "So what's happening with this law about dikle? Just like the majority on new laws here in Italy, it will take a long time for it to start working. Dikle look for the work themselves via their friends [according to the new law, the role of intermediary should go to specialized agencies]." See Anonymous, "Emigrantske rimese" [Remittances of the Emigrants], *Matajur* 9, no. 21/187 (1958): 2.

62. Luigia, interview by the author, September 19, 2001, Cepletischis/Čeplečišče, Italy, written transcript in possession of the author. The phrase "to be a part of the family" used by maids, their employers, and in general in the different contexts of their work and of life among employing families has been critically analyzed by a number of researchers of this phenomenon. Rhacel Salazar Parreñas, *Servants of Globalization: Women, Migration and Domestic Work* (Stanford, CA: University Press, 2001), 179–78, who put together an overview of the critique of this phrase, says that it is rooted in the feudal understanding of maids as master's servants, blurs the status of maids as paid workers and thus makes negotiations with the employer more difficult for the employee, enables the employer to use the "family" ideology in negotiations regarding payment to the employees, and finally marginalizes the existence of the maids' families.

63. Silvana, interview by the author, October 20, 2001, Mersino Alto/Gorenji Marsin, Italy, written transcript in possession of the author. Barbič and Miklavčič-Brezigar, "Občasne migracije podeželskih žena na Goriškem," 46, differentiate two kinds of employer-family attitudes toward household help. The traditional attitude was determined by a strict separation of the master or madam and the servant or in cases where the maid was treated as one of the family. The contemporary attitude is characterized by the relationship between the family and the employee as a relationship between the employer and worker regardless of whether this relationship is hierarchical or democratic. The authors found that the servants in wealthier middle-class families were more likely to encounter the hierarchical method, while servants in working-class families were more often accepted as family members.

64. Over the years, the attitude of dikle toward their families changed. If between the two world wars and a decade or two afterward the majority of the girls still sent money home, this practice has become increasingly rare since 1960, as the interviews show. It is only to the later dikle that the income could mean also (at least partial) economic and social independence.

65. Marina, interview by the author, November 7, 2001, Clodig/Hlodič, Italy, written transcript in possession of the author.

66. Mladen Dolar, *A Voice and Nothing More* (Cambridge, MA: MIT Press, 2006), 12.

67. Listening to the stories of housemaids brings a number of interpretative difficulties. These touch on knowledge and of course authority. Were they are a helpless and exploited workforce, or do we have to understand them as emancipated women, to name just two of the potential extremes? Following the thinking of Bojan Baskar, *Dvoumni Mediteran: Študije o regionalnem prekrivanju na vzhodnojadranskem območju* [The Ambiguous Mediterranean: Studies on the Regional Overlap in the Area of the Eastern Adriatic] (Koper: Zgodovinsko društvo za južno Primorsko, Znanstveno-raziskovalno središče Republike Slovenije, 2006), 28, about the different interpretations of the *šavrinke* (female peddlers from Slovenian Istria), we could talk about at least two: the optimist-feminist one (emphasis on woman power, agility, and decision making) and the pessimist-feminist one (emphasis on gender inequality and the economic exploitation of women).

68. Marina, interview by the author, February 16, 2002, Clodig/Hlodič, Italy, written transcript in possession of the author.

References

Anonymous. "Dikle—Domestiche" [Maids]. *Matajur* 8, no. 8/150 (1957): 1.

Anonymous. "Dikle so postale osigurani delavci" [Dikle Have Become Insured Workers]. *Matajur* 9, no. 9/174 (1958): 1–2.

Anonymous. "Emigrantske rimese" [Remittances of the Emigrants]. *Matajur* 9, no. 21/187 (1958): 2.

Anonymous. "Emigracija v Nadiški dolini" [Emigration in the Natisone Valley]. *Matajur* 12, no. 8/238 (1961): 1.

Anonymous. *Fotoalbum izseljencev iz Benečije/Fotoalbum degli emigranti della Benecia* [Photo Album of Emigrants from Slavia Veneta]. Trieste: Založništvo tržaškega tiska, 1986.

Anonymous. "Prebivalstvo Nadiških dolin živi v skrajno težki mizeriji" [The Population of the Natisone Valley Lives in Great Misery]. *Matajur* 7, no. 19/141 (1956): 1.

Barbič, Ana, and Inga Miklavčič-Brezigar. "Občasne migracije podeželskih žena na Goriškem: Gospodinjsko delo v tujini—nuja in priložnost nekoč in danes" [Occasional Migrations of Rural Women in Goriška: Domestic Work Abroad—Necessity and Chance, Past and Present]. *Glasnik Slovenskega etnološkega društva* 39, no. 3-4 (1999): 39-38.

Baskar, Bojan. *Dvoumni Mediteran: Študije o regionalnem prekrivanju na vzhodnojadranskem območju* [The Ambiguous Mediterranean: Studies on the Regional Overlap in the Area of the Eastern Adriatic]. Koper: Zgodovinsko društvo za južno Primorsko, Znanstveno-raziskovalno središče Republike Slovenije, 2006.

Bruner M., Edward. "Introduction." In *The Anthropology of Experience*, edited by Victor. W. Turner and Edward M. Bruner, 3-30. Urbana: University of Illinois Press, 1986.

Dolar, Mladen. *A Voice and Nothing More.* Cambridge, MA: MIT Press, 2006.

Ehrenreich, Barbara, and Arlie Russell Hochschild, eds. *Global Woman: Nannies, Maids and Sex Workers in the New Economy.* New York: Metropolitan Books, 2003.

Henshall Momsen, Janet. "Maids on the Move." In *Gender, Migration and Domestic Service*, edited by Janet Henshall Momsen, 1-22. London: Routledge, 1999.

Kalc, Aleksej. "Selitvena gibanja ob zahodnih mejah slovenskega etničnega prostora: Teme in problemi" [Migratory Movements along the Western Borders of the Slovenian Ethnic Territory: Issues and Problems]. *Annales* 7, no. 10 (1997): 193-214.

Kalc, Aleksej, et al. *Poti in usode: Selitvene izkušnje Slovencev z zahodne meje* [Paths and Destinies: The Migration Experiences of Slovenians from the Western Border]. Koper and Trieste: Zgodovinsko društvo za južno Primorsko, Znanstveno-raziskovalno središče Republike Slovenije and Narodna in študijska knjižnica, 2002.

Kalc, Aleksej, and Majda Kodrič. "Izseljevanje iz Beneške Slovenije v kontekstu furlanske migracije s posebnim ozirom na obdobje 19. stoletja in do prve svetovne vojne" [Emigration from Slavia Veneta in the Context of Friulian Migration, with Particular Attention to the Period of the Nineteenth Century until the First World War]. *Zgodovinski časopis* 46, no. 2 (1992): 197-209.

Kodrič, Majda. "Življenjska zgodba izseljenke varuške" [The Life Story of an Emigrant Nanny]. *Jadranski koledar 1991* (1990): 99-102.

Komac, Miran. "Politična kultura, narodnostna identiteta, migracijski procesi in etnorazvoj: Protislovja narodnostnega razvoja Slovencev v Videmski pokrajini" [Political Culture, National Identity, Migration Processes and Ethnic Development: Contradictions of the National Development of Slovenians in the Province of Udine]. PhD dissertation, University of Ljubljana, 1990.

Lorenzon, Onorato, and Pietro Mattioni. *L'emigrazione in Friuli* [Emigration in Friuli]. Udine: Pellegrini, 1962.

Makuc, Dorica. *Aleksandrinke*. Gorizia: Mohorjeva družba, 1993.

Marx, Karl. *The Eighteenth Brumaire of Louis Bonaparte*. Moscow: Progress Publishers, 1979.

Mlekuž, Jernej. "Izbrani vidiki zaposlovanja beneških deklet v gospodinjstvih italijanskih mest: Tiha, grenko-sladka, nikoli povsem slišana zgodba" [Selected Aspects of the Employment of Girls from Slavia Veneta in Households of Italian Cities: Quiet, Bittersweet, a Story Never Completely Heard]. *Dve domovini/Two Homelands* 19 (2004): 141–64.

———. "Proučevanje učinkov migracij na vrednotenje prostora med izseljenci iz Nadiške Beneške Slovenije" [Examining the Effects of Migration on the Evaluation of the Space among the Emigrants from the Natisone Valley in Slavia Veneta]. Master's thesis, University of Ljubljana, 2002.

Orehovec, Martina. "Ženske in delo v Istri v 20. stoletju" [Women and Work in Istria in the Twentieth Century]. Master's thesis, University of Ljubljana, 2001.

Pagani, Bianca Maria. *L'emigrazione friulana dalla metà del secolo XIX al 1940* [Friulian Emigration from the Mid-Nineteenth Century to 1940]. Udine: Arti Grafiche Friulane, 1968.

Peacock L. James, and Dorothy C. Holland. "The Narrated Self: Life Stories in Process." *Ethos* 21, no. 4 (1993): 367–83.

Prešeren, France. *Poezije doktorja Francéta Prešérna: Z Dodatkom* [The Poetry of Dr. France Prešeren: With Supplement]. Ljubljana: Cankarjeva založba, 1982.

Salazar Parreñas, Rhacel. *Servants of Globalization: Women, Migration and Domestic Work*. Stanford, CA: Stanford University Press, 2001.

Stupca, Antonija. "O oskrbi za posle in kolodvorskih misijonih" [On the Care for Servants and Railway Station Missions]. In *Slovensko-hrvaški katoliški shod v Ljubljani, 1913* [Slovenian-Croatian Catholic Jamboree in Ljubljana, 1913], 183–87. Ljubljana: Katoliška bukvarna, 1913.

Verginella, Marta. *Ženska obrobja: Vpis žensk v zgodovino Slovencev* [Women on the Margins: The Inscription of Women in the History of Slovenians]. Ljubljana: Delta, 2006.

III | Active, Skilled, Ambitious

Chapter 5

Slamnikarice Abroad and at Home
Ladies and Entrepreneurs

Saša Roškar

These enterprising straw hat makers started to expand their activities into the world. They were opening a factory in America, in New York; in 1908 they sent 196 sewers and supervisors to start the production there and train the workforce. My husband's grandmother Francka left with this group. Over there, she met her husband, a fellow Slovenian, who'd emigrated before to make a living. They were married in 1910, and a year later their son Janko was born. Her plan was to stay there. However, Francka had to return home and travel to Lvov, in today's Ukraine, to open another factory. So her husband returned home, too. They intended to go back to America after Francka had finished work, and they left their son there with a nanny temporarily. Unfortunately, this is not how the story ends. Francka became gravely ill in Ukraine and died of tuberculosis. She's buried there. The Red Cross sent her son Janko to Slovenia a couple of years later to be reunited with his father, who had by then remarried and started a new family.[1]

The story told by Marina Lenček,[2] the wife of Francka's grandson, meant a new dimension in the history of straw hat making in Domžale,[3] at least to me, because my roots are not in the region. I knew about the migration statistics but did not know about the personal fates hiding behind them. Straw hat makers, *slamnikarice* as they are known locally, were people who worked in the straw hat–making industry. In accordance with the production process, they were responsible for different tasks. Some—and they were the majority—sewed hats, some put them into presses, and some equipped the finished hats with sweatbands, decorative ribbons, and other accessories. Most of them were sewers[4] who used braids of wheat straw or other materials to make a side band that then through the manufacturing process became a hat. At the end of the nineteenth century and the beginning of the twentieth century, the slamnikarice of Domžale left as seasonal workers to large cities of western and central Europe and also temporarily or permanently to the United States, primarily to New York. They left as skilled workers to large hat-making factories. Slamnikarice left as young women, most of them unmarried, and for the large part worked until they were married.

These stories of seasonal workers and emigrants began to raise many questions: other than some dry statistical data and lists, nothing concrete had been written about them, despite the fact that we can recognize their involvement in family and social networks, their acceptance of life as charted by the social and economic circumstances of the time,[5] and the vivaciousness, the curiosity, and also the tragedies of individual life destinies, similar to the ones we have so far mostly known through our discovery of the legacy of the *aleksandrinke*.[6] Slamnikarice and aleksandrinke share not only the historic period but also another important trait, namely that the migration was mostly female.[7] The latter is mostly the consequence of the technological process in straw hat making, which for the most part needed female sewers of straw hats. Men held managerial positions or did heavy physical tasks, which didn't demand a large number of employees.

Today, the straw hat makers who left to work in other countries are no longer around. The stories we have left are the memories of their children, relatives, and neighbors. Correspondence with their families and photographs are also preserved. The stories that we are rediscovering today tell us about young women's search for better income and economic independence, the informal education they achieved, survival strategies, social networks that represented security, and often an additional impetus for leaving: women left to stay with their aunts, neighbors, and fellow villagers. Those women who had children left them in the care of relatives for the most part.

The main reason for emigration was financial: the earnings were several times higher than those that hatmakers would get for the same work at home. However, there must have been other motives hiding behind this, such as leaving home and thus the departure from several more or less conflicting situations, finding economic independence, learning languages and other skills, and responding to invitations from relatives and friends to come abroad. And we must not neglect the attitude that women encountered at home and abroad: "Over there, we were ladies, but as soon as we glimpsed the hayracks, we were wenches."[8]

Although straw hat making was a phenomenon that included the wider rural areas of Domžale and Kamnik, the manufacturers and industry were concentrated in Domžale and Menges. Since the fieldwork so far has concentrated mostly on the Domžale area, the historic overview will also be mostly limited to this area.

The period in which slamnikarice were coming and going lasted between 50 and 60 years, from the last two decades of the nineteenth century to roughly the mid-1930s. Straw hats and straw hat making had been significantly present in Domžale and surrounding areas for at least 150 years before that. The sources available today show that making straw hats and selling them at fairs near and far existed in the Domžale area already in the first half of the eighteenth century.[9] At the time, straw hat making was a craft. Wheat straw of suitable quality was carefully selected from the rest of the harvest and kept; in winter, braids were plaited and hats were sewn in many households. The legend says that the knowledge about the craft was brought to the nearby village of Ihan by a man who served in Florence as a soldier, but there are not any precise facts and data about when the craft expanded to Carniola. In addition to the locals who sold hats at the local fairs and in Ljubljana, the peddlers from Kočevje and the Kočevska region also traded with them and peddled all over the Austrian land, as did the sellers from Bled who mostly sold them in the Carinthia. From the beginning of the nineteenth century, the Tyrolean peddlers also joined the straw hat–selling chain and sold them in Carinthia and Tyrol. The straw hats at the time were either wheat-colored or black and were only intended for the lower strata of the society. Some decades later, the sources list more than fifty different shapes of straw hats intended for sale in Styria, Carinthia, and other parts of Austria all the way to Salzburg and Bavaria and praise their quality.[10] However, they still differed greatly in the quality of straw and the quality of manufacture from the Florentine straw hats, made in and around Florence.

Hat making brought important additional income in the part of the year when there was no work in the field, as the season of braiding and sewing straw hats was from late autumn to early spring. Because many of the locals were cottagers, it is quite possible that not all of them could find employment as farmworkers, and there must have been many who depended on work in transporting and freighting goods or in various crafts.[11] For the semirural population, who often depended on working the land of rich landowners for which they were paid in produce, braiding and sewing hats brought monetary income.

The system of seasonal work in the straw hat–making factories outside the place of residence was introduced to Domžale and its surroundings by the Tyrolean factory owners who arrived in the region in the 1860s. The reasons for this were economic. In the war with Italy (1866),[12] Austria lost Veneto. The unified economic territory shrunk, so the owners moved their factories from Marostica and other parts of Veneto to Domžale. They already knew the area, and they brought with them some experienced Italian sewers as well as sewing machines.

The local hat-making entrepreneurs had workshops that were much smaller and were no competition for the Tyrolean factory owners in terms of capital and the development of the market. However, they always called and named them factories, and this is the reason we use the both terms as synonyms throughout this chapter. In terms of production, the local hatmakers surpassed the Tyroleans before the end of the nineteenth century, but the latter bought hats from the local makers and dressed and finished them for the market. Thus, they reaped a large part of the profits,[13] and they opened their subsidiaries in large cities (Vienna, Prague, Budapest, Lvov, Linz, Bucharest, etc.). In the beginning of the twentieth century, there were around twenty large and small millinery workshops and factories, which until World War I employed around 1,000 workers. Around 1923, 250 men and 600 women were employed in the millinery factories.[14] "In wintertime everybody in Domžale and around, even the daughters of the wealthiest landowning families, is in factories."[15]

Millinery brought about the general development of the place and a quick growth of the population. In 1856 the Domžale parish had 1,126 inhabitants. In 1920 there were 2,156 and another 40 temporarily making hats in Europe and 390 in America, altogether 2,586.[16]

The golden age of industrialized hat making ended with World War I and the dissolution of the common Austro-Hungarian market. Due to new political and economic circumstances, the effectively organized production and business politics of Tyrolean factory owners within the old monarchy lost important markets and connections to subsidiaries as each of the newly formed countries introduced import duties for foreign products. The subsidiaries, spread all over Europe, became independent. At the same time, the companies could not pay off substantial loans that they took out to modernize production before World War I.[17] The Tyrolean companies were economically weakened and mostly went bankrupt; the majority of Tyroleans emigrated. In the 1920s and 1930s, straw hat making again became a trade practiced mostly by Slovenian entrepreneurs in their small workshops, and their market shifted from central and western Europe to Slavonia and Dalmatia. An additional factor for the demise of braiding[18] was the import of quality straw from Italy and China: the local farmers, despite appeals and instructions,[19] never grew cereal exclusively for straw; the straw was a by-product. The second important reason was the change in fashion trends and style. Jerica Moder, a straw hat maker who sewed and sold straw hats by herself from her home until the early 1930s, said to her son: "I also don't know how come everything came to nothing; the factories went even earlier, I don't know if it was because other places produced more, or because people went about with bare heads."[20]

After World War II, the demand for straw hats grew. The factories that restarted production (Univerzale and the Straw Hat–Making Cooperative in Menges) sold men's hats mostly to Slavonia, Vojvodina, and the coastal cities.[21] Even before World War II, these factories started making other types of hats in addition to straw hats and later branched out into clothing. The quantities of hat production varied, but the decade of the 1960s was the most successful. Later the production kept falling until in 2002 Univerzale, the last millinery factory, closed its doors.

Seasonal Work in European Cities and America

Franc Bernik, the priest who established the Domžale parish, left us extraordinary records. For the first three decades of the twentieth century, he kept a detailed record of migration processes with names and numbers.[22] It is interesting that he was a lot more pedantic in recording straw hat makers who went to America than he was in recording those who were doing seasonal work in European cities; he only mentions the latter in individual censuses and only in numbers, without names, although they were far fewer than those who went to America.

In this way, a number of girls grew in the parish and the surrounding area—girls who, like swallows, fly to big cities every autumn and return home around the Pentecost. They go not only seconded by the order and as employees of the Domžale industrialists but also on the request of others who want to have them because they sew well. In the winter of 1908, for example, among sewers from the Domžale parish were 21 in Vienna, 11 in Bucharest, 6 in Prostějov, 5 in Budapest, 4 in Prague, 4 in Lvov, 2 in Kronstadt, and 2 in Breslau.[23]

To understand the issues of slamnikarice, these female straw hat makers must be divided into those who left for seasonal work in European cities and those who left for America. The nature of seasonal work is tied to a limited period of time, in this case from late autumn (and sometimes even after Christmas) until spring; the seasons are fixed and predictable. For the rest of the year, the straw hat maker was a part of her primary family. Bernik does not have the exact data when such seasonal work started in Domžale and the surroundings areas as he does for the first departures to America, nor does his data tell us when this era was finished. Arnez states that around 1890 Slovenian straw hat makers were already working in Ladstätter's subsidiary in Bucharest.[24] The era was certainly largely over with World War I and the gradual demise of the Tyrolean straw hat–making companies; however, the narrators tell us that their relatives were leaving as late as the 1930s.

The departures for America were in a way the exact opposite. The workers who left for America did so for a longer period, many forever (although seasonal workers too sometimes stayed permanently in the European cities they went to for seasonal work). Bernik recorded the departure of slamnikarice from Domžale and the surrounding area with the preciseness of a record keeper.

In 1882, a local hat-factory owner, Krizant Ladstätter, and Menkov, a representative for a sewing machine factory, wanted to open together a straw hat–making factory in New York in America. They sent two sewers over: Ivana Šme from Zgornje Domžale, house number 2, and Marička Štraser, residing in

Zgornje Domžale. These two were the first Domžale Americans. However, Ladstätter and Menkov went their separate ways in about a year. Ladstätter called Štraser back home, while Ivana Šme stayed with Menkov in New York.[25]

The following year Menkov and Ivana Šme wrote home for three more slamnikarice to come, and indeed the following year Marija Zajec, Marija Flerin, and Marija Rojanec migrated as well. One of them soon returned home, while two stayed in America. Anna Praček Krasna cites the writings of Ignac Mušič,[26] who was allegedly a straw hat maker himself, in which he describes a discussion with Marija Ganser, one of the first straw hat makers who came to New York from near Domžale. He talked to her when she had been in New York for forty years. "We were here alone, without any friends; we were afraid to even go out. And we saved up, three hundred dollars in three years each one of us." After three years she returned home, where she stayed for three months only and then took two of her sisters and another girl with her to America.[27]

For the next twenty years only rare individual migrants left, but in 1905 a so-called American epidemic was triggered in Domžale. In 1908 there were 196 persons in America, and Bernik listed in his chronicle the names of all Domžale parishioners who were in America in 1923: 238 (62 percent), of whom were women[28] and 146 were men, altogether 384. The breakdown by the city was as follows: New York, 305; Cleveland, 37; Chicago, 30; and elsewhere, 12. The report of the Slovenian parish of St. Cyril in New York for 1922 lists 90 families and 75 single people as parishioners, among them 35 families and 33 single persons from Domžale.[29] Bernik writes that the Ave Marija Koledar for the year 1928 wrote "very honorable words" for Domžale—"New York–American Domžale"—and that the Domžale people in New York mostly worked in straw hat making, lived in small apartments in tall buildings. The flats were tastefully decorated and comfortable, and slamnikarice earned well, "comparatively best in America." Because he visited America himself that year, he was full of praise for the diligence of the people and their piousness. For 1939 he claims that there were 339 people from Domžale parish in the United States.[30]

Besides Krizant Ladstätter, who had a straw hat factory in Domžale, there were a few other Slovenians in New York who started straw hat and felt hat millinery workshops. Most people employed in these workshops were their fellow countrymen.[31] At first the Domžale straw hat makers settled in Manhattan, close to the factories where they worked, but later families started moving to Ridgewood in Brooklyn, where flats were cheaper and far from factories and city noise.[32] In 1916, Slovenian Catholics in New York established their own parish and the Church of St. Cyril, which became and remains today one of the centers of religious and social life. People from Domžale, together with other Slovenian immigrants, established choirs, drama societies, music groups, support organizations, and their own gazettes. Bernik also wrote that "Without any plea from the priest many contributed to the great work that took place in these years in their home church, on their own accord, completely voluntarily, and with a lot of good will."[33]

What separates slamnikarice from other Slovenian female migrants is that they were skilled workers, while the rest of the female migrants were mostly agrarian workers, maids, or housewives.[34] Bernik had positive and even admiring words for these women, the straw hat makers:

> Women are dressed more smartly than can otherwise be observed on a workday in the countryside. Naturally! They are coming straight from a factory where they do a relatively good and clean job. And then many of them have seen some more world than the village steeple. Many a skilled straw hat sewer spent one or more winters in Vienna, Prague, Budapest, or elsewhere. But it didn't go to their heads. You see them, how they are! Some natural, unforced kindness shines from their faces and behavior. They're all laughter.[35]

Bernik does not condemn them for leaving home or judge them for striving for better incomes, and he values them as skilled workers who are valued elsewhere too because of the quality of their work. "Straw hat sewers from Domžale have long been famous as the best and they were eagerly accepted in the finest straw hat–making factories in world metropolises. This fame they kept to this day."[36]

Bernik's enthusiasm about hat makers who left to work abroad is not exactly in line with the church doctrine of the time, which at first warned of the dangers of foreign lands and later recommended that to avoid breaking up families, entire families should migrate and of course remain faithful to the Catholic Church.[37] Straw hat makers were skilled, hardworking, diligent, and for the most part pious and loyal with ties to family, neighborhood, and professional associations. They kept in touch with their relatives back home and also with their home parish. In most major projects that the home parish undertook in Domžale, such as building a cultural home, a children's shelter, and a cooperative, the Domžale emigrants significantly contributed with their money.

Bernik nowhere mentions how many hat makers returned home from America and how many never returned from seasonal work and instead stayed abroad for various reasons (most likely marriage or permanent employment). Other sources so far do not provide us with this data. The Austro-Hungarian monarchy did not limit emigration,[38] and the church considered emigrants to be in the first place a church problem, so the Slovenian Catholic Church established St. Raphael's Society to help emigrants. Its subsidiary in New York—St. Raphael's Society for Slovenian Settlers in the United States—was established in 1908 with the intent of providing people with shelter, offering them advice, helping them find employment, and helping them in dealings with authorities. Later, a section for the protection of girls was also established.[39]

Through different forms of organization, the immigrants in America offered important help to their fellow countrymen and women after World War I and especially after World War II. The help came in the form of money, food, and clothing. The postwar packages are still a part of the memory of this era, and many families in Domžale and around received them.

So far, I have not managed to establish contact with descendants of Domžale straw hat makers in America. What the next generation remembers about the lives of straw hat makers in New York remains a topic for further research.

The Voice of Slamnikarice and Intimate Memories

Because straw hat makers can no longer convey their own memories, feelings, and knowledge, we can only base our research on the memories of those who shared their life destinies or followed them through family correspondence and legacy. I have collected some very different life stories from different periods relating to both the American and the seasonal experiences. Despite that, some questions remain open, mostly those related to the everyday life of straw hat makers—where exactly they lived, what they did in their free time, what they ate, etc. My narrators were children when the stories were taking place, and their interests were those typical of children: when the slamnikarice would come again and what they would bring. Today we do not know if women just didn't discuss life abroad when they were at home or whether such conversations simply weren't interesting for young people at the time. It appears that the slamnikarice did not describe their lives abroad in detail. Their voices will therefore be a memory of them based on the curiosity of children and the reality that became lost somewhere in time and also acquired the veneer of something valuable. I imagine that in the past the life stories of emigrants were ordinary in and around Domžale because there were hardly any families who did not have at least one relative abroad. Today they are a curiosity, as many inhabitants of Domžale, a place that developed as a characteristically industrial and artisanal town with a large number of people who moved there from other parts of Slovenia and former Yugoslavia, do not have these stories in their family chronicle, just as they do not have local straw hat–making stories.

Ship Journal

Frančiška Kos went to America in 1905, and her brother Andrej followed her a year later. In 1915 at age twenty-one, Tereza Kos joined Frančiška. The family owned a rather large farm in Študa, and their mother also worked as a seasonal straw hat maker in Vienna. More details are not known. I heard their story from Roman Kos,[40] Frančiška's great-nephew, who owns the homestead today. Andrej, who went to Chester (a town apparently in America), disappeared without a trace, but Tereza and Frančiška worked as straw hat sewers in New York City and years later returned to Domžale separately. There is little information about their lives and their work. They went abroad as unmarried girls and did not marry while in America. In 1929 Tereza came home for a visit, and a couple of years later she returned for good and married. Frančiška returned home immediately after World War II and died soon after. Neither ever had children.

Roman Kos says that "We have to look at it in the spirit of the time; no one had a problem going away from home. There were too many hungry mouths anyways, because all the families, especially rural ones, had many children. Well, in this family, there were nine. And on the farm, there was usually one who stayed, and maybe an unmarried aunt." He believes that families helped to buy ship tickets for those who went to America and that this was often part of an agreement regarding demand for the dowry or part of the farm, because based on the information from America, they were convinced that the income there would be a lot better. "I think they were relying on those who were already there. They always went to someone. Because of this encouraging, positive news... I think it was easier. And also, here it was really hard. It could have hardly been any worse." Roman Kos also doesn't know whether they sent money home, but he does know that they gave money to the Domžale priest Franc Bernik for his projects. "But I have to say that when she [Tereza] came home, when she stayed home, she helped a lot here. Her husband Matevž acted as a confirmation sponsor for all my brothers and myself. My

Figure 5.1. Tereza Kos. *Courtesy of Roman Kos*

mother took care of her when she became old, and after she died, she left the house to my mother."[41]

Tereza left a journal[42] written in 1929 that describes the sea voyage home for a visit, some weeks of life at home, and the first couple of days of her return journey to America. She also left photos of her birth house, the family, and the graveyard that she took with her own camera during this visit; at that time personal cameras were very rare in Domžale. Other material documents of her or her sister from the time of emigration have not been preserved.

Tereza started writing her journal on June 8, 1929, and finished on October 10 of the same year with the second entry during the return to America. The voyage from New York to Trieste took twelve days. Mostly she uses the feminine plural form, but we do not know who traveled with her. The feminine plural is used to describe ship routines, food, etc. Personal remarks are in singular.

The first entry is as follows:

> 8 June 1929 sobota (*Saturday*)[43]
> Took off from New York at 12 at night. In the morning at 7 there

was breakfast without spoon coffee and bread a bit poor then we went to the deck and it rained a little and was cold then we went to *Ladies Salon* and Slovenian women sang Slovenian songs and from there we went to lunch we had. We had minestrone *steak* cabbage cake black coffee wine and after lunch we sat down and then went on the deck sea was beautiful and calm sky cloudy and cold at half past two tea and rusk and then *moving picture* for dinner bean soup with *macaroni* salad fish [the edge of the notebook has been torn off] black coffee....
lunch at 11 *o'clock*
dinner at 5 *o'clock p.m.*
raining at 6 *p.m.*[44]

With this first entry she set the pattern for further writing with date and daily routine interrupted by the meals she describes in detail:

June 9. nedelja (*Sunday*)
We slept brilliantly breakfast at 7 cocoa, *butter,* salami at half past eight we went to mass and then on the deck we walked for 1 hour and then it was lunch. Spaghetti meat beans gherkins *ice cream* and black coffee wine. After lunch we went back to the deck and there sang Slovenian songs and my cotravelers danced and played harmonica sky cloudy rain now and then air clean and good and not too cold. Dinner minestrone with *macaroni* roast meat with potatoes wine, cheese, raw apple, black coffee. Rolls hard. 6 p.m. weather already nice sky cloudy air windy.[45]

Below the line she wrote curiosities: "In the morning I trapped my little finger in the door and then put ointment and bandage on it. Today 10. Monday it's better already and now I will another one...??"[46] She describes the social life and new encounters:

June 10. ponedeljek (*Monday*)
...Enough party, enough boys. Half past two tea on the deck and then we went to the top deck again and had fun with the boy from the island and laughed so that I hurt all over and then dinner at five minestrone, goulash banana wine black coffee bread. Then back to the lower deck to have fun and time flew by I almost forgot what we ate I feel fantastic.[47]

Over the next couple of days Tereza writes that they met Croatians, Dalmatians, and a Czech man and that nobody was sick. They danced folk dances and sang Slovenian songs. She writes what kind of ships they met—cargo and passenger ships—and about the fish that jumped out of the water.

On June 15 Tereza writes that at 10 a.m. they saw the first land—Portugal and Africa on the right: "They sailed fast and in the middle of the sea so that we could tell apart houses or villages a little with a naked eye and then we saw the world famous fortress 'Gibraltar' a great view of the giant." On June 17 she writes that they passed Sardinia, but she didn't see it because she was asleep. She also writes that "Today the Italians will disembark in Naples and then it will be nicer they're so dirty." From her entries we can conclude that she mostly associated with Slovenian women and other Slavs on the ship; once she mentions an Englishman but no other nationalities. "In the afternoon at 4 we started approaching Naples beautiful mountains houses villages on the hills on the right hand we saw Vesuvius that spits fire and at 8 we stopped in Naples and the Italians disembarked left mail and cargo and we Slovenian girls had good fun until twelve thirty. Left Naples at 2 at night." The next day they passed Sicily, and she also writes that they saw villages and towns and that the decks are empty because "the polenta people went down."[48]

On June 19 she writes that they arrived in Patras: "people went down to small boat and we left luggage and at 9 we turned toward Trieste to the Adriatic sea lovely view of the harbor, hills, mountains, and islands.... Today we can see the mountainous Albania on the right then comes Dalmatia and then the last stop Trieste."[49]

June 20 was the last day on the ship:

> The last day on water got up early weather beautiful sea completely calm. We started approaching the port. Beautiful places can be seen all around everybody is happy and healthy and glad that we will soon be on land nothing bad happened but a person still feels better on mother earth in the afternoon at three we stopped and the rich ones went out to Venice and then we went for a while really quickly so we arrived at 8 in the much desired

Figure 5.2. Tereza Kos and her relatives in front of her birth house, 1929. *Courtesy of Roman Kos*

> Trieste. There we disembarked quickly and found someone to take our suitcases to the station and at the customs we had to open our suitcases they weren't even too annoying. From there we went to the train station from where we started off at 1 o'clock at night on 21 June.[50]

This entry is interesting, because it deviates from the established pattern of recording waking up, the food, and walking on the deck and is more personal. For the first time and in passing, Tereza mentions the division of passengers according to social class—the rich and "us."

At first Tereza describes coming to the border in Postojna. They checked their passports and then continued their journey without problems. Then she writes that "In St. Peter in the Karst it was difficult to part with Mister Peter Samanič," which indicates that the entire group of returnees who met and got to know each other really well on the boat must have continued the journey by train together. In Rakek they checked their hand luggage again. "At seven thirty we arrived in the White Ljubljana and had breakfast at the Stari Tišler."

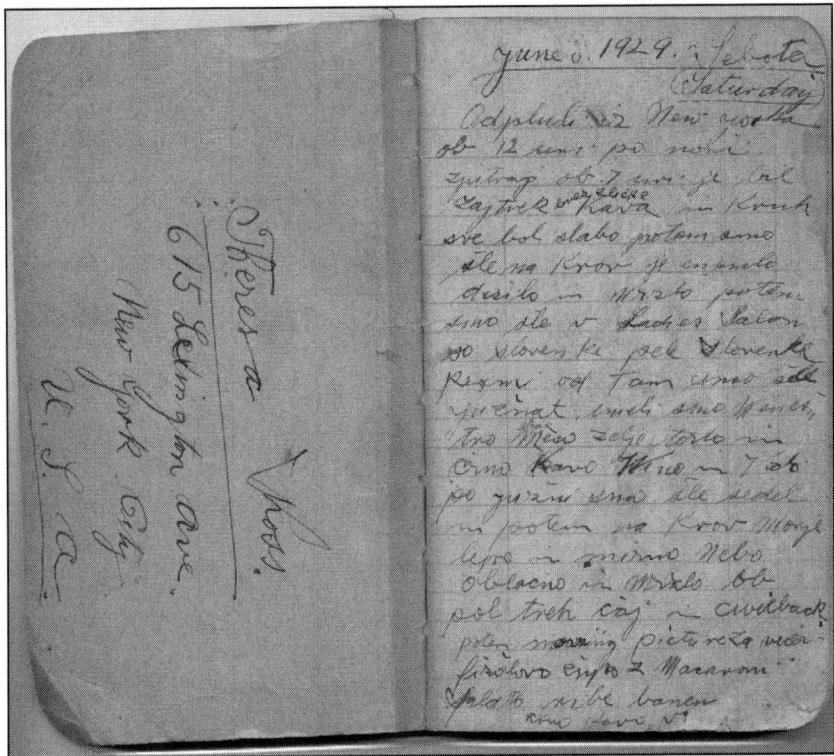

Figure 5.3. Tereza's ship journal. *Courtesy of Roman Kos*

Here the entry switches to the feminine form again. Can we assume that she was traveling with a group of female friends? At the station they had to open their luggage again. "Then we went for lunch and on this occasion bade goodbye to our Slovenian cotravelers then back where we went to our birthplace Domžale. The second day 22 June we were at home all day and went to sleep for a bit and in the evening we went to see Kristina's house."[51] Here, it becomes clear that two women arrived home: Tereza and possibly Frančiška. Roman Kos believes that Tereza visited her home country alone, but from her journal it is clear that she was traveling with another woman and that after visiting relatives and home locations they moved around together a lot.

The next day the women went to church and the graveyard and visited various people. Tereza may have also gone visiting on her

SLAMNIKARICE ABROAD AND AT HOME   187

own in the following days, because some of the entries are in the singular form:

> On Tuesday 25th I was in Študa at my brother's in the birth house and everything is still just as it was inside, only the stable is now covered and the manure heap moved but otherwise it's more or less misery[.] The children I didn't know at all in the evening my brother went with me it was rain and we were completely wet.[52]

This entry is interesting. After the arrival Tereza and her friend thus did not stay at home in the birth house; they stayed somewhere else. Her remark about the "more or less misery" tells us that the things in her birth house haven't really changed since her departure, that is, for fourteen years. Her birth house is still standing today. It is a one-story partly wooden house with a fireplace in the hall and is a testimony of a living culture at least three hundred years old. Poverty ensured the preservation of one of the last wooden houses in the Domžale area.

Besides visiting relatives, the next day the women enjoyed a trip to Kamnik. They went for a drink, visited the monastery church and Šutna, and then went back to Domžale. The following days were again dedicated mostly to visiting friends and relatives. The last dated entry before the return to America is from July 3, when they went to Ljubljana to run some errands. The next day Tereza was home and went for a walk and to church.

The final part of the journal, which is very brief, is titled "Back to America" and describes only six days of the voyage, from October 5 to October 10, 1929:

> On 5 October at 9 o'clock in the evening we drove from the white Ljubljana and went to... until 7 October at 3 in the afternoon. We slept there for two days the weather was windy and raining. On 9 October at seven we drove to the ship Ile de France on board we took off at half past two with a heavy heart but god pains us with a wish to return soon to the Beautiful Yugoslavia. Sea rough raining and windy.[53]

The beginning of the voyage back to New York is described in a far drier manner than the beginning of her journey to the homeland, and we can sense her desire to return home.

The last entry is as follows:

> 10 Oct. We slept well at night we arrived in Plymouth. In the morning the ship was rocking I went to the deck but it was too windy I had breakfast and lunch but brought it all back up other than that I'm quite well others are sick too and look like lemons or are in their cabins.[54]

Her journal ends here. It is clear that because of the bad weather, the voyage back to America was far more difficult than coming home. Whether this was the only reason to stop writing we cannot tell.

There is a gap of about three months between her last entry describing activities and the return to America. There are several dry four-leaf clovers between the pages of the journal. Which meadow are they a memory of? The journal of Tereza Kos gives us insight into activities and partly into the thinking of a woman who came (together with her sister?) from New York to visit her relatives and friends. We learn about social life on the ship, the ship menus, and also the fact that her family home is poor and that nothing had changed since she left. The journal is a precious document of a travel—an integral part of any individual migration route.

As we have already mentioned, Tereza Kos returned to her homeland permanently a few years later. Roman Kos doesn't know the exact date of her return. She bought a house in Študa and got married, and together with her husband, who was a retired financial inspector, lived a rather comfortable life off her savings, according to the perceptions of the surrounding people. In relation to the circumstances from which she came, she progressed on the social scale. She was distinguished from her fellow villagers by her prestigious objects and her clothes, which were designed following American fashion, and particularly in that she no longer had to work after returning home. She joined in the family life again. She was the godmother of all four boys of her nephew (Roman Kos's father) who inherited the homestead. Roman Kos's mother took care of Tereza when she got old.

Roman remembers that Tereza had a gramophone. "I know they would set up the gramophone and then had parties. Because they were the only ones who had it. And they had Slovenian music from America. Šubelj, Columbia records."[55] He also remembers that his parents and neighbors went to play cards with Tereza and her husband. Her emigrant life was a given fact in the family, but Roman never asked about any details because at the time he wasn't interested.

> This was the mistake that I didn't ask her more when she was still alive.... I was the only one then.... When she was our godmother I was about thirteen years old... [and] at that age, you're not interested.... We were interested [in] what she'd give us.... And I knew she had that radio... and they played cards.... And I have almost all her glasses, from the pincer-specs to the later ones.... [I] have her gramophone, photos, records... and there were a number of other things... and they were, so to speak, mine for the taking.[56]

From memories and photos, today Roman is trying to form a picture of Tereza's life. "It's interesting, she bought a camera, but the photos are only from free time, and none from what she did and where she worked. Just in this garden with this friend, and another friend, and the view through the window... And then, when she came home, this was... of course, who had a camera then."[57] This reasoning can be applied to other photographic records from America in that time that we have available, because they usually show family members on various occasions, while the photographs showing work—production or other work—are rare.

Tereza Kos cashed in on her migrant experience in a way that enabled her to have a safe and comfortable old age. She did not lose contact with her family at home when she was abroad, and after her return she reestablished active social contact with the members of her primary and extended family; they regularly visited and helped each other.

Mother and Father Went to Bucharest Together for Years

Antonija Plevel, the mother of our narrator Frančiška Koračevič,[58] lost her own mother as a child and grew up with her Aunt Reza in Zgornje Domžale, and her father remarried. As a girl, Antonija worked in the Kurtzhaler straw hat factory in Domžale as a sewer and went to Vienna, Prague, and Budapest as a seasonal worker. After she was married in 1925, she and her husband Franc Šubelj, a milliner who was a widower with six children, left every year for nine months to go to Bucharest, where Antonija worked as a straw hat sewer, and they came home over the summer. They had two daughters together.

Antonija had an aunt with whom she lived when she was in Vienna, which was her first experience of living abroad:

> The aunt lived in Vienna for a long time. She had one daughter born in Vienna, who died [at] three months old. Then she had another one that my mother brought here, to this aunt who later took care of us, when she was six weeks old.... And the neighbor said, Reza, you're not going to bring this one up. And she said, maybe I will. And she was such a great girl. When she was ten or twelve her parents came from Vienna, and they built a house in Ljubljana. The husband was from Dolenjska somewhere.[59]

The eldest three children from Franc Šubelj's first marriage left home soon after their father remarried. Two daughters who worked as straw hat makers at the Kurtzhaler factory in Domžale left as minors to go to New York (one was age sixteen and the other was age seventeen) to work as straw hat makers, married men from Domžale there who also made straw hats, and stayed in America. They lived in Brooklyn. "I have many photos of them," Frančiška said, "probably more than her daughters. Mama corresponded with them almost religiously."[60] They never came to visit. The daughter of one of them came in 1985.

While the parents were away doing seasonal work, Aunt Reza took care of the other children as well as the daughter of a relative who sewed straw hats in Vienna with her husband. The children from the two marriages were very close to each other. Aunt Reza was also a

Figure 5.4. Antonija and Franc Šubelj. *Courtesy of Frančiška Koračevič*

straw hat sewer and worked in the Oberwalder factory in Domžale. Antonija Plevel left her daughters in her aunt's care when they were very small (less than a year old) and went with their father to do seasonal work in Romania. "Mama never said that she felt bad about this," Frančiška said. "She left us without care. The aunt was terribly meticulous about upbringing, and she never married. She had us as if we were hers. She really looked after us. And she didn't have just us. She also had three children from my father's first marriage."[61]

The aunt never received any pension and kept her savings at home, as was the custom at the time.

> Mama used to say that when the aunt was elderly she no longer went to work but had a lot of money saved. She used to say, I have to have money for old age; who will give anything to me? The house from the uncle who lived in America was for sale. But

the aunt wouldn't buy. She said, how will I stay without money? How will I live? And then all the money came to nothing. She had enough to buy a house. But then the money became so worthless that for all that money she could buy a stove with it. Mother said she thought she'd die of sadness. Then she was here with us. She and my mother lived here.[62]

The intertwining of the roles within the extended family and the intergenerational codependence were common at that time because of poorly functioning or nonexistent social institutions. In Domžale the Braid-Weavers' Cooperative was established, which meant the beginning of social security, and a nursery and an old age home were established for the most vulnerable; all of this was the doing of the priest France Bernik. Still, the distress of the working class was great, and the older generation's fear of a time when they would no longer be able to work was real. Older people depended on the care provided by their children.

Frančiška believes that in other towns, the factory owners provided flats or rooms for the straw hat makers. Her parents took a train to Bucharest and had a flat there. There were a number of people who traveled together from Domžale and the surrounding villages, and there were a good number of married couples among them. Her father worked in the factory as a master; he managed the workshop. Her mother sewed straw hats. "Father never liked talking about these things [work in Romania]. What we learned, we learned from mother." Her mother also knew how to braid but never did it at home. "Those who worked on several machines and finer things, were paid better." When her parents were on seasonal work, they corresponded with their family back home. "When we were at home, we always sent them reports." The parents had good memories of Bucharest. They went on excursions on Sunday, which was not a habit at home. "Mama was curious; she was interested in everything." She was also deeply religious, but Frančiška does not know where they went to church. "Oh, how happy we were when they came home. They brought toys, dresses.... You couldn't buy so many things here then. We were so glad."⁶³ Frančiška also states that

> They never put the money in the bank; they always brought it home with them. Once someone reported that they had money. And Mother said that they were looking for it for more than three hours, undid their entire luggage—you have money, you have money. And Father said, then find it, if I have it. Mother wore braids at the time. She had to undo them too. They made her take all her clothes off. They said you have money. And they had a lot. But they didn't find it. Mother said, "I was walking up and down the train and the controller who was looking for it said, 'Well, madam is all nervous, madam is all red-faced.... We're close now.'" And it was Father who had it, in his suitcase, put away I don't know where, sewn in somewhere. And then they let them go. That was when, Mother said, she felt awful. That she thought that they both worked in vain for a year, unable to bring anything home.⁶⁴

They brought not only their money but also the money from other Domžale people who worked in Bucharest and didn't come home regularly. Often, the money went to the Domžale church. "As soon as Bernik heard that our two were home, he was at the door."⁶⁵

With the money they brought home, they settled family debts. "Ložar Romana had a tiny little shop next to Jarc's shop, and we did all our shopping there and took everything on credit. And when they came home they went to pay. So, in effect, the merchant financed us through the entire year."⁶⁶

Franc Šubelj and Antonija Plevel returned to Domžale in 1939. Franc worked in Romania for thirty-two years, but because there was no convention regulating pension insurance, he received no pension after he returned and was too old to find other employment. He set up a workshop at home and repaired hats. Mother, who was eleven years his junior, continued to work for five years after World War II in Univerzale as a straw hat sewer. She died in 1954, and her husband died eight years later.

Franc was the second of ten children born to Franc Šubelj and Mariana Pirnat from Rodica. One child died as a baby, and of the rest four were straw hat makers (two sisters, Frančiška and Johana, and two brothers, Jožef and Avgust), two were milliners (Franc and Johan), and one was an internationally acclaimed opera singer (Anton). Jožef and August worked as straw hat makers in Vienna and Bucharest, and then both of them and the sisters Frančiška and Johana went to New York. Later Anton joined them, first on a visit and then permanently, and he stayed and worked in America as an opera singer and teacher until his death.

The homestead went to Johan. The sources aren't quite clear here as to whether the house was rented or under a mortgage, but his wife Amalija Janežič went to America twice to earn enough to buy the homestead. "Grandma Amalija went to America to sew straw hats, and with her earnings she bought this house."[67] This information is interesting because it confirms that straw hat makers went to America for shorter periods as well and then returned, not only after years of active employment but also after they judged that they had earned enough to buy what was their goal at home.

A letter from Anton Šubelj to his sister Marija Kompare states that "I'm now with Francka and Peter. It's very pleasant. They both love me very much, they have a lovely flat and I have a lovely room, and over the day, the entire flat. Especially now in the summer, when Francka is at home, we're having a really nice time."[68] From the fragment of the letter we find out that the sister and her husband have their own flat (possibly rented). Because Frančiška Šubelj was a straw hat maker, we can presume that she was working in the same industry in America. We understand from the letter that in America the work was seasonal as well. We also gather that people abroad helped the newly arrived relatives by taking them in and helping them establish social and professional contacts. They provided emotional and material support for each other. "Sisters and brothers in New York were of course indescribably happy to see me. After 21 years, we gathered again."[69]

From the description of the professions and migrations in which Frančiška Koračevič's extended family circulated, we can understand the importance of straw hat making, which significantly influenced at least three generations in Domžale and the surrounding area. The relatives maintained contacts by letters, packages, sending money, and visits. (Johana came to visit in 1936; Anton came to visit three more times after 1928, when he emigrated permanently; and the granddaughter of Franc Šubelj came to visit once.) In this story, family ties appear to be most important and made it easier to leave home; they went abroad but to their own people. Besides that, another important factor was that they knew the work and the technology. They did not go into the completely unknown.

From today's perspective it may seem unusual that mothers left their children with relatives for extended periods of time and looked for work elsewhere. The daughter of a straw hat–making mother tells us about this but not with bitterness; she doesn't judge her mother and understands that the children were cared for. The unmarried aunt who acted as their guardian replaced the parents excellently and brought up first their mother and then their father's three children, a cousin, the narrator, and her sister. Within this system of tight family ties that signifies some sort of social corrective, there was the extended family or even wider family. Because women in their childbearing years are at the same time also at the peak of their work abilities, they used to and continue to choose between work obligations and family. What the choice meant to them personally we can only learn indirectly, from the narratives of their children. Was the perception of the children at the time a consequence of the good care provided by the relatives, or does it really reflect the mothers' perceptions?

One Woman's Straw Hat Was Worth a Cow

Marija (in some documents Marijana) Svetlin, born in Študa, was first married to Grčar and then was married to Kokalj. She was not a straw hat maker but instead was an entrepreneur. Her life story also comes to us in fragments, told by Ludvik Kokalj[70] and Valentin Hribar,[71] the grandsons of her second husband. Ludvik knew her better because his mother lived with Marijana after her second wedding, and he spent a lot of time with her and inherited her house and workshop, while Valentin only knew her through family gatherings.

When Marija was a very young girl, her parents, who had a smithy, sent her to Vienna to school. According to Ludvik, she was training to become a model. She went to school for three years and lived and worked as a model in Vienna for several years after school. "She was always different from everybody else. She always wanted to be a little different." She learned five or six languages and also lived and worked in the Czech Republic and in Budapest. When she earned enough money, she went to America. "She said she brought so much money from Europe that she could start her own business immediately."[72]

Marija came to New York to her relatives, and there she met her future husband Grčar. She gave birth to their two sons, Franc and Karol. She opened a store and a repair shop for straw hats under her own name. Because quality straw hats were expensive, people took them to be repaired. Her two brothers Johan and Francelj joined her; they later started families there and remained. With this part of the family, Ludvik Kokalj still corresponds.

Just before World War I, Marija and her husband came home for a visit. The war prevented them from returning to America, so they built a house in Ihan, and Marija opened a straw hat–making workshop. The sons, who were still in school, stayed with Grčar's aunt in New York and never followed them. The husband and one son had hemophilia. The husband died a year or two after they returned home, and the son died a couple of years after that. Marija maintained regular correspondence with the other son, who lived in Brooklyn, and Ludvik Kokalj later kept up these contacts. After the war, the son sent money in letters and packages and came to visit once.

After the death of her first husband, Marija Grčar married his cousin, a rich landowner named Janez Kokalj Goropeški who had previously given her and her first husband the land on which to build a house and the hat-making workshop. His farm was big. They had nearly five hundred acres of arable land, meadows, and woods. Janez was a widower with six children. Two eldest daughters were already married.

Janez took one son and one daughter—Ludvik Kokalj's mother—with him to Marijana's and left the farm to the other son. Valentin's mother remained on the farm with her older brother and looked after her brother's children, who were barely a few years her junior.

The workshop in Ihan also carried Marija's name—the seal said "Marija Kokalj, tovarna slamnikov, Ihan št. 60, p. Domžale" [Marija Kokalj, straw hat factory, Ihan no. 60, Domžale]—and she managed the business and made all the decisions. She had between twelve and sixteen employees, mostly women and two men, who pressed hats in special presses.[73] They made new straw hats and other types hats and repaired and renovated old ones. Marija imported the braids for women's straw hats, machines, and other materials from America. This was unusual for Domžale, which was mostly tied to Italy and central European cities. She made men's straw hats from local braids, particularly later when the demand for straw hats went down and it was difficult to import raw materials. Marija brought different patterns for braids from Bavaria; she also bleached and dyed the straw herself. She sold her straw hats to twelve women's milliners from Ljubljana as well as to milliners in Belgrade, Vienna, and Budapest. The employees transported the hats themselves, with horses and a carriage specially adjusted to transporting light loads, such as straw hats packed in special cardboard boxes. Ludvik Kokalj remembers that a particularly fine and elegant women's straw hat was worth the price of a cow. Marija's workshop operated until 1932, when it closed because of the crisis in the straw hat market; her husband then made better money selling cattle than she did selling straw hats. Some of her workers later found jobs at Oberwalder in Domžale.

Ludvik remembers Marija as a strict and extraordinary woman; she also dressed differently from the other local women. Marija put on smart clothes on Sunday night, and she and her husband went to Domžale to Keber's tavern with their cart. "She really did take care of her appearance when she left home."[74] According to Ludvik, she also participated in public life, where she was a competent counterpart to other Domžale factory owners and entrepreneurs.

The local people accepted Marija because she gave them work, but she was conspicuous among village life. The legend goes that because of the connections she made when she was a model in Germany, she managed to save her husband's granddaughter from prison in Begunje during World War II, where she was imprisoned for working with the partisan resistance.

Valentin Hribar also remembers her as a special lady. "She seemed special, although I was not particularly aware of that at the time, but I noticed that she was different from others. She thought differently.... She dressed differently. Not like a peasant. She had her own clothes." His memories of her are memories as a child. He doesn't remember them ever speaking about her life story at home, and he never knew her as an entrepreneur. "But it is a fact that after the war, in the 1950s, we made braids. But that had nothing to do with Marijana. Our grandmother taught us, my father's mother, so the three of us were braiding, mother, my father, and I. For several years.... So we earned something."[75]

Valentin knew Marijana as an old lady who came to the house on his mother's birthday and name day and on such occasions talked to his parents. Several times, his mother sent him to her house because they lived in the neighboring village, and he remembers that even her home was different from the local houses:

> In short, everything was a bit different. Once or twice it happened, although she was pretty holed up in that house, that she invited me there. She showed me different things. I remember very well that she once gave me a little horse. A cardboard one. I really liked it. But it wasn't a part of a Christmas crèche. She had a special collection, maybe from her children in America. She

never spoke of these children. This is the first I read about them. Maybe my mother, who was a living chronicle, knew more. But I didn't; I was very pleased about the gift, though. Of course I took care of it, but then in the end I did put it in my pocket. And when I got home, it was broken. I was so disappointed.[76]

Although Marija Kokalj's story is put together from the childhood memories of two grandsons of her second husband, it shows a woman who had two straw hat–making workshops—one in New York and one in Ihan—which was unusual for women at the time. In her article, Katarina Kobe-Arzenšek does name two more entrepreneurs who had their own straw hat–making companies registered in the 1920s—Milka Kos in Mengeš and Angela Pekolj—but we know nothing more about them.[77] In any case, women who had straw hat–making workshops registered in their names were rare.

Going abroad gave Marija Kokalj the breadth that allowed her to enter business life confidently. She had her own business connections that were not tied to the Tyrolean business networks, and she took care of the entire business process chain: organizing production, purchasing machinery and material, manufacturing and controlling half-products by introducing novelties from abroad, and handling distribution and sales. Marija was said to have made excellent straw hats from the finest and most exacting imported materials; she found the market for such hats herself and didn't leave the hats to the Tyrolean factory owners as partially finished products. In the statistical overviews of the hat-making entrepreneurs, her name is not found.[78] She is briefly mentioned only by Stane Stražar in his chronicle of Ihan.[79] Was the production in her workshop too small, or is there another reason?

A Straw Hat Maker until Marriage

Angela Kavka went to Munich to sew straw hats in 1927 at age sixteen. She lived with her aunt, who had married a German in Munich and stayed there. Later Angela worked in Lille, France, and in cities around Yugoslavia—Zemun, Sisak, and Split. Her sister, Bernarda Kavka, remembers that in wintertime Angela would receive mail and then leave until April or May, that is, for the entire hat-making season. Three of their aunts used to go to Bucharest to sew straw hats as unmarried girls; one of them married an Italian there and stayed. The other two stopped seasonal work when they were married. "Because those with husbands, they didn't go. They had to be single, so they could work all day."[80] All the female relatives went abroad for money. They earned significantly better than at home. Angela did seasonal work for almost fifteen years, but after her wedding this part of her life was over, just as the era of seasonal straw hat making was ending. She then worked in a metalware shop in Šiška in Ljubljana and then after her wedding worked with her husband in a garden nursery.

The Kavka family had a small farm in Šentpavel and nine children. The father was a cobbler and repaired shoes during winters to provide extra income for the family. At home the family made braids but didn't sew the hats, and no other girl worked in straw hat making. When Angela Kavka was at home, she didn't work in the hat making industry. In the part of the year when she wasn't doing season work, she worked in the metalware shop. What she earned abroad she brought home in cash. She and her mother would go to the bank in Ljubljana the day after she returned and put the money into the bank. "All I know is that they so mysteriously counted that money, she and mother, and that she put it in the bank after that. And they went to a bank in Ljubljana, where she then kept what she earned.... It was important that she earned something, because she was preparing her own dowry." She didn't give her money to the family; she kept it to start her independent life. "When she got married that house needed to be fixed a little bit. She bought a new stove, a built one. They made it, and then she bought furnishings; she loved buying mugs.... She loved pretty mugs."[81] Angela did contribute for her younger sister's clothes and was also her sister's confirmation sponsor and bought her clothes until she got married.

Bernarda Kavka was significantly younger than her sister and followed her comings and goings through the perspective of a child. Bernarda remembers Angela telling her how thin the thread was that they used abroad, how fine and thin the straw was, and how much they had to work. Bernarda remembers almost nothing about her sister's life abroad because she wasn't interested at the time. "The children where the happiest if she brought us chocolate and sweets, because this was something we didn't have. What joy when they told us 'Angela is coming home,' when she wrote a letter."[82]

Angela traveled with one suitcase. She let the family know by mail when to pick her from the Domžale train station so they could help her roll the suitcase home on a trolley. She corresponded with her family regularly, but Bernarda doesn't remember that she would ever send photos or other objects. Angela carefully kept her money and only spent it on the most essential things. Bernarda remembers that for years after Angela stopped doing seasonal work, they kept receiving New Year's greetings from a factory owner from Split.

The girls who went to work abroad were viewed with admiration and approval because they knew how to keep themselves out of the difficult circumstances at home. They brought home new things such as fashion, foreign languages, and new tastes. Bernarda remembers that Angela brought tomatoes home and assured the family that they were good; her family was not familiar with them. And Angela learned how to cook jam at her aunt's home in Germany, which they did not do at home. "They were esteemed! My sister liked to dress well and put a straw hat on her head. Because, for example, in our village no other woman wore a hat, but she did. Shoes with heels and a hat. They used to say she looked 'schimmy.'" She used to wear a large ladies' straw hat, the kind the rural women didn't wear. It meant a lot to her that she saw the world and learned languages—she spoke good German and Serbian. She saw her knowledge as an advantage and as something other people envied her for. "She had a gift for languages, and this helped her when she traveled. But French, she said, she found very hard to learn; French she couldn't do and so she didn't really like going to France. I don't know, she was only twice or so in the city of Lille." By working abroad, slamnikarice created an important social status for themselves at home because they were economically independent and could also afford to buy things that others couldn't buy. "We kind of considered them to be something more. We looked up to them, like this.... I know my sister had a bike.... How important this was, that she bought herself a bicycle! They said 'Angela has a bike' and came to look at her."[83]

The girls abroad also had more freedom in terms of social contacts and less social control than at home. They could go to town in the evening and carouse a little bit. The narrator saw them as merry, joyful, and at times mischievous. After returning home, they were forced to go back to the old customs. "This was the fruit of the upbringing. Once you get married, you get married; you accept it and you have to sacrifice yourself. That was their point of view."[84] This is another reason why they went so happily: they were economically independent, they had their own friends and coworkers, and got a different view of the world. And through this experience, they were valued at home. At the same time, the narrator didn't forget to stress the important attribute that we see in all the stories of slamnikarice: their diligence.

The family had relatives in America—Bernarda's mother's sister and two brothers—and corresponded with them. "Mother had problems getting herself to write letters; only for holidays." Bernarda does not know what the relatives did; they lived in Cleveland and Los Angeles. "Oh, after the war they sent us packages. But I have to say that they rescued us. They did really send us clothes and food. My sister, who was a dressmaker, made clothes for all of us. We used everything. So we never lacked anything."[85]

The story of Angela Kavka is an almost stereotypical story of a seasonal straw hat maker—she was diligent, hardworking, and liked by her employers. With work she earned enough to give herself a head start into adult life, and with her wedding she stopped her girlhood wandering around the world. At the same time, through her sister's memories we see a young, independent woman who at least in one part of her life could step over the boundaries of control in the small community from which she came, and even in a material sense she offered herself things that were considered luxuries in that environment. The knowledge and skills that she acquired abroad were important mostly to her, and it seems that as a married woman she never managed to use them to the same degree.

Public Memory

Where in the collective social memory of Domžale is the place for the migrant female straw hat makers? Right now it is in the chronicles of the priest Franc Bernik and, of course, in the family heritages that include stories of grandmothers, mothers, and sisters in big European cities and in America and the many memories of postwar packages that the relatives from America sent. The historic framework and the hat-making theme were also used in Breda Smolnikar's novel *When the Birches Up There Are Greening*,[86] but there hasn't been a serious overview of hat makers' migration despite the fact that the female straw hat makers, the slamnikarice, in addition to the aleksandrinke, are recognized as a particularity of Slovenian migration of the first half of the twentieth century and despite the fact that they had a significant influence on the local economy.

We can also ask ourselves why we should even bring up finished stories of some past lives, stories to which their protagonists can no longer add. We do not know how much the slamnikarice questioned the urgency of their departures. Judging from the stories of their descendants, the slamnikarice viewed departure as a challenge and as an opportunity to change their own lives and the lives of their family members for the better. They had strong support in their relatives and local communities, but at the same time departure was something inevitable that life brought to them. We do not have enough testimonies today to reveal the extent that family and professional support eased the everyday distress of these women and also the men and children. The lives of those who returned to Slovenia went back to the standard customs. The departure of the girls was accepted and praised in Domžale. In that time, the step from the farming class to the working class meant important social and personal progress, and slamnikarice did just that with their mass entry to the factories.

I believe that the testimonies we have collected are valuable and important because they shed light on the straw hat-making history of Domžale in terms of production issues and economic and social changes as well as the personal lives of slamnikarice and their families.

Notes

1. Marina Lenček, interview by the author, October 11, 2007, Domžale, Slovenia, camera recording in possession of the author.

2. In 2007, twelve interviews connected to straw hat making in the Domžale area were recorded by camera. For the present chapter, three interviews were added. All audio and video material is owned by the author.

3. Straw hat making—making braids and sewing hats and also baskets—was a cottage industry that employed around twelve thousand people from the region of Brdo and Kamnik at the end of the nineteenth century. The annual output was about eight hundred thousand hats and in the best years about a million hats. Families in all the villages around Domžale made braids that were then sewn onto hats in factories in Domžale and Menges. Many hats were sewn at home and were finished and dressed for the market in the factories.

4. Today we talk about slamnikarice and use the word to mean all the female workers in the straw hat-making industry, regardless of the work they did in the factory. In the period of straw hat making there was an expression for every specialty: sewer (*šivalka*), dresser (*aperterka*), etc.

5. About the case of aleksandrinke, Daša Koprivec, in "Aleksandrinke—Življenje v Egiptu in doma" [Aleksandrinke—Life in Egypt and at Home], *Etnolog* 16 (2006): 101, points out that women who stayed in Egypt for a long time conformed to the accepted way of life, and in one way or another all the adult members of the family accepted it. We could say something similar about slamnikarice. Often, young

girls were sent abroad by their mothers and earned their trousseau themselves, while mothers kept going abroad for several years and sent the money for the upbringing of their children to their relatives.

6. See also chapter 3 in this book.

7. At the turn of the nineteenth century, marked in Slovenia by the first large wave of emigration, male emigrants were the majority. In Slovenia, we know two migrant waves in which the majority of migrants were women: one to Egypt and the other involving slamnikarice migrating to America. Marjan Drnovšek, "Emigration of Slovene Women: A Short Historical View," *Dve domovini/Two Homelands* 17 (2003): 31.

8. Bernarda Kavka, interview by the author, January 5, 2011, Domžale, Slovenia, tape recording in possession of the author.

9. Franc Bernik, *Zgodovina fare Domžale* [The History of Domžale Parish] (Domžale: Printed by the author, 1923), 22; Vlado Valenčič, "O slamnikarski domači obrti" [The Craft of Straw Hat Making], *Kamniški zbornik* 5 (1959): 165–93.

10. Valenčič, "O slamnikarski domači obrti," 171–72.

11. Marjanca Klobčar, *Občina Domžale: Etnološka topografija slovenskega etničnega ozemlja—20. stoletja* [The Municipality of Domžale: An Ethnographical Topography of the Slovenian Ethnic Territory—20th Century] (Ljubljana: Znanstveni inštitut Filozofske fakultete, 1989); Valenčič, "O slamnikarski domači obrti," 168; Jože Žontar, "Domžalsko območje v prvi polovici 19. stoletja" [The Domžale Region in the First Half of the 19th Century], *Zbornik občine Domžale* (1979): 95–96.

12. See also chapter 4 in this book.

13. Katarina Kobe-Arzenšek, "Iz preteklosti slamnikarstva v domžalski okolici s poudarkom na domačih proizvajalcih" [From the Past of Straw Hat Making in the Domžale Area with an Emphasis on Local Manufacturers], *Zbornik občine Domžale* (1979): 106.

14. Bernik, *Zgodovina fare Domžale*, 220.

15. Ibid., 220.

16. Ibid., 22.

17. Miroslav Stiplovšek, *Razglasitev Domžal za trg leta 1925: Ob razstavi v počastitev 80 letnice* [The 1925 Proclamation of Domžale as a Market Town: An Exhibition in Honor of the 80th Anniversary] (Domžale: Kulturni dom Franca Bernika, 2005).

18. This refers to braiding made from cereal straw.

19. Matija Oberwalder strove to improve the quality of the straw for braiding and was the initiator of braiding courses. See Matija Oberwalder, "Navod za pridelovanje slame za pletenje" [A Guide to Cultivating Straw for Braiding], *Kmetijske in rokodelske novice* 54, no. 40 (1896): 396, and "Pridelovanje pletilne slame" [The Cultivation of Braiding Straw], *Kmetijske in rokodelske novice* 55, no. 26 (1897): 253.

20. Janko Moder, "Kitarji in slamnikarji v Dolu pri Ljubljani" [Braiders and Straw Hat Makers in Dol pri Ljubljani], *Slovenski etnograf* (1962): 83.

21. Valenčič, "O slamnikarski domači obrti," 189.

22. I believe that we can trust Bernik's numbers, because he knew his parishioners extremely well and at the same time kept records of all the events in the parish. The precise statistics of the period for Domžale is also exceptional because the official statistics for Carniola are incomplete and unreliable. See also Marjan Drnovšek, "Nekatere evidence o izseljevanju v Ameriko pred prvo svetovno vojno" [Some Records about Emigration to America before World War I], *Kronika-časopis za slovensko krajevno zgodovino* 36 (1988): 205–17.

23. Bernik, *Zgodovina fare Domžale*, 232.

24. John Arnez, *Slovenci v New Yorku* [Slovenians in New York] (New York: Glas naroda, 1966), 95.

25. Bernik, *Zgodovina fare Domžale*, 245.

26. Ignac Mušič, "Slamnikarska obrt in slovenski slamnikarji" [The Craft of Straw Hat Making and Slovenian Straw Hat Makers], *Slovensko-amerikanski koledar* (1928): 19–43.

27. Anna Praček Krasna, "Domžale v New Yorku" [Domžale in New York], *Slovenski koledar 1981* 28 (1981): 253–57.

28. Despite inaccurate data, we can claim that the number of female migrants from Domžale and the surrounding areas deviated greatly from the Slovenian average in the period when people migrated for jobs in the straw hat-making industry. The Slovenian average in the period 1876–1910 is estimated at 35 percent. Drnovšek, "Emigration of Slovene Women," 29–46.

29. Bernik, *Zgodovina fare Domžale*, 245–53.

30. Franc Bernik, *Zgodovina fare Domžale: Druga knjiga* [The History of Domžale Parish: Volume Two] (Domžale: Printed by the author, 1939), 266.

31. Praček Krasna, "Domžale v New Yorku," 255.

32. Arnez, *Slovenci v New Yorku*, 117; Praček Krasna, "Domžale v New Yorku," 254.

33. Bernik, *Zgodovina fare Domžale*, 252.

34. Drnovšek, "Emigration of Slovene Women," 32.

35. Bernik, *Zgodovina fare Domžale*, 8.

36. Ibid., 223.

37. Marjan Drnovšek, "Izseljenec: Življenjske zgodbe Slovencev po svetu" [Emigrant: Life Stories of Slovenians around the World], in *Izseljenec: Življenjske zgodbe Slovencev po svetu* [Emigrant: Life Stories of Slovenians around the World], edited by Monika Kokalj Kočevar et al. (Ljubljana: Muzej novejše zgodovine Slovenije, 2001), 16. See also chapter 3 in this book.

38. Drnovšek, "Nekatere evidence o izseljevanju v Ameriko pred prvo svetovno vojno," 205–17.

39. Arnez, *Slovenci v New Yorku*, 9.

40. Roman Kos, interview by the author, January 12, 2011, Domžale, Slovenia, tape recording in possession of the author.

41. Ibid.

42. Tereza Kos's journal is in the possession of Roman Kos.

43. The transcripts are exact, with all the language inconsistencies. It is interesting to note the use of both languages, Slovenian and English. For the purpose of translation, the parts that were originally in English are in italics.

44. Tereza Koz's journal, in the possession of Roman Kos.

45. Ibid.

46. Ibid.

47. Ibid.

48. Ibid.

49. Ibid.

50. Ibid.

51. Ibid.

52. Ibid.

53. Ibid.

54. Ibid.

55. Roman Kos, interview by the author, January 12, 2011, Domžale, Slovenia, tape recording in possession of the author.

56. Ibid.

57. Ibid.

58. Frančiška Koračevič, interview by the author, November 20, 2007, Domžale, Slovenia, camera recording in possession of the author.

59. Ibid.

60. Ibid.

61. Ibid.

62. Ibid.

63. Ibid.

64. Ibid. The event took place at a border crossing.

65. Ibid.

66. Ibid.

67. Vilma Vrtačnik Merčun, Nika Grošelj, and Lara Tekavc, *Operni pevec Anton Šubelj z Rodice: Njegovo prvo potovanje v Ameriko (1928–1929)* [The Opera Singer Anton Šubelj from Rodica pri Domžalah: His First Journey to America (1928–1929)] (Domžale: Kulturno društvo Gorblje, 2012), 105.

68. Anton Šubelj to his sister Marija Kompare, August 18, 1928, the archives of the Museum of Mengeš, quoted in Vrtačnik Merčun, Grošelj, and Tekavc, *Operni pevec Anton Šubelj z Rodice,* 46.

69. Ibid., 46.

70. Ludvik Kokalj, interview by the author, December 11, 2007, Ihan, Slovenia, camera recording in possession of the author.

71. Valentin Hribar, interview by the author, January 4, 2011, Tomišelj, Slovenia, tape recording in possession of the author.

72. Ludvik Kokalj, interview by the author, 11 December 2007, Ihan, Slovenia, camera recording in possession of the author.

73. Stane Stražar, *Svet pod Taborom: Kronika Ihana* [The World under Tabor: Chronicles of Ihan] (Ihan: Odbor za praznovanje 750-letnice Ihana, 1974), 183–90.

74. Ludvik Kokalj, interview by the author, 11 December 2007, Ihan, Slovenia, camera recording in possession of the author.

75. Valentin Hribar, interview by the author, January 4, 2011, Tomišelj, Slovenia, tape recording in possession of the author.

76. Ibid.

77. Kobe-Arzenšek, "Iz preteklosti slamnikarstva v domžalski okolici s poudarkom na domačih proizvajalcih," 111.

78. Bernik, *Zgodovina fare Domžale*; Kobe-Arzenšek, "Iz preteklosti slamnikarstva v domžalski okolici s poudarkom na domačih proizvajalcih"; Valenčič, "O slamnikarski domači obrti."
79. Stražar, *Svet pod Taborom*, 183–90.
80. Bernarda Kavka, interview by the author, January 5, 2011, Domžale, Slovenia, tape recording in possession of the author.
81. Ibid.
82. Ibid.
83. Ibid.
84. Ibid.
85. Ibid.
86. Breda Smolnikar, *When the Birches Up There Are Greening* (Depala vas: Printed by the author, 2005).

References

Arnez, John. *Slovenci v New Yorku* [Slovenians in New York]. New York: Studia Slovenica, 1966.
Bernik, Franc. *Zgodovina fare Domžale*. Domžale: Printed by the author, 1923.
———. *Zgodovina fare Domžale: Druga knjiga* [The History of Domžale Parish: Volume Two]. Domžale: Printed by the author, 1939.
Drnovšek, Marjan. "Emigration of Slovene Women: A Short Historical View." *Dve domovini/Two Homelands* 17 (2003): 29–46.
———. "Izseljenec: Življenjske zgodbe Slovencev po svetu" [Emigrant: Life Stories of Slovenians around the World]. In *Izseljenec: Življenjske zgodbe Slovencev po svetu* [Emigrant: Life Stories of Slovenians around the World], edited by Monika Kokalj Kočevar et al., 9–17. Ljubljana: Muzej novejše zgodovine Slovenije, 2001.
———. "Nekatere evidence o izseljevanju v Ameriko pred prvo svetovno vojno" [Some Records about Emigration to America before World War I]. *Kronika-časopis za slovensko krajevno zgodovino* 36 (1988): 205–17.

Klobčar, Marjanca. *Občina Domžale: Etnološka topografija slovenskega etničnega ozemlja—20. stoletje* [The Municipality of Domžale: An Ethnographical Topography of the Slovenian Ethnic Territory—20th Century]. Ljubljana: Znanstveni inštitut Filozofske fakultete, 1989.

Kobe-Arzenšek, Katarina. "Iz preteklosti slamnikarstva v domžalski okolici s poudarkom na domačih proizvajalcih" [From the Past of Straw Hat Making in the Domžale Area with an Emphasis on Local Manufacturers]. *Zbornik občine Domžale* (1979): 103–30.

Koprivec, Daša. "Aleksandrinke—Življenje v Egiptu in doma" [Aleksandrinke—Life in Egypt and at Home]. *Etnolog* 16 (2006): 97–115.

Moder, Janko. "Kitarji in slamnikarji v Dolu pri Ljubljani" [Braiders and Straw Hat Makers in Dol pri Ljubljani]. *Slovenski etnograf* (1962): 73–84.

Mušič, Ignac. "Slamnikarska obrt in slovenski slamnikarji" [The Craft of Straw Hat Making and Slovenian Straw Hat Makers]. *Slovensko-amerikanski koledar* (1928): 19–43.

Oberwalder, Matija. "Navod za pridelovanje slame za pletenje" [A Guide to Cultivating Straw for Braiding]. *Kmetijske in rokodelske novice* 54, no. 40 (1896): 396.

———. "Pridelovanje pletilne slame" [The Cultivation of Braiding Straw]. *Kmetijske in rokodelske novice* 55, no. 26 (1897): 253.

Praček Krasna, Anna. "Domžale v New Yorku" [Domžale in New York]. *Slovenski koledar 1981* 28 (1981): 253–57.

Smolnikar, Breda. *When the Birches Up There Are Greening.* Depala vas: Printed by the author, 2005.

Stiplovšek, Miroslav. *Razglasitev Domžal za trg leta 1925: Ob razstavi v počastitev 80 letnice* [The 1925 Proclamation of Domžale as a Market Town: An Exhibition in Honor of the 80th Anniversary]. Domžale: Kulturni dom Franca Bernika, 2005.

Stražar, Stane. *Svet pod Taborom: Kronika Ihana* [The World under Tabor: Chronicles of Ihan]. Ihan: Odbor za praznovanje 750-letnice Ihana, 1974.

Valenčič, Vlado. "O slamnikarski domači obrti" [The Craft of Straw Hat Making]. *Kamniški zbornik* 5 (1959): 165–93.

Vrtačnik Merčun, Vilma, Nika Grošelj, and Lara Tekavc. *Operni pevec Anton Šubelj z Rodice: Njegovo prvo potovanje v Ameriko (1928–1929)*

[The Opera Singer Anton Šubelj from Rodica pri Domžalah: His First Journey to America (1928–1929)]. Domžale: Kulturno društvo Groblje, 2012.

Žontar, Jože. "Domžalsko območje v prvi polovici 19. stoletja" [The Domžale Region in the First Half of the 19th Century]. *Zbornik občine Domžale* (1979): 95–102.

Chapter 6

Eurocrats in Brussels
Contemporary Career Women

Tatiana Bajuk Senčar

Sitting at a table in Place du Luxembourg, one is able to watch the bustle of activity that makes this plaza one of the liveliest in all of Brussels. Cafés line its boundaries, and their tables spill out onto the sidewalks, particularly at the first sign of sunny weather in a city notorious for its gray drizzle. From these tables one can appreciate the extent to which this plaza is a nexus for people coming from all over the city. Numerous buses go by in different directions, the noise of their passing an inevitable backdrop that marks the passing of time. Taxis wait patiently in line for their customers. People hurry by, going in different directions; some have come from the nearby train station that also links the plaza directly to train lines that lead out of the city and connect Brussels to the rest of Europe.

In addition to being a significant urban nexus and meeting place, Place du Luxembourg is also a particularly important social landmark for a group of people who help make Belgium's capital also the center of the European Union (EU): European officials, or Eurocrats. Place du Luxembourg is centrally located in the European Quarter and faces the grand buildings of the European Parliament, one of the major institutions of the EU and also the workplace for a number of the Slovenian Eurocrats I spoke to during my stay in Brussels. On the other end of the plaza is the end of Rue du Luxembourg, a relatively short street along which one can find a number of European Commission buildings. Together with Schumann Circle, Place du Luxembourg represents the key points on the map of the European Quarter. While the plaza itself is not a location for the EU institution buildings, it is important because it is one of the central meeting places for countless Eurocrats, including EU interns making their way in what is for them a new world, as well as experienced officials meeting colleagues for lunch or for a beer after work.

Place du Luxembourg is one of the central places where I met the women who formed part of the first generation of Slovenian Eurocrats. Slovenia's accession to the EU in May 2004 together with nine other countries meant that Slovenians also had the right to become employed in the EU institutions. Since that time, the first generation of Slovenian Eurocrats has been slowly taking shape, one person at a time. In my time in Brussels I met with Slovenian Eurocrats across the European Quarter in their offices, at their homes, and in cafés and restaurants, including those in Place du Luxembourg.[1] As the wife of a Slovenian diplomat who was stationed in Brussels, I also formed part of the broader EU Slovenian diaspora in Brussels, experiencing daily life as it was informed by work in conjunction with the EU institutions and participating in the travel between Brussels and Slovenia multiple times each year. Slovenia's EU diaspora also includes those Slovenians (and their families) working either at the EU institutions themselves or interacting with them on a daily basis as part of their duties as employees of the Slovenian Permanent Representation to the EU.[2]

The Question of EU-Centered Migrations

This Slovenian EU diaspora that has been developing and taking shape roughly since just after the turn of the millennium is particularly interesting given the European project that forms the ideological foundation of the EU as well as the idea of Europe as a particular postnational space. Do these EU-centered migrations differ in any way from previous waves of migration within Europe? Is it possible to identify a specific manifestation of Europeanization in this specific wave of migration, and what implications does this potential manifestation of Europeanization or European integration have for these Slovenians' sense of identity and belonging within Slovenia, within Belgium, and within Europe? What can the first generation of Slovenian Eurocrats tell us about the emergent social reality of the EU?

Until now, researchers have explored questions concerning the social formation and identity construction of Eurocrats (no matter the nationality) by focusing primarily on their activities within the EU institutions, at their workplace.[3] One of the key questions that has structured such inquiries has been the degree to which these new Eurocrats have adapted to the working culture of the EU institutions and the effects that such socialization has on the identity of these Eurocrats. Analytical questions of this kind are often formulated in relation to the degree to which new Eurocrats presumably take on an official European identity linked to the European project (as defined by the EU) and the effects that such an identification has on feelings of nationality, which are often reduced to the issue of national loyalty.

Inquiries constructed in this manner are self-limiting, given the presumptions made about the social actors who are the subject of such analysis. These social actors are divested of any pertinent cultural formation and agency, and their European life narratives presumably begin with their first arrival in Brussels as EU officials. In effect, to a great degree their own experiences of integration are ignored, and with this a great deal of important data is neglected. In order to understand the reality of European integration that is currently developing, it is crucial to bring to light the European stories of these actors wherever they might begin and wherever they might take us. This implies not only filling in certain holes in the grander narratives of integration but also using these stories to continually reassess the way that Europeanization is conceptualized, narrated, and analyzed.

Incorporating into the integration analyses the in-depth stories of the migrations of these cultural actors is an important step, as this provides a more grounded understanding of the broader context in which each person's experience in Brussels may be placed. More specifically, this would also involve broadening the analytical focus to include a person's agency and activities that brought her or him to office within the institutions of the EU. Ideally, this would include the entirety of this person's Brussels or European story, the reasons for migrating to Brussels, and the person's actions, decisions, history of travel, and plans for the future or for a possible return to Slovenia.

Women, of course, form a crucial component of this diaspora in terms of their roles in the productive and reproductive economies and often by their roles in both. By this I mean that the women who travel to Brussels are not solely the spouses of those who are employed in the EU institutions, although these women form an important segment of the population that is often ignored not so much in migration studies but in studies of EU integration that are focused on the EU institutions. This chapter does not strive to focus on women and their roles in the reproductive economy but instead focuses on those women who are Eurocrats themselves. While the highest-ranking Slovenian Eurocrat is a man, more than half of all Eurocrats with permanent positions within all the EU institutions are women, and at least two women hold higher-level positions accorded to Slovenians across the EU institutions. In fact, according to the information we received at the time of our research, there were more Slovenian women than men employed in the European Commission.[4]

The Roots of EU-Centered Migration

As mentioned earlier, Slovenia became a member of the EU in 2004, and most of the women we spoke to had started sometime after that, although a fair number of them had started earlier as contractual or short-term agents who then received permanent positions. While a fair number of the women explained that upon looking back they felt as if they wound up in Brussels by chance, analytically speaking their presence in Brussels could be understood as the result of certain experiences, certain social connections that opened up a particular path. Despite the great heterogeneity among the women interviewees, one of the things that linked them together was the fact that each to some degree or another had a European story before she set out for Brussels in terms of previous travel to Brussels, previous academic or professional experience, previous contacts, etc. None of these women could be considered to have been a blank slate upon beginning their work within the EU institutions. So what do the roots of such EU-centered migration look like? How do these stories begin?

The interviewees for this project include Slovenian women of different ages who had varied levels of schooling, worked in a range of grades and positions and a scope of different professions across the EU institutions, and had a diverse set of reasons for coming to Brussels. The result is a set of stories, each of which at first seems to be distinct from all others. This of course also means that the European stories of these women varies greatly due to a number of factors. The one factor that links these stories is that the lives of these women changed in conjunction with the course of Slovenia's accession process. Moreover, when Slovenia became a member of the EU, these women were positioned in such a way that employment in the EU became for them a logical and feasible step.

Helena

Some of the stories of these women also included family experiences of travel within Europe, family stories that speakers defined as part of their own life experiences insofar as they informed their own views on the possibility of living abroad. One of our narrators, Helena,[5] a younger woman who works in the European Commission, is from a family who spent a significant time abroad in various countries across Europe because of her father's profession. She relates that this is one of major factors that predisposed her to living abroad:

> Essentially in my case a number of factors played a role in my coming here, because I grew up in a family in which the parents worked abroad, so that maybe this also influenced me.... This was in my opinion one of those reasons... I was embedded in such an environment, that... I did not think so much about whether or not going abroad was a possibility because it was self-evident to me, that... it is possible to go abroad and work there and stay in touch with one's homeland and parents and so on.[6]

The life story that Helena relates is not punctuated by occasional travel but in effect is structured by it. She carried out a significant part of her university study abroad, taking advantage of the possibilities offered by the Erasmus Programme when it was set up in Slovenia.[7] Upon working for a few years in Slovenia, she decided to pursue a master's degree and received a scholarship for the College of Europe, which was at that time announced by the then Government Office for European Affairs. At that time she had not decided on pursuing a career specializing in European affairs in her profession, but she decided to take the scholarship and go to the College of Europe in Bruges, Belgium.[8] This was a crucial decision in her European story:

> I got the scholarship for the College of Europe in Bruges, which is in essence a breeding ground for EU officials, and then it is understood that you at least try, not that you go but that you at least try to find a job in Brussels; this was probably another important reason.[9]

According to Helena, before then she had not really thought about working in the EU institutions; however, she equated going to the College of Europe with getting on the European train, that is, the path that led to work in Brussels. In addition to completing a master's degree in Bruges, Helena, together with many of her colleagues, tried to find a job in Brussels. For her as well as for her colleagues from the then accession states, this meant taking the first *concours* (competition) that was set up to select those persons who would become the first Eurocrats from member states. The concours is a lengthy selection process that lasts approximately one year and begins with a rigorous written exam. If one succeeds in passing the written exam, there follows an oral exam or interview. It is important to note that passing the concours does not mean that you are guaranteed a job. Instead, this means that your name is placed on the list from which candidates are chosen for concrete positions across all the EU institutions.

Upon completing her master's degree and before completing the concours, Helena returned to Slovenia, where she worked in the office of an EU institution that was located in Ljubljana, the capital of Slovenia. During her work in this office she began the concours process.

As in the case of the College of Europe, work in the offices of the EU institutions located in Ljubljana represents an important stepping stone for a number of the women interviewed. Not only do they represent a workplace where one acquires a great deal of basic and necessary knowledge concerning the EU institutions, but they also represent an important network of persons circulating between Ljubljana and Brussels as well as a crucial source of EU-related information. While working in this particular position in Ljubljana, Helena learned of the fact that EU officials in Brussels were looking for persons to assume positions in their EU institutions from the date of accession onward, and she was among those Slovenians who applied. Thus, Helena formed part of the group of Slovenians who assumed positions in the EU on the day that Slovenia became a full member of the EU.[10]

The first generation of female Eurocrats of any country represents a singular challenge to researchers because these women do not have the strongly established paths or models of operation at their disposal to aid them in attaining a position within the EU institutions. Eurocrats from older member states benefit from the existence of multiple generations of EU officials from their home countries as well as an established infrastructure and set of social networks. This differs substantially from the case of those persons who are among the first professionals to take on positions from new member states.

While of course they have the same aid and the same infrastructure of the EU institutions themselves that is at the disposal of all potential applicants, they do not have the benefit of informal networks, cultural infrastructure, or mentors from their own state. In a manner of speaking, one can liken our narrators to *bricoleurs* as understood by Claude Levi-Strauss, persons who manufacture a particular professional path from a number of disparate elements and skills as well as sets of social contacts.[11]

In the case of Helena, one can begin to understand her social positioning as a Eurocrat and her sense of identity by linking together her family and personal history of travel across Europe, the structure of her professional career, and the changes occurring at the level of Slovenia's accession to the EU. Her story as a Eurocrat consists of a combination of these elements that unfolded for her at a particular juncture in time and put her in an ideal position to pursue a career as a Eurocrat. Helena is among the younger women I spoke to, although at her age she already had a master's degree and was an accomplished professional with eight years of work experience. In addition to having a significant group of interviewees who fit a similar profile, among the women who participated in the research project there was a group of older women who were further along in their profession at the time of accession. Some of these women in effect had spent a significant part of their careers working on Slovenia's accession process itself and EU affairs before 2004.

Veronika

As mentioned above, another important group of women among the Slovenian Eurocrats are those who were able to construct an EU-focused career before accession. The women in this group were at the time mainly Slovenian civil servants, and their EU careers go as far back as the mid-1990s. Having an EU career not only implies simply learning about the EU or having EU-related tasks in Ljubljana but can also consist of systematic travel between Ljubljana and Brussels as a representative of the Slovenian government in diverse meetings and other forms of institutional dialogue. This particular form of short-term and periodic travel is quite distinct from the travel mentioned in the case of Helena and consists of some of the key experiences of a very particular group of social actors whom anthropologists refer to as "national Eurocrats"—that is, those persons employed at the national level but whose tasks include systematic interaction with the EU institutions.[12] In this context I will introduce the case of Veronika, whose particular career story can serve as an example for this second group of Slovenian women. In the following passage, she describes her first of numerous trips to Brussels as a civil servant:

> I came to Brussels for the first time in '95; that was during the preparations. These were essentially preparations for the accession of the candidate countries in the field of... These preparations were very important for the candidate countries because it was very important for them to establish systems that would be...compatible with the system of the member states. As you can imagine, for example, in the field of...we are dealing with issues that affect our everyday lives in concrete ways.... At that time I attended for the first time a seminar for candidate countries. I went with a colleague of mine...though at that time there was no systematic approach to this in the civil service because we did not become a candidate country until '97, '98.... We began to cover these issues more systematically from '96, '97 onward. In fact, I followed developments in this area very, very closely—how the market is organized... the organization of the joint market in the area that I was covering. We tried to approximate our work as much as possible to the organization that was valid at that time in the EU, knowing at the same time that of course this organization was shifting constantly. We would talk about a sort of, a sort of shifting target that is constantly on the move, and you try to keep up. Basically I was participating in these preparations, these so-called screening processes, in '98 and '99, in a number of areas. These were in fact intense meetings during which we would go through the entire sets of legislation in great detail.[13]

Veronika first came to Brussels in 1995 to participate in preparations for potential accession state countries as a member of the Slovenian civil service, where she worked from 1994 to 1999. The meeting that she described above for potential accession countries was the first in this field, and as she goes on to say, it was the first such meeting to which that particular ministry sent a representative. Upon accession, Veronika continued working on the screening process through 1999 from within the civil service. During this time, she also completed her postgraduate studies focused on Slovenia's accession to the EU. In 2000 Veronika's movements between Ljubljana and Brussels shifted significantly because she took a position within an international nonprofit organization focused on the EU institutional network. This was her first longtime stay in Brussels, albeit less directly linked to the EU institutions. In 2003 she returned to her position in Slovenia's civil service and was then assigned to Brussels to work at the Slovenian Permanent Representation to the EU to help in the initial preparations for Slovenia's presidency.

This sort of position enabled Veronika to become a national Eurocrat employed at the Slovenian Permanent Representation of the EU, where she engaged the EU institutions on a daily basis. National Eurocrats who fit into this category do not travel periodically between their capitals and Brussels, or what Renita Thedvall terms "pendulum movements," but instead are stationed in Brussels for four years or more at a time.[14] While each direct professional contact, however brief, aids civil servants in better understanding the working of the EU institutions, being stationed in Brussels marks an important distinction between different groups of national Eurocrats. Veronika describes this distinction in terms of her own personal experience, marking a distinction between those who are stationed in Brussels and those working from Ljubljana:

> In short, during that time basically it was possible to...gain a great deal of information, while for example our colleagues in Slovenia were not so involved in this.... They did not...invest

so much time, energy, I don't know, interest or motivation to get so caught up in that which already existed... what was available also to them, right. But yes, we represented a sort of mediator, intermediate link... something that I saw later in the civil service itself, in the years 2004, 2005, when our civil service became more flexible and they started to establish their own set of connections with their... colleagues from other member states.[15]

During the time that Veronika was a national Eurocrat based at the Slovenian Permanent Representation, she also participated in the concours and took on a position at the European Commission in 2007. When she assumed her position within the EU institutions, she had been working for more than ten years in EU affairs, sometimes directly with the EU institutions and other times less so. Given that her professional experience coincided with the first steps of Slovenia's accession process, Veronika had amassed a crucial amount of knowledge, expertise, and connections that put her in an ideal position when Slovenia finally became a member of the EU. Given the professional trajectory made possible by the accession process, working in the EU institutions would be a logical step in an EU-centered career. Veronika is among the group of persons (male and female) who have the highest positions assumed by Slovenians within the EU institutional network.

Hana

As mentioned earlier, one of the things that links together the life experiences of these women is that each had to some degree a European story in which they would place their EU or Brussels experiences. At one end of the spectrum are extensive professional histories, such as in the case of Veronika. On the other end of the spectrum are young administrative assistants whose EU-related professional experiences were relatively minimal but who acquired connections and information that enabled them to take part in the selection process for EU-related positions. In the case of Hana, we have someone who through her work in an EU-related office in Ljubljana was able to find out about the possibility of employment in the EU institutions at the right time. Hana was in the proper position to find out about a call of interest for positions made available shortly before accession:

> What brought me to work in the EU institutions? Basically my ex-boss in the...in Ljubljana told me about this possibility. Before working here I had worked as a...in Ljubljana, and because it was 2002, that is, two years before the expansion of the European Union, the institutions in Brussels were apparently looking for people who would like to come to Brussels as soon as possible. This means with a one-year or eighteen-month short-term contract. I think that it was to also get a feel for the kind of people we are in Eastern Europe.... So in 2002...they advertised a test, a concours of sorts, a call for interest they called it, a test for those who would be interested in work in the European institutions from the new member states before accession.... I applied to take that test because...my ex-boss warned me "Go, go, you have nothing to lose. Here this office may close, it may be completely reorganized, and it is not clear whether or not you would be able to stay on."[16]

As mentioned earlier, there was a group of Slovenians who had been hired by the European institutions before accession on short-term contracts. These persons took quite a risk because they traveled to Brussels with only a letter of invitation that would presumably lead to a contract upon arrival. Many of the persons who came to Brussels before accession were relatively young and had decided to accept a challenge of sorts. Hana describes her decision in the following terms:

> Well, I went to take the test and I passed it. The test was made up of two parts, written and oral. The whole thing took two, three months. And I received a reply in the year 2003, and...at that time they called me from Luxembourg, that is, from the administrative center of the European Parliament, asking if I was interested in coming to work here in the parliament. Yes, I of course accepted, because what did I have to lose, right? I was single, I think—yes, I was single. And the work would in any case

be over in a year or two, so I accepted the position and came with my suitcase to Brussels. And it was like that.... It is funny; when you get here you don't have a contract, you don't know where you are going to live, you don't know anything. You don't know what you will be working on; you only know... that someone will give you a contract for a year or two, a temporary contract. You come here basically with a suitcase in hand; you come here to the main office and [laughs] and here they offer you a contract. You get a draft [letter] a week in advance, but of course you never know if they will sign the draft or not.[17]

Migration and the Issue of Integration

The women in this particular group are unique in that they are not defined in accordance with their moving to a specific country or even to a specific city. Their identifying characteristic lies in their moving to work in a specific set of institutions that are multicultural and presumably European in nature, a heterogeneous but specific social landscape that lies primarily in the European Quarter that I described at the beginning of this chapter. Their experiences in this social landscape overlap to varying degrees with their daily lives that they experience outside the quarter and in greater Brussels, but it is the professional and personal experiences that unfold for them on a daily basis within the EU-based environment that to a great degree structures their daily lives in Brussels as well as the experience of their migration. In addition, their European stories also serve to portray the extent to which their EU-based environment not only is centered on the EU institutions but also extends geographically and socially—given their travel, experiences, and sets of connections. All of this informs the EU postnational social landscape in terms of which each woman constructs and makes sense of her own integration experience.

Upon assessing the European stories gathered from this group of women, one can observe that through the course of their academic and professional career experiences they had constructed a set of contacts and relationships. These life trajectories suggest progressions between work in Ljubljana and/or work in Brussels or Europe at large, though not in terms of Thedvall's pendulum movements, which are meant to refer to the binary movements that Eurocrats often make between their home capital and Brussels. Instead, in these progressions social actors shift positions or roles with each geographic shift. These geographic shifts are also social shifts as each person becomes embedded in additional networks and sets of contacts through time.

On the one hand, these professional and academic progressions structured in terms of long- and short-term travel provide these women with some of the basic knowledge and experiences that facilitate their professional integration into their workplace, a level of integration that is not the central focus here. Instead, integration here is understood more broadly as the development of ways of living and belonging that are linked to the move and work in Brussels. What happens to the positioning of this group of women upon their establishment within the EU institutions as Eurocrats? Despite the wide range of experiences that these women recounted, the most accurate way to categorize this vision of integration was in effect described by one of our informants as living long-distance. This is akin to the concept of simultaneity argued by Levitt and Glick Schiller in migration studies, which refers to a transnational way of life in which persons in essence maintain ties to the social world he or she leaves behind.[18] Living long-distance implies that our narrators continue to remain embedded in a continually shifting set of networks and that this embeddedness is evident in the understanding of their own identity as well as in their daily lives. For example, in my interview with Helena I asked her to tell us her life story. She begins with the following words:

> In essence a lot of factors came into play in my decision to come here, because I grew up in a family in which the parents worked abroad, so that maybe this was already a factor, knowing that going abroad is an alternative, that it is not...an option that is closed off but that it is possible and that one can...live long-distance and be connected.[19]

Living long-distance does not imply that the women interviewed did not go through a process of adaptation to their new work environment or to the new city in which they lived. Quite the contrary. In many of the stories there are passages about the different stages of adaptation that they experienced and about the activities or thought processes that each employed to make a space for herself in Brussels. Katarina, one of the women interviewed, narrated such a process as she began to think more long-term about Brussels:

> And so, if I actually got the job, then I will go, right. Especially if it is for a year and a half.... Maybe I will save some money.... Everyone talks about how much money is to be had up there.... So I said, okay, let's go see, it can't hurt, right. And so then you move and then all of a sudden you are here... and you think, in any case after a year and a half I go back. And then you extend the contract.... You say, I will go after the contract expires; in any case you always plan that, then you go back to Slovenia. And then there is the concours that is held in the meantime... in any case you will not pass.... And then I passed, right. And then okay, okay, then I will stay, what else, if I passed the concours. And then you have to tell everyone at home. First, they think you will go for a few years... and... then it looks like you will stay here. So that... then the final decision is then that.... But then you always say that you can always come back, right.[20]

Besides passing the concours, other potential stages of adaptation include broadening one's circle of friends beyond the Slovenians one meets at the very beginning of one's stay, making friends with work colleagues, and buying an apartment, which represents a decision to stay more long-term beyond a succession of short-term contracts. Another significant step that is mentioned concerns minimizing the number of trips back to Slovenia. Given the high salaries of Eurocrats and the possibilities of flying on low-cost airlines such as Ryanair and Wizzair, flying back and forth to Slovenia represents a minimal expense. Thus, it was financially feasible to return home every weekend at very little cost.

Among the women interviewed there is a range of forms of living long-distance. There are a few cases of persons who are actually living long-distance, meaning that during the week they live in Brussels and on the weekends they go home, where their families or significant others await them. This is relatively rare among Slovenians of either gender, though it is a more common practice for certain Eurocrats from member states neighboring Belgium, where distance is not that much of an issue. Whether or not one can classify this as a typical Eurocrat practice that is also slowly gaining ground among Slovenian Eurocrats is an important question that unfortunately transcends the boundaries of the research carried out in Brussels.

On the other end of the spectrum there are persons who have come to Brussels and married Belgians, forming personal ties outside the narrow bounds of the EU institutions in Brussels but also forging a connection between these personal ties and the networks that link them to Slovenia. These women are the ones who are most well integrated into life in Brussels or Belgium in general, something that is not necessarily the case with Eurocrats who are otherwise presumed to be caught up in what is the so-called EU bubble. An analogous situation is that of Slovenian women who have married Eurocrats of another nationality. These are women who meet their partners in the EU institutions themselves or in their studies and travel through Europe. For such a couple, Brussels can represent the ideal middle ground between two homelands and the center of a broad transnational set of networks.

Living long-distance implies that even before moving to Brussels, these women lived to varying degrees embedded in transnational or European networks that serve to outline the social and geographic landscape in which they live and operate. In addition, these networks serve as the basis for developing ways of living transnationally—in Brussels as well as through shifting ties in Slovenia. Just as there exists a progression that these women's life trajectories represented in a shifting and growing set of relations that link a person to Brussels, the women interviewed also narrate shifts in the social relations that tie them to Slovenia. Slovenia as home can become reconfigured, with certain ties becoming less important and others more important.

One of the most important aspects of Slovenia as home that is consistently reconfigured concerns Slovenia as a possible professional option. Many of the women interviewed related that they became Eurocrats by chance; they did not plan to take on permanent positions as Eurocrats. Given the newness of EU membership and the professional possibilities that this represented for Slovenians as well as for persons from the remaining new member states, it is not surprising that when they decided to transfer to Brussels to take on a new job in the EU institutions, a professional return to Slovenia was for the most part an option. Leaving open the option to return did not take away from the fact that for many of these people, the opportunity to work in the EU institutions meant a great step forward professionally and financially. Hana describes the feeling that she and her colleagues from other new member states had when they began to work in the European Parliament. In her group there was one person from each member state:

> There were ten of us when I arrived. A Latvian, a Lithuanian woman, an Estonian woman, a Slovak, me from Slovenia.... There was one person from each country. Actually, it was all extremely interesting...every person was extremely enthusiastic and expectant, wondering what they will be doing, where will they go, what tasks will be assigned...and what to do after work, and what will the work be like, and what are the people like.... I think that it was an intense time.[21]

However, integration is not a seamless process, and there was a range of issues that the women who were interviewed had to deal with in their first days, weeks, or months on the job. It is not possible to generalize across experiences, because the women are so dispersed across the EU institutions that no one woman can be identified as being representative in nature. Some women found it much easier than others to fit into their work environment, and some women faced more difficult challenges than others, all of which affected the way they looked upon a professional return to Slovenia and the sorts of strategic contacts they would maintain back home. One possible factor in this regard concerns the kinds of positions that have been made available to potential Eurocrats from new member states. The vast majority of the concours held for potential Eurocrats from new member states have been for entry-level positions.[22] While at first the move to the EU institutions is described in extremely positive terms, by the time these interviews were conducted, many of the interviewees had begun to question—directly or indirectly—their long-term job prospects in the EU institutions, in which it is very difficult to move ahead. The Slovenian national civil service, due to its smaller size, is much more flexible and allows for the construction of successful professional careers. One of the major themes that is problematized in the narratives is the range of professional options open for these women who left Slovenia mainly for professional reasons, who identify with their work in the institutions but deliberate about the direction of their professional future. Responses range from forging and maintaining strategic professional ties in Slovenia to defining Slovenia more as the setting of friends and family that one systematically visits and the homeland to which one will eventually retire.

The experiences of this first generation of Slovenian Eurocrats are ongoing, and the compilation of their European stories of travel and migration aid us in shedding light on the shape of these emergent processes. This may potentially affect living long-distance as a potential model of Europeanization. A relatively short period of time has elapsed since Slovenia's accession to the EU, and institutionally speaking, Slovenians who have become Eurocrats have had a relatively short period of time in which to make a space for themselves in a postnational context, regardless of gender. Is it possible that the living long-distance approach is simply a manifestation of the lack of time that Slovenians have had to settle in? Or are they in essence developing a specifically

European or transnational way of living that reflects the contours of a new specifically EU-based social reality? Despite the variety that exists among the women's stories that have been gathered, at this particular juncture the argument can be made that living long-distance is not a simple result of the short period of time that has elapsed since Slovenia's accession, although this thesis needs to be tested over time.

Notes

1. The interviews that I conducted formed part of a research project with Dr. Jeffrey David Turk funded by the Slovenian Research Agency titled the Anthropology of European Integration. This research project centered on the integration experiences of the first generation of Slovenian Eurocrats and includes the gathering of approximately fifty life stories of Slovenian Eurocrats, of which approximately half were women. For discussion of research results, see Tatiana Bajuk Senčar, "The Integration of 'East' and 'West': Slovene 'Eurocrats' and the Politics of Identity within the Institutions of the European Union," *Traditiones* 38, no. 2 (2009): 153–66; and Tatiana Bajuk Senčar and Jeffrey David Turk, "Following European Stories: An Anthropological Study of European Integration," *Traditiones* 40, no. 2 (2011): 139–51.

2. Slovenia's bilateral embassy to Belgium and Luxembourg is also stationed in Brussels, as is Slovenia's embassy to the North Atlantic Treaty Organization. There are also other Slovenian organizations, such as the Slovenian Business and Research Association, as well as other networks of Slovenians who live across Brussels and Belgium but are not subjects of the research, as it was focused solely on EU-centered Slovenian migrants.

3. See Marc Abélès, "Identity and Borders: An Anthropological Approach to EU Institutions" (Online Working Paper No. 4, Center for 21st Century Studies, University of Wisconsin–Milwaukee, 2004); Irène Bellier, "A Europeanized Elite? An Anthropology of European Commission Officials," *Yearbook of European Studies* 14 (2000): 135–56; Maryon MacDonald, "Identities in the European Commission," in *At the Heart of the Union: Studies of the European Commission*, edited by Neill Nugent, 51–72 (New York: St. Martin's, 1997); and Renita Thedvall, *Eurocrats at Work: Negotiating Transparency in Postnational Employment Policy* (Stockholm; Intellecta Docysis, 2006).

4. The EU institutions consist primarily of the European Commission, the European Parliament, and the Council of the EU. The information that we received from the European Commission gave us an overall view of the commission's permanent staff broken down by grade, nationality, category, and gender. Unfortunately, the data we received did not break down the population of Slovenians by gender and grade, so it is not apparent from the data the grades at which Slovenian women work as opposed to Slovenian men. Dr. Janez Potočnik serves as a commissioner and is the highest-ranking Slovenian Eurocrat in the EU institutions.

5. All of our interviewees were granted complete anonymity. In order to protect their identities, each woman has been given a code name, and great care has been taken not to disclose the particulars of their life stories. This means that certain specificities of each life story mentioned in this chapter have been concealed or slightly changed.

6. Helena, interview by author, February 5, 2009, Brussels, Belgium, tape recording in possession of the author.

7. The Erasmus (European Community Action Scheme for the Mobility of University Students) Programme is an EU student exchange program established in 1987 and represents the operational framework for the European Commission's initiatives in higher education. The program operates in thirty-three participating countries, primarily member states and accession state countries.

8. The College of Europe is an independent postgraduate university institute of European studies with the main campus in Bruges, Belgium. Since 1993, the college has also had an additional campus in Natolin, Poland. The College of Europe is considered to be the elite postgraduate university for European studies and the breeding ground for Eurocrats.

9. Helena, interview by author, February 5, 2009, Brussels, Belgium, tape recording in possession of the author.

10. There was a small number of Slovenians who took on temporary positions within the EU institutions in mid-2003 and were thus already working in the institutions by Slovenia's accession in May 2004. These persons had gained important working knowledge of the EU institutions from within and were asked to stay on after accession.

11. Claude Lévi-Strauss, *The Savage Mind* (Chicago: University of Chicago Press, 1966).

12. For more on national Eurocrats, see Renita Thedvall, *Eurocrats at Work: Negotiating Transparency in Postnational Employment Policy* (Stockholm: Intellecta Docysis, 2006); and Karin Geuijen et al., *The New Eurocrats: National Servants in EU Policy Making* (Amsterdam: Amsterdam University Press, 2008).

13. Veronika, interview by author, January 20, 2009, Brussels, Belgium, tape recording in possession of the author.

14. Renita Thedvall, *Eurocrats at Work*, 198–206. The Permanent Representation of the Republic of Slovenia to the EU is in effect the embassy that each member state has in Brussels. However, it is an embassy that has a broader range of duties than a regular bilateral embassy, with civil servants assigned to Brussels from virtually every single ministry within the Slovenian civil service. Furthermore, it is worth noting that Brussels represents a certain exception in the diplomatic world, as civil servants stationed at the Permanent Representations have a greater chance of staying longer than the standard four years.

15. Veronika, interview by author, January 20, 2009, Brussels, Belgium, tape recording in possession of the author.

16. Hana, interview by author, June 23, 2009, Brussels, Belgium, tape recording in possession of the author.

17. Ibid.

18. Peggy Levitt and Nina Glick Schiller, "Conceptualizing Simultaneity: A Transnational Social Field Perspective on Society," *International Migration Review* 38, no. 145 (2004): 595–629.

19. Helena, interview by author, February 5, 2009, Brussels, Belgium, tape recording in possession of the author.

20. Katarina, interview by author, March 12, 2009, Brussels, Belgium, tape recording in possession of the author.

21. Hana, interview by author, June 23, 2009, Brussels, Belgium, tape recording in possession of the author.

22. There have of course also been concours processes for higher-level positions within the EU institutions, but the majority are entry-level positions.

References

Abélès, Marc. "Identity and Borders: An Anthropological Approach to EU Institutions." Online Working Paper No. 4. Center for 21st Century Studies, University of Wisconsin–Milwaukee, 2004.

Bajuk Senčar, Tatiana. "The Integration of 'East' and 'West': Slovene 'Eurocrats' and the Politics of Identity within the Institutions of the European Union." *Traditiones* 38, no. 2 (2009): 153–66.

Bajuk Senčar, Tatiana, and Jeffrey David Turk. "Following European Stories: An Anthropological Study of European Integration." *Traditiones* 40, no. 2 (2011): 139–51.

Bellier, Irène. "A Europeanized Elite? An Anthropology of European Commission Officials." *Yearbook of European Studies* 14 (2000): 135–56.

Geuijen, Karin, et al. *The New Eurocrats: National Servants in EU Policy Making.* Amsterdam: Amsterdam University Press, 2008.

Lévi-Strauss, Claude. *The Savage Mind.* Chicago: University of Chicago Press, 1966.

Levitt, Peggy, and Nina Glick Schiller. "Conceptualizing Simultaneity: A Transnational Social Field Perspective on Society." *International Migration Review* 38, no. 145 (2004): 595–629.

McDonald, Maryon. "Identities in the European Commission." In *At the Heart of the Union: Studies of the European Commission,* edited by Neill Nugent, 51–72. New York: St. Martin's, 1997.

Thedvall, Renita. *Eurocrats at Work: Negotiating Transparency in Postnational Employment Policy.* Stockholm: Intellecta Docysis, 2006.

Turk, Jeffrey David. 2009. "Slovene Integration and EU Environmental Policy Impact: Using Narratives for Social Science." Paper presented at the 41st National Convention of the American Association for the Advancement of Slavic Studies, Boston, Massachusetts.

Conclusion
Jernej Mlekuž

The concept of this book, which focuses on the subjective, experiential, and lived-through dimension of events and occurrences, provides stories of people who are not favorites of political, national, and other important histories. As indicated by the heroines of these chapters, the stories, memories, and records tell us more about the sense and experience of events and phenomena than about the very events and phenomena themselves. Moreover, those senses and experiences create a bond across the continents—the points of departure and arrival—creating intricate emotional landscapes and weaving feelings of transnational proportions, which overcome and contextualize political boundaries and systems, economic and social differences, cultural traits, values, creeds, and beliefs. As Paul Thompson thoroughly demonstrated, this is a project of the democratization of history and knowledge in general as we finally give voice to those who were silenced, who often had neither the opportunity nor the right to speak out.[1] Hence, such a project should not be deprived of researchers' self-reflection—those who discover the stories, select them, record, process, and place them within a theoretical or conceptual frame and, last but not least, nest them through interpretation within their own concepts. In other words, such a project is by no means free of political, social, and other researchers' viewpoints.

What counts is not merely the storytellers' contexts but also the contexts of those who produce knowledge and power on the basis of those stories.² The biographical method thus raises the issue of knowledge itself. Instead of great events and great political and military actors, biographical methods place in the limelight the ostensible everywoman and everyman and what she or he can tell about the events, that is, what they mean to her or him. Thus, it is not hard to understand why biographical methodology has become important for the development of women's studies: it was with its help that "half of humankind," by and large utterly ignored by academic studies, has begun to speak out.

Who speaks in this book? That "half of humankind" without which, as Gisela Bock says, there is "less than half of history."³ Women, especially women from the professed yet highly inaudible category of little people, were hushed in the field of social-historical memory and knowledge. They were not given a voice, as it was considered insignificant. Their stories usually didn't reach farther than the kitchen, although in most cases they were seemingly of existential significance for male family members, too. Women didn't leave the kitchen because they were not important enough, they couldn't match the fascists, the El Alamein battle, and other so-called great and loud male stories.

Why, then, tell the stories of *slamnikarice, aleksandrinke, dikle,* contemporary Eurocrats, Pepice, Francke, and all other various ordinary and allegedly plain women? Stories, experiences, and testimonies of women carry an important message, mission, and plan. In this book, in this site of knowledge, this workshop and storage of social and historical memory, women have been given a voice: they have not only been allowed to speak but have also been called upon to speak out, thus becoming historical and social subjects. It is through this act that they have inscribed themselves in the field of historical and social memory and knowledge. Women, who have long been denied any significance in the field of knowledge and historical and social memory, have been (re)invigorated—they have become important.⁴

What else is important about those stories, experiences, and testimonies? First, they are brought to us as a version different from those the variants that are considered to be real, true, eternal, or official. The personal stories, memories, experiences, and testimonies collected in this book dare to question the official, dominant, compulsory knowledge. And even when these narratives doubt, they often do so unconsciously. We might say that they always carry within them a torch of resistance that may easily trigger fires of larger proportions, and the flames of these fires may terminally devour stereotypical notions, humiliating images, and fallacious scientific arguments on poor, ignorant, exploited, and misfortunate women who set off to seek their fortune. Yet this book is not merely about looking for the torch of resistance or hot stories that spark fires and stand loud and clear against this or that kind of obduracy. The concept of the stories collected in the book is essentially simple—tales, experiences, and testimonies speak for themselves. And by speaking, they question the obduracy of the word.

Women's stories, testimonies, and experiences are not to be understood merely as an invigoration of the ignored half of humankind but also as a project of breaking the image of single-gender processes, actions, and history. Presenting women as helpless victims—conscientious, quiet, and meek companions of male actions and male history—denies not only their ability to oppose and rebel but also their actions.

Active, skilled, and ambitious women have existed throughout history, although history textbooks teach us differently. Women migrants departing to every corner of the world are among the numerous examples of history, which deconstructs the passive nature of women and migration as male actions in which women are merely male appendages, following men in their migration decisions and providing them with various services. Slamnikarice, aleksandrinke, dikle, Eurocrats, Francka, Pepica, and all the others like them who left and came back (and also remained for good), worked and played, saved and spent, wrote letters and ran farms, took care of their families, and boisterously strolled across world metropolises tell us that migrations represent neither a male domain nor a single-gender or genderless castrated activity. Moreover, they teach us that gender is not a static category, an unchanged attribute of individuals of both sexes, but instead is a process of continuous transformation and redefining that is especially often manifest through migration processes. Migration does not inherently mean emancipation, liberation, or diminishing gender dichotomy and inequality but can also be a step in the opposite direction, into an even greater submissiveness and dependence, into worsening and hardening relations, and/or can have ambiguous meanings for those involved. Moving to another environment may equally bring to migrant women emancipation and a renewed submissiveness, as it was experienced by many domestic workers who freed themselves from the control of family and village communities but in turn fell under the control of the employer and the new family situation and acquired a dependent position. But not necessarily.

This book does not deal with discovering and writing about merely female migration—some kind of female migration—but instead mainly deals with understanding the complex, multilayered, and multigender nature of migrations. This was possible only through putting forward the missing yet constitutive part of migration processes—women's migration—and making visible that which was, or what the title of one of the most famous feminist books refers to as "hidden from history"[5] in order to inscribe women into the migration knowledge and knowledge in general. This inscribing must not be only a matter of complementing and reshuffling thus far overlooked events, phenomena, and occurrences but instead must be a project of critical analysis involving the entire corpus of migration studies and within it the reproduction of gender-determined knowledge.

Such a concept means that women cannot be viewed as a unified category sharing a universal experience. Experiences, stories, and tales of women are shaped by numerous highly complex factors such as class, age, and ethnicity as well as ideological and other beliefs.

The experiences of contemporary Eurocrats are very different from those of dikle, and the individual experiences of dikle can be very different, often opposing one another, which does not mean that we cannot find parallels and similarities with other migration phenomena in the group. The positions, roles, and probably the experiences of aleksandrinke are in many aspects similar to the positions, roles, and experiences of today's largest number of domestic workers, the maids in world metropolises. Much like today's Filipina women, aleksandrinke often left their children at home. Their money was often the main source of family and household income, while at the same time they were the targets of moral condemnation in their original environment.[6] Homesickness, the husband's alienation, taking care of the family and the farm, chicanery in the local environment—all of what Francka reveals to us in her letters—is probably the experience shared by numerous women from Mexico as well as Central and South America whose husbands are working in the United States. Nor is Pepica a single example of a migrant bride in time and space.

While today's communication technology helps migrants to condense time, thus helping to diminish the feeling of distance and homesickness, the emotions that come with separation from one's family, friends, and culture are nonetheless still strong. Pepica and Francka used to have to wait days or weeks, even months, for the delivery of a letter; today's migrants can send an e-mail that is received immediately or use the telephone and other technologically sophisticated means of communication to stay in touch. But regardless of the era in which they lived or are still living, dikle, Francke, Pepice, slamnikarice, aleksandrinke, and Eurocrats are examples, cutouts, and fragments of the history of a small European nation and at the same time are lives comparable to lives in other times and in other parts of the world. They are women who moved and still move the Earth with their work, love, emotions, letter writing, remembering, and caring. They are, to borrow the title of a highly influential book on contemporary migrants, "global women."[7]

Notes

1. Paul Thompson, *The Voice of the Past: Oral History* (Oxford: Oxford University Press, 1988).
2. See Liz Stanley's thorough and lucid study *The Auto/Biographical I: The Theory and Practice of Feminist Auto/Biography* (Manchester, UK: Manchester University Press, 1992).
3. Gisela Bock, *Women in European History* (Oxford, UK: Blackwell, 2002), 13.
4. This book by all means does not pretend to take over any honorable or special place within the project of inscribing women and their stories, experiences, and testimonies in the field of knowledge and social and historical memory. Yet as Slovenian historian Marta Verginella concludes in *Ženska obrobja: Vpis žensk v zgodovino Slovencev* [Women on the Margins: The Inscription of Women in the History of Slovenians] (Ljubljana: Delta, 2006), 189, "the shift has taken place indeed, but it remains to be seen in the future how far-reaching it is and whether it will contribute to the final cut and an improved affinity toward inscribing women in history."
5. Sheila Rowbotham, *Hidden from History: Rediscovering Women in History from the 17th Century to the Present* (New York: Vintage Books, 1976).
6. See Rhacel Salazar Parreñas, *Servants of Globalization: Women, Migration, and Domestic Work* (Stanford, CA: Stanford University Press, 2001).
7. Barbara Ehrenreich and Arlie Russell Hochschild, eds., *Global Woman: Nannies, Maids and Sex Workers in the New Economy* (New York: Metropolitan Books, 2003).

References

Bock, Gisela. *Women in European History.* Oxford, UK: Blackwell, 2002.
Ehrenreich, Barbara, and Arlie Russell Hochschild, eds. *Global Woman: Nannies, Maids and Sex Workers in the New Economy.* New York: Metropolitan Books, 2003.
Rowbotham, Sheila. *Hidden from History: Rediscovering Women in History from the 17th Century to the Present.* New York: Vintage Books, 1976.
Salazar Parreñas, Rhacel. *Servants of Globalization: Women, Migration, and Domestic Work.* Stanford, CA: Stanford University Press, 2001.

Stanley, Liz. *The Auto/Biographical I: The Theory and Practice of Feminist Auto/Biography.* Manchester, UK: Manchester University Press, 1992.
Thompson, Paul. *The Voice of the Past: Oral History.* Oxford, UK: Oxford University Press, 1988.
Verginella, Marta. *Ženska obrobja: Vpis žensk v zgodovino Slovencev* [Women on the Margins: The Inscription of Women in the History of Slovenians]. Ljubljana: Delta, 2006.